Writing Baseball

THE SOUTHERN ILLINOIS UNIVERSITY PRESS SERIES

Other Books in the Writing Baseball Series

THE ST. LOUIS CARDINALS

Series Editor's Note

In 1943, G. P. Putnam's Sons began a series of major league team histories with the publication of Frank Graham's history of the New York Yankees. From 1943 to 1954, Putnam published histories for fifteen of the sixteen major league teams. The Philadelphia Athletics ball club was the only one not included in the series, though Putnam did publish a biography of Connie Mack in 1945. Of the fifteen team histories, only one, the St. Louis Cardinals history, originally published in 1944, was expanded for a later edition.

Thirteen of the fifteen team histories in the Putnam series were contributed by sportswriters who were eventually honored by the Hall of Fame with the J. G. Taylor Spink Award "for meritorious contributions to baseball writing." Three Spink recipients actually wrote eleven of the team histories for the series. The famed New York columnist Frank Graham, after launching the series with the Yankees history, added team histories for the Brooklyn Dodgers and the New York Giants. Chicago sports editor and journalist Warren Brown, once dubbed the Mencken of the sports page, wrote both the Chicago Cubs and the White Sox team histories. Legendary Fred Lieb, who, at the time of his death in 1980 at the age of ninety-two, held the lowest numbered membership card in the Baseball Writers Association, contributed six team histories to the Putnam series. He also wrote the Connie Mack biography for Putnam.

For our reprints of the Putnam series, we add a foreword for each team history by one of today's most renowned baseball writers. The bibliography committee of the Society for American Baseball Research has also provided an index for each team history. Other than these additions and a few minor alterations, we have preserved the original state of the books, including any possible historical inaccuracies.

The Putnam team histories have been described as the "Cadillacs" of the team history genre. With their colorful prose and their delightful narratives of baseball history as the game moved into its postwar golden age, the Putnam books have also become among the most prized collectibles for baseball historians.

Richard Peterson

THE ST. LOUIS CARDINALS

THE STORY OF A GREAT BASEBALL CLUB

FREDERICK G. LIEB

With a New Foreword by Bob Broeg

Southern Illinois University Press
Carbondale and Edwardsville

First published 1944, 1945 by G. P. Putnam's Sons. Copyright © 1944, 1945
Frederick G. Lieb.

Writing Baseball series edition published 2001 by Southern Illinois University
Press. Reprinted by arrangement with G. P. Putnam's Sons, a member of
Penguin Putnam, Inc.

Series editor's note and foreword copyright © 2001 by the Board of Trustees,
Southern Illinois University

Printed in the United States of America

04 03 02 01 4 3 2 1

Library of Congress Cataloging-in-Publication Data

Lieb, Fred, b. 1888.
    The St. Louis Cardinals : the story of a great baseball club / Frederick G. Lieb ;
  with a new foreword by Bob Broeg.
        p. cm. — (Writing baseball)
    Originally published: New York : Putnam, 1944.
    Includes index.
    1. St. Louis Cardinals (Baseball team)—History. I. Title. II. Series

GV875.S3 L5 2001
796.357'64'0977866—dc21

                                                                00-061222

ISBN 0-8093-2366-4 (paper : alk. paper)

The paper used in this publication meets the minimum requirements of American
National Standard for Information Sciences—Permanence of Paper for Printed
Library Materials, ANSI Z39.48-1992. ♾

CONTENTS

ILLUSTRATIONS

FOREWORD

I F FRED LIEB wasn't the first to write a full-fledged history of the colorful Cardinals, he certainly was, as Dizzy Dean would say, "amongst 'em." Lieb, who looked as if he would live forever, was past ninety-two when he checked out in 1980, only a month after he had penned a final piece in a controversy over Ty Cobb. You see, longevity as well as talent was a charm of this tall, trim, thin-mustachioed man, who looked like a handsome refugee from Rudyard Kipling's British best about Victoria's generals.

Polite and proper, Frederick George Lieb knew all the words because most certainly he had heard them—from Babe Ruth, who led the league in vulgarity as well as in belting, belching, booze, and broads. Yet Fred never used vulgarity himself in conversation, much less in the millions of words he wrote. After all, when he wrote this book about St. Louis's Redbirds—the first of seven he would do for the distinguished G. P. Putnam big-league ball club series—he already had lived much of the life of the Cardinals' colorful rags-to-riches history. Further, he had a close personal relationship with Sam Breadon, the owner who profited from his own audacity and Branch Rickey's wisdom.

The center cut of the Cards' success—nine pennants and six world championships in a twenty-year period—helps a skilled writer considerably in this first full history of the St. Louis Nationals. To write it, Lieb had the added charm of the files of the *Sporting News,* a treasure trove of research. With New York papers folding then as many did over the years, Mr. Lieb had the smarts to step back into jobs he could afford to take.

As one who could turn a deaf ear to the profanities of J. G. Taylor Spink, dynamic editor-publisher of the St. Louis baseball weekly, Lieb summered in the gateway city for many years. He and his wife wintered in St. Petersburg, Florida, where he'd fallen in love with the baseball center of the sunshine state and built a home there. Ultimately, St. Pete, where the Yankees first trained in 1925, became the final vehicle for the delightful codger's pen. He wrote a weekly column for the *St. Petersburg Times* and displayed his nostalgic touch and fabulous memory in obituaries the *Sporting News* now sorely misses.

His credentials as one of the first two living writers elected to Cooperstown's writing wing in 1973 included many unusual accolades. He was the young man—in 1920—who persuaded baseball to count all runs on a game-winning homer, not just the one that created the game's difference. He also was the man who labeled Yankee Stadium exactly what it was—"The House That Ruth Built."

Lieb also shepherded an incredible all-star team to Japan after the 1931 Cardinals' World Series victory over the powerful Philadelphia A's—duly described in this book—and made a nifty twenty-seven thousand dollars personally. At the time, the Depression made a dime look like a manhole cover.

Benefiting from several years on the Hall of Fame's veterans committee with Lieb, I felt like a callow kid in my fifties when Fred told nifty stories about that trip on which he had future Hall of Famers Lou Gehrig, Frankie Frisch, Mickey Cochrane, Lefty Grove, Al Simmons, and Rabbit Maranville. For instance, Frisch was a close acquaintance when the Flash was a New York Giants infielder and Fred a baseball writer there. Lieb knew, too, that Frisch, a hero in his Redbirds book, was my boyhood idol and later a good friend and Cooperstown colleague. En route by train to San Francisco, where a Japanese luxury liner waited, Frisch needled catcher Cochrane, unhappy victim of Pepper Martin's steals, though the Wild Horse actually stole against great pitchers, Grove and George Earnshaw. Finally, Lieb begged Frisch to ease off, noting that Cochrane also just lost heavily in the stock-market crash. "Frank gave in," said Fred, "and the refreshing sea air helped calm Cochrane."

The Athletics were Lieb's boyhood favorites in Philadelphia, his hometown. Early, he fell in love with baseball, though he worked a few years as a junior railroad clerk. An early story written as a teenager for national *Baseball Magazine* got him his first job in New York with the *Press,* one of four papers for which he worked.

Covering the World Series his first year in New York in 1911, an early member of the Baseball Writers' Association of America, he ultimately carried the BBWAA's number one card. He covered every World Series for a half-century and more than eight thousand games. With his penchant for picking pennant and Series winners and writing personality pieces, as reflected in this and other books, Fred was ahead of his time when writing his dozen books, capped by one at age eighty-nine in 1977. The title told it all, including the old-timer's ability to gossip without malice—*Baseball As I Have Known It*.

Lieb and dear wife Mary Ann, whose death preceded his by a dozen years, acquired an interest in the occult, as evidenced in two books on metaphysics. Fred's favorite player was the captain of the Yankees, slugging first baseman Lou Gehrig, a tragic hero. The Liebs and Gehrigs were social friends. Lou's road roommate, Bill Dickey, and Fred were the only baseball men at the star's marriage to Eleanor Twitchell. That last spring, 1939, the Gehrigs were guests at the Liebs' St. Petersburg home. Eleanor urged Mary Lou to reach her Ouija board "entity," called "Marc Antony" by the Liebs. Would "it" have a message for Mrs. Gehrig? The Ouija spelled it out for Eleanor: "You soon will be called on to face the most difficult problem of your life." Within weeks came Gehrig's diagnosis of fatal amyotrophic lateral sclerosis, a nerve degenerative illness shortened in name to ALS and best known as "Lou Gehrig disease."

Fred Lieb was an honorary pallbearer when Babe Ruth died six years after the guy Babe called "Buster." The man who wrote about both of baseball's great stars had been an honorary pallbearer for Gehrig, too.

Bob Broeg
April 2000

PREFACE

IN THE NINETIES—and they weren't gay for St. Louis baseball lovers, and in the early years of this century, the river town on the Big Muddy was represented by a ball club in the National League, but that's all it was—a ball club. Its role was to play out the schedule, while more opulent teams fattened on their visits to St. Louis. In a baseball sense, the town took a brutal beating; there was one dreary spell of fifteen years in which the Cardinals once rose as high as fourth. Why, when the mite, Miller Huggins, lifted the club as high as third place in 1914, it was a miracle. Unlike New York and Chicago, St. Louis then didn't think in terms of pennants; all the city asked was an occasional spot in the first division.

The late John McGraw, who spent one season of his tempestuous career as a Cardinal, once let fall this pearl of wisdom: "A St. Louis ball club, because of the city's summer climate wearing down the players, 'must be 25 per cent stronger than any other major league club to win." McGraw was a very wise man in baseball; maybe he had something, or they just had an awfully hot summer when he played in St. Louis in 1900. But old timers, who lived in memories—or those who listened at their grandpappy's knees, knew there once was a St. Louis ball club—Chris Von Der Ahe's and Comiskey's Browns, who had won four successive pennants in 1885-6-7-8 in the old American Association, the National League's major rival of that day. If those old Browns did it, there was hope it could happen again.

It did happen! A quarter of a century ago, two bright fellows as different as night is from day—Branch Rickey and Sam Breadon, came into the club and completely revolutionized the picture. Rickey, a genius for organization, who severed his Cardinal connections in October, 1942, devised a new system whereby a poor club could compete with its richer rivals, and Breadon brought the acumen of a successful automobile business into a baseball office.

Instead of the Cardinals being one of the poor pennantless waifs of baseball—a Patsy for all to kick around, they now are the top club of their League. In the National League for years, if McGraw's Giants didn't win, they were the team to beat. And now, despite McGraw's ideas on the enervating effects of St. Louis' summers on its ball players, the Cardinals are the club which wins the pennants, or the team the other seven managers must figure how to subdue. Since 1926, St. Louis' famous Redbirds have won seven league championships, and four of the six World's Championship buntings won by the National League during that time have fluttered from the Cardinals' center field flagpole at Sportsmans Park. And Cardinals Rogers Hornsby, Frankie Frisch, Pepper Martin, Dizzy Dean, Ducky Medwick, Mort Cooper, Terry Moore and Stan Musial have written sprightly chapters in the nation's sport annals.

However, even in their most dire days, the Cardinals were an interesting, colorful crew. Certainly no tailender in baseball's history ever kicked up the commotion of Chris Von Der Ahe's team after it was taken into the National League. In St. Louis baseball, things just always happened.

In writing this story of the Cardinals, dating back to 1876, when St. Louis first was represented in the National League, I wish to give thanks to J. G. Taylor Spink, publisher of *The Sporting News,* for his kind permission to use *The Sporting News* files, going back to 1886, and that newspaper's valuable clippings. Also to Sam Breadon and Branch Rickey, the main characters in this powerful baseball drama, and to Bob Connery, former scout of the club, the man who discovered Hornsby, and Miller Huggins' most intimate associate in the five years the midget manager held the reins.

For old-time St. Louis baseball, I wish to thank Edwin J. Rickart, also his son, Paul Rickart of *The Sporting News.* I also acknowledge the kind assistance of such St. Louis sports editors and baseball writers as Sid Keener of the *Times-Star,* Ed Wray and Roy Stockton of the *Post-Dispatch,* Martin Haley of the *Globe-Democrat* and Ellis Veach of the East St. Louis, Ill. *Journal,* also of Dr. Robert F. Hyland, club physician to both St. Louis clubs; John A. Heydler, former president of the National League; Bill DeWitt, General Manager of the Browns—a former Cardinal official; Scout Pat Monahan of the Redbirds, and Arthur Feltzner, of the St. Louis club's farm organization.

BILLY SOUTHWORTH

THE ST. LOUIS CARDINALS

I ⊜ A CHARTER MEMBER

THAT COLORFUL, picturesque word, Cardinals, so typical of the modern flamboyant Redbirds, the National League championship club which won 211 league games in 1942 and 1943, goes back only to 1899, when Willie McHale, then a cub St. Louis baseball writer, suggested it in his column in the old *St. Louis Republic*. St. Louis National League clubs then were the Browns, as are the city's American Leaguers of today, and Willie thought some of the brownish taste of years of second division baseball might disappear with a new, more vivid nickname. Frank DeHaas Robison, the St. Louis clubowner at the turn of the century, figured: "What can I lose?" and the team has been the Cardinals, or Redbirds, ever since.

However, St. Louis representation in the National League goes all the way back to 1876, the nation's centennial and the year the old National was born. In fact, it was a St. Louis jurist with a baseball bent, Judge Orrick C. Bishop, who drew up the young league's first constitution and wrote the first player contract. With a few changes here and there, that early constitution and style of player contract remain in force today. Though a charter member, St. Louis' sojourn in the league has not been continuous. There were two breaks; from 1878 to 1884 and 1887 to 1891.

While the Breadon-owned Cardinals of this century didn't move to their present location at Grand Avenue and Dodier Street until 1920, when they became tenants of Phil Ball, then the owner of the St. Louis American League club (both clubs now rent the grounds from the Phil Ball estate), that first St. Louis National League club of 1876 played on the same field on which Terry Moore, Stan Musial, Whitey Kurowski, Marty Marion and Mort Cooper romped and did their stuff the last few years.

While St. Louis fans frequently have held their fingers to their noses as they beheld some of the teams which followed, they had no need to apologize for their first National League club. It won 45 games and lost 19 in a 64-game schedule. There was only one better team in all the land, Al Spalding's Chicago White Stockings. The Chicagoans rolled up a percentage of .788 against .703 for the

St. Louis Nationals, called the Browns. It was to be exactly 50 years later, when Rogers Hornsby's inspired club crashed through to a sensational pennant, before another St. Louis National League club would finish that high.

No 25-player St. Louis roster, with an additional 15 rookies, was mailed to big league reporters of 1876—a pre-World War II procedure, by the early secretary of St. Louis' first National League entry. Most of the players had come to St. Louis the year before, when a group of Mound City sportsmen, headed by John R. Lucas, put the Browns in the National Association, an early quasi-major of which the present National League is the offshoot. As players went in the 70s, there was some pretty smart talent on the 1876 St. Louis aggregation. George Washington Bradley and Joe Blong did the pitching, and John Clapp and Tom Miller, known as "Little" Miller, caught their deliveries bare-handed from the old catching position some distance behind the home plate.

The St. Louis infield was made up of Herman Dehlman, first base; Mike McGeary, second base; Joe Battin, third base; and Dickie Pearce and Denny Mack, shortstop. Edgar Cuthbert played left field; Lipman Pike center field and Joe Blong right field, when he wasn't pitching. In those days the fifth wheel of a ball club was stuck in right field. John Lucas was president of the club and Mason Graffan was manager, though Captain Dehlman directed the Browns on the field.

Bradley was one of the early pitching wizards of the game, and tossed the first no-hitter into the National League records, throwing back Hartford (yes, they were once in the league) without a hit on July 15, 1876. Bradley liked to have "Little" Miller work with him as his battery partner. Bradley, Al Spalding of Chicago, later the big sporting goods manufacturer, and Bobby Mathews of the New York Mutuals were considered the "Big Pitching Three" of the first National League season.

Lip Pike was one of the early fence-busters of baseball, while Cuthbert, along with Al Spink, an early St. Louis sports writer, were the chaps who later introduced Chris Von Der Ahe, Der Poss Bresident, to St. Louis baseball. Joe Blong, the alternate pitcher, probably was ahead of his time. Whenever a 1944 baseball writer speaks of a hypothetical pitcher, he always is Joe Blotz—perhaps a lineal descendant of Joe Blong.

4

The National League cut down to six clubs in 1877, and the St. Louis club didn't do itself or its fans much good, slipping to fourth with a .467 percentage. John R. Lucas, the president, also took over the management. Dehlman was reduced to substitute roles, as Arthur Croft took over first base, while Jack Remsen, who had played with the famous Atlantics of Brooklyn, and Mike Dorgan of the Syracuse Stars were outfield acquisitions.

No-Hit Bradley moved to Chicago to help Al Spalding on the White Stocking staff, and Fred "Tricky" Nichols, a former New Haven star, took his place as No. 1 St. Louis boxman. Before the 1877 St. Louis National League season got under way, the Browns played a 15-inning 0-0 tie on May 1 with the Syracuse Stars, a strong independent team, which for days was the talk of the town. Tricky Nichols was such a trickster that day that the Stars made only two hits; St. Louis garnered only eight off McCormack, the Syracuse pitcher.

Lucas and his fellow St. Louis boosters weren't satisfied with their 1877 showing and for the 1878 season signed the cream of the second-place Louisville club of the preceding campaign, Captain and Shortstop Charley Snyder, Pitcher W. H. Craver, Third Baseman James A. Devlin, Pitcher A. H. Nichols and Left Fielder G. W. Hall; also Shortstop Johnny Peters of the Chicago club. Pennant hopes were running high for 1878, when the roof fell in on the St. Louis baseball structure. Four of the Louisville contingent—Craver, Devlin, Nichols and Hall, were accused of throwing games in 1877 and were permanently barred from professional baseball in the first of the two great scandals to rock the game, the second being the Black Sox World's Series scandal of 1919.

What stung Lucas and his fellow St. Louis organizers to the quick were intimations that they had knowledge of the nasty business when they acquired the players and were about to let them practice their wiles on unsuspecting St. Louis fans. In a huff, John Lucas and his associates resigned from the league, ending the first chapter of St. Louis in the National League.

2

St. Louis was without league baseball for several years, but in 1882, the original American Association, then a major league, put a club in St. Louis. Chris Von Der Ahe, one of the legendary characters of the game, was the backer, assisted by Al Spink, who with his brother, Charles, founded *Sporting News,* the baseball bible, in 1886. Al was uncle to Mr. Baseball of today, the high-powered J. G. Taylor Spink, present publisher of *Sporting News.* Von Der Ahe took over the name of the original St. Louis National League club, the Browns, and at Al Spink's suggestion engaged Charley Comiskey, a former Chicago sand-lotter, as first baseman and playing manager. Comiskey later organized and owned the Chicago White Sox of the American League and was the founder of the Chicago baseball fortune. Commy, as he was affectionately called, was the pioneer of the great first basemen, the first player in that position to play away from his bag. Up to Comiskey's time, the first basemen were heavy-buttocked fellows, who packed a healthy wallop at the plate, but who played their position with their left foot glued to the bag—even when no runner was on base.

Comiskey's Browns became the most famous club in the country, winning their association pennants four successive years, 1885, 1886, 1887 and 1888. In World's Series with the National League Champions, they won one series and tied another (it broke up in a fight) with Anson's great Chicago White Stockings, and lost to the Detroits of 1887 and Jim Mutrie's "We are the People" Giants of 1888.

The Browns of the American Association also played at Grand Avenue and Dodier, the site of St. Louis' present-day Sportsmans Park. Originally baseball was only a side issue with Chris, a means of getting customers to his beer gardens and amusements, especially on Sunday, for St. Louis, with its population made up largely of German, Irish and early French, always was a friendly open town, and had Sunday baseball when that still was considered wicked and sinful by more sedate cities. The Browns' ball games were played between Von Der Ahe's beer tables. St. Louisans of the eighties said rather truthfully: "The Browns were built around a keg of beer and a barrel of pretzels." Well, between selling a scuttle of suds for a nickel and a baseball admission ticket for two bits, Chris did a thriving business, and eventually "paseball" became his first enterprise.

Von Der Ahe was one of those characters who could have existed only in St. Louis of the eighties and nineties. Chris gets quite a little attention here, as he later became the president and owner of the St. Louis National League club and almost wrecked it. He was pudgy and had a nose on which Jimmy Durante and W. C. Fields would have looked with envy; as Chris seldom passed when drinks were on the house his proboscis usually was lit up like a red bulb on a Christmas tree. While he eventually lost his ball club, and operated a small frowsy saloon in his later years, in the eighties he was one of St. Louis' best known citizens. He wore a stove pipe hat, gaudy waistcoats and in his flush days almost as many diamonds as Jim Brady, who dazzled New York around the same time.

Where other clubs went to the ball park in prison van-like buses, Chris made a parade of his team's trip from hotel to the ball grounds. Nothing less than open barouches, with St. Louis Brown blankets on the horses, were good enough for Comiskey and his "poys." Chris was a lavish entertainer, and every night was party night. Like most of St. Louis' sporting fraternity, he loved the ladies, and never was squeamish about their social standards. He had a well-trained horse who knew the way home in the early hours of the morning without the benefit of "Whoas," "Ghees" and "Giddy-upps." One morning faithful Dobbin drew the buggy to the curb of Chris's house. He was asleep on one side of the front seat, as was his lady friend on the other, while Dobbin, having done his job, vainly tried to drown out Chris's snores with his impatient neighs. An old *Sporting News* cartoon shows Von Der Ahe with a buxom blonde on one knee and a shapely brunette on the other.

3

While the Browns flourished, St. Louis had another brief spell of National League baseball. In 1884, a league, terming itself the Union Association, invaded the field in various National League and American Association cities. Its platform was that the reserve clause, put into the contracts by the St. Louisan, Judge Orrick Bishop, was undemocratic, unAmerican and made serfs of the ballplayers. And, hadn't Lincoln freed the slaves only two decades before?

The backer of the club in St. Louis was Henry V. Lucas, a wealthy realtor and club man and nephew of John R. Lucas, the first

St. Louis National League president. The Lucases came of a prominent, well-to-do St. Louis family; one of the downtown streets is named after an earlier Lucas. Henry Lucas called his team the Maroons, and they played at Jefferson and Cass Avenues, in the heart of the Kerry Patch, once a famous hotbed for St. Louis home-grown ballplayers. Under the management of Arthur Irwin, a crack early shortstop, the Maroons won the Union Association's only pennant hands down, as franchises were shifted during the season to such smaller cities as Wilmington, Del., Altoona, Pa., and St. Paul.

The Union Association's brief career aroused considerable bitterness. Not respecting the reserve clause, the league had raided freely in the two established leagues and lured some good players. But when it blew up after one season, animosities soon were forgotten, and the National League voted a franchise to Henry Lucas and his pennant-winning Maroons. Henry managed his own club, and moved it to Vandeventer and Natural Bridge Avenues, which also became the home of later-day Cardinals.

The two seasons the Maroons were in the National League, 1885 and 1886, were an evil augury of the many lean Cardinal years before the sun was to shine through the clouds years later during the Breadon-Rickey reign of plenty. In 1885, Lucas's team won only 36 games, and the Union Association champs of '84 finished behind the 8-ball in the National League cellar. It was the first of many St. Louis tailenders. Lucas won seven more games in 1886, and boosted the club to sixth, but it was rough and hard going.

Von Der Ahe's Browns won the first two of their string of pennants in those two years and the city went into the seventh baseball heaven when Comiskey's club defeated Anson's Chicagos in the 1886 World's Series, four games to two. The city was Brown-conscious; Von Der Ahe, Comiskey and the Browns were kings and could do no wrong; the Maroons were poor baseball relatives who ate scraps at the second table. Henry Lucas took a bad financial licking. He sold the St. Louis franchise to John T. Brush of the When Department Store of Indianapolis, and John moved the club to the Hoosier capital. Brush later moved up the baseball ladder, buying bigger and better clubs, as his trail led to Cincinnati and New York. He was the wealthy and influential owner of the Giants when he died in 1912.

However, Lucas had several pretty fair ballplayers on his team, including Fred Dunlop, a second baseman, and Jack Glasscock, one of the early shortstop greats and later a National League batting champion in New York. Stage and radio funster Phil Baker may be amused to know the Maroons had a catcher by that name, and in 1886, Sam Crane, who for many years wrote baseball for the *New York Journal*, was the Maroon second baseman.

II ⊝ DER POSS BRESIDENT

I

S T. LOUIS was back in the National League in 1892, and has been represented in the oldest major ever since, but the next seven years in the old 12-club National League were the darkest, dankest and direst in St. Louis baseball history. In those seven years the St. Louis club—they still were the Browns—dug through the league cellar into the subcellar and then excavated even below that level. In the seven lean years, St. Louis had two twelfth-place clubs, three elevenths, one tenth, and once rose as high as ninth. It was difficult to stay under the misfit teams which represented Washington and Louisville, but bad as they were, the Brown National Leaguers succeeded in being just a little worse.

But, we've got to hark back to the previous decade. The present Cardinal club actually is the direct lineal offspring of the American Association Browns of the eighties, rather than of the St. Louis National League clubs of 1876-77 and 1885-86. While the National League and the old American Association usually respected each other's territory and players, there was little love between the two leagues. The animosity and bitter feeling was even more acute than that which frequently existed between the two majors, the National and American Leagues, of today.

In 1885, when the Browns played the Chicago White Stockings in the World's Series, two of the games were played in Cincinnati and Pittsburgh to spread around the interest. In the second game, played in Chicago, Comiskey took exception to an umpire's decision in the sixth inning and marched his club off the field. The game was forfeited to Chicago, and the series later was called off in an air of bitterness with each club having three victories. The incident only heaped coals on the fires of animosity and ill will between the two circuits. Anson accused Comiskey of quitting in the series; the then not-so-Old Roman replied in kind; while Al Spalding, president of the Chicago club, vowed he never again would have anything to do with the Association, or any of its clubs, particularly Von Der Ahe and Comiskey.

However, a year later—1886, the same clubs won again in their respective leagues. Von Der Ahe, who didn't let grudges interfere with business, sent Comiskey to Chicago to see Spalding and Anson and to challenge them to a World's Series for the baseball championship. The Chicagoans were cool, and Anson snapped: "We will play you under only one condition, and that is winner take all, and by all, I mean every penny that is taken at the gate." Spalding and Anson thought that would dispose of the St. Louis managerial upstart, but to their surprise Comiskey accepted.

Commy then was afraid to break the news to Von Der Ahe; he knew Chris liked to see the money coming through the gate, and didn't know whether he would gamble on such high stakes. But Chris expressed his pleasure at the success of Comiskey's mission. "Sure, we will take them up and teach those fellars a lesson. No club is goot enough to beat the Browns."

No club was goot enough that year. The Browns won the series, four games to two, on one of the great plays of the eighties, always referred to later by Comiskey as "Curt Welch's $15,000 slide." With the Browns leading three games to two, the score was 3-3 in the ninth inning of the sixth game, with the famous White Stocking battery, John Clarkson and King Kelly, working for Anson. Welch was taking quite a lead off third, and Kelly signaled for a high pitch—out of the reach of Bushong, the St. Louis batsman. However, Curt came in with the pitch and when the great Kelly slightly juggled the ball, Welch slid home in safety with the run which made the Browns World's Champions.

The entire gate of the series was far below that of the first game of a present-day World's Series. However, after expenses, including champagne for everyone after it was over, Von Der Ahe had some $15,000 left. He shared it liberally with his players. The two clubs also had put up $500 to wager on themselves; Von Der Ahe had offered to bet Spalding another $10,000, which the Chicagoan ig, nored. Chris, who had his generous side, even helped out quite a few of the Chicago players who went broke backing the White Stockings with side bets.

The Browns continued to win pennants, and despite his liberal spending—and squandering, Von Der Ahe made lots of money in baseball and beer. Starting in with a little German grocery store at Spring and Sullivan Streets, just north of the present Sportsmans Park, Von Der Ahe built rows of houses, with space for saloons on the corners. His own saloon and expanded grocery business also showed substantial profits. After each game, Chris's grocery wagon backed up to the ball park and hauled the dollars to the bank. He went deeply into politics and was reputed to be a millionaire.

He was well pleased with himself, frequently patted himself on the back and once told interviewers: "I am the smartest fellar in baseball." Once he even boasted: "I have the largest diamond in baseball," when Comiskey reminded him that all baseball diamonds were of the same size. "Vell, Charley, maybe I vas mistaken dis time, but I got de biggest infield, anyway." Some one sold him the idea that a great man like Chris Von Der Ahe should be preserved for posterity. He had a life-size statue of himself sculptured; later it was placed over his grave.

2

When the Chicago White Stockings sold the great Mike "King" Kelly, then baseball's most colorful star, to the Boston Nationals in the winter of 1886-87 for $10,000, Von Der Ahe was much impressed. In the following winter, Chicago sold the King's battery mate, John Clarkson to Boston for another $10,000, and that gave Chris ideas. Why not do the same; sell some of the good players, pay less salaries, and have Comiskey develop some new ones. Charley could do it. Without consulting Commy, he sold Pitchers Dave Foutz and Bobby Carruthers and Catcher Doc Bushong to Brooklyn for $10,000 and Outfielder Curt Welch and Shortstop Gleason to the Philadelphia Athletics for $5,000. Comiskey saw red when he heard of it; he threatened to resign, but his Brown salary was $8,000, a princely sum in the eighties, and he reconsidered.

St. Louis fans also were wild with rage; the indignation spreading to nearby cities and towns, where the menfolk had been loyal supporters of the Browns. It was much like the turmoil thirty-nine years later, when Sam Breadon, the present Cardinal owner, outraged St. Louis fans by trading Rogers Hornsby, his World's Championship manager of 1926, to New York for Frankie Frisch. There was talk of boycotting Chris's club, and many predicted a last-place finish for the 1888 Browns. But Comiskey had amazing luck with sand-lotters and minor league replacements. Silver King, Chamberlain and Devlin turned into winning pitchers; Big Milligan took Bushong's place behind the plate; a youngster, Shorty Fuller, filled the shortstop gap, and Tommy McCarthy was so sensational in center field that he made the fans forget Welch of the $15,000 slide. And, to the surprise, not only of St. Louis but the entire nation, the Browns won another pennant, making it four straight. It would be thirty-eight years before pennant lightning again would strike in St. Louis!

But Von Der Ahe was supremely happy. His club had lost the World's Series to the New York Giants; a predecessor to the four St. Louis (Cardinal)—New York (Yankee) Series of present day baseball. It was a well-attended, profitable series, and if the Browns lost, they made a good showing, winning four games to New York's six. Even in defeat, Chris rubbed his hands with glee. "They talked of poycotting my team," he laughed. "I made more money than with my old wonder poys. I guess I am a pretty smart fellar."

Chris engaged a special train to take the team and loyal St. Louis fans to New York, Der Poss Bresident paying all expenses, even hotel bills. He had Al Spink put big streamers from the windows of the Special, reading: "St. Louis Browns; Four Time Pennant Winners."

But, he wasn't so smart a fellar. Though he won the 1888 pennant and his teams were in the race the next three seasons, his downfall really started with the sale of his stars to Brooklyn and the Athletics the winter before, for from that time things never again were quite the same.

3

The Browns finished a close second in 1889, the new Brooklyn club, built around Carruthers, Foutz and Bushong winning the championship. Then came a year, 1890, which wrecked many early baseball fortunes. The crack players of the National League and American Association, claiming they were tired of grasping owners getting all the money in baseball, formed an association called the Players' Brotherhood, which procured backers for their own circuit, the Players League. The great bulk of stars and top ranking players went to the new league, feeling they were the drawing cards and the fans would support them against their old greedy bosses. They were to divide the profits equally with the backers.

Even such later-day wise men as Connie Mack and John K. Tener, later Governor of Pennsylvania and president of the National League, fell for it. Tener, who had been a great pitcher for Anson in Chicago, jumped to the Pittsburgh Players League team and was treasurer of the Brotherhood. The new league put clubs in New York, Brooklyn, Philadelphia, Boston, Buffalo, Chicago, Pittsburgh and Cleveland. Von Der Ahe was spared Brotherhood competition in St. Louis, but his crack manager, Comiskey, went over to the Players League as manager of the Chicago club. After one season, the backers of the new league went broke, and the club owners of the established leagues were only one jump behind. Many fans became disgusted, lost their regard and esteem for big-named players, and there was such general ennui after the 1890 World's Series ran into some bad weather, it was called off because of lack of interest, with each contending club, the Brooklyn Nationals and Louisville A. A. Colonels, having won three games, a seventh resulting in a tie.

The Players League lasted only one season, and in 1891 the players, hats in hand, were glad to return to their former employers. Comiskey returned to the management of the Browns, but his relationship with Von Der Ahe was not the same. The game had been rocked to its very foundations, and it was some time before baseball regained its former hold on the American public. The season of 1891 was a lean one, especially for Chris's League—the battered American Association.

With the Players League war out of the way, the two leagues again got to bickering and fighting among themselves. Two Association stars, Louis Bierbauer and Harry Stovey, had jumped from the Athletics to the Brooklyn Players League club. Jumping players were ordered back to their former clubs, but through an oversight the American Association had neglected to place Bierbauer and

Stovey on their reserve list; the Pittsburgh Nationals signed the former and the Boston club the latter. The American Association charged the conduct of the Pittsburgh club was "piratical," and ever since the Pennsylvania team has been known as the Pirates. A board of arbitration awarded the disputed players to Pittsburgh and Boston, whereupon the Association withdrew from the National Agreement, and another baseball war was on.

The upshot of the matter was that after a season of scrapping, player-snatching and name-calling, the two leagues agreed to merge into one 12-club organization. At a special meeting in Indianapolis in December, 1891, the National League purchased the Association clubs in Chicago, Boston, Columbus, Milwaukee and Washington for $135,000. The Washington franchise was awarded to George Wagner of Philadelphia, and the St. Louis, Baltimore and Louisville Association clubs were admitted to the National League.

It was in this manner that Chris Von Der Ahe and the Browns came into the National League, an unhappy experience for both Chris and the League.

III ☻ THE NATIONAL
LEAGUE BROWNS

I

V ON DER AHE'S FIRST ACT was to move his newly acquired National franchise to the field used by Henry Lucas's St. Louis National League Maroons of 1885-86 at Vandeventer and Natural Bridge Avenues. He still called it Sportsmans Park; later under the name of League Park and Robison Field, it was to become the home of the St. Louis Nationals until 1920, when Sam Breadon moved the present-day Cardinals back to modern Sportsmans Park, the site of Chris's American Association baseball beer stube of the eighties. Judge Landis never would have approved Vondy's move to Natural Bridge. The ball park was located right across the street from the Fair Grounds race track, and the ineptitude of later day St. Louis players frequently was due to the fact that their thoughts were on five bucks riding on some nag across the street rather than the baseball business on hand.

After winning their four straight pennants, the Association Browns continued to be strong contenders and made a little money for Chris. The 1889 club finished a good second, only a game and a half behind Brooklyn; in 1890 the Browns dropped to third, but in 1891, the team was a strong runner-up to Boston. However, before the merger, raids and reprisals had sent the best of Von Der Ahe's players to other clubs, and Chris's worst break came when his manager, Charley Comiskey, signed to manage the Cincinnati Reds. It was in Cincinnati that Commy became intimate with a young baseball writer, Ban Johnson, and the two later organized the American League. But Commy's shift to the Reds took away Chris's right arm; the able energetic Chicagoan, one of baseball's really great men, might have brought order out of his mess; without Commy everything was chaos. The man who ran a corner grocery store and beer garden even tried to run his National League club himself. The 1892 outcome need not have occasioned any surprise; it was almost a complete failure as the St. Louis Nationals came home a poor also ran, in the eleventh slot. Only one club, Baltimore, finished lower than the Browns' record of 56 victories, 94 defeats, and a percentage of .373.

The club did have several pretty good players, including the Pretzel Battery, Theodore Breitenstein and Heinie Peitz—both very popular with St. Louis fans, especially those of Germanic origin. Breitenstein, a native St. Louisan, was a left hander, and they called him The Breitenstein. He pitched in organized baseball for twenty-eight years. Bill "Kid" Gleason, the later-day White Sox manager, Frank Dwyer, Jimmy Galvin and Charley Getzein, formerly a great pitcher in Detroit, were other members of the staff.

Perry Werden at first base, Charley "Jack" Crooks at second, George Pinckney at third, and Jack Glasscock at shortstop, made a pretty fair infield. Glasscock was the same player who had been with Henry Lucas's St. Louis Maroons. Bob Carruthers, the former pitcher, Cliff Carroll, Walter "Steve" Brodie and a host of others played the outfield. Brodie was one of the sluggers of his day, and two years later, Von Der Ahe heaped more coals of fire on his battered head by selling Steve for $1,000 to Baltimore, where he became center fielder of Ned Hanlon's famous Oriole champions of 1894, '95 and '96.

Brodie could hit the ball a terrific wallop, but he wasn't so quick on the mental trigger. When he was with Baltimore, those fast Irish thinkers, John McGraw, Hughie Jennings, and Joe Kelley induced the groundkeeper to let the grass grow long in the outfield, especially in left field and left center. The trick was to plant balls in the thick grass, field planted balls, and let long balls hit by the opposition disappear in the thick underbrush. One afternoon when the Browns were playing in Baltimore, Tommy Dowd hit a sharp drive to left center. Kelley cut across the path of the ball, apparently scooped it up, threw the ball to McGraw, who nailed Joe Quinn going into third base. The single umpire was just about to call the runner out, when Brodie, who had pursued the real ball, threw it in from deep left center, and gave away another of Baltimore's famous inside plays.

In 1894, Bill Watkins ran the St. Louis Nationals, and achieved a moral victory. This time two clubs, Louisville and Washington, finished below the Browns, who advanced to tenth place. In 1894, under the leadership of George "Calliope" Miller, a rollicking catcher, and A. C. Buckenberger, St. Louis reached its peak in the 12-club National League, coming home ninth, ahead of Cincinnati, Washington and Louisville.

2

The season of 1895 was Chris's year of years, when he engaged no less than six managers. It wasn't baseball; it was *opera bouffe*. The procession started with Joe Quinn, formerly a great second baseman, and even then running an undertaking business on the side. Joe still is alive, but long since moved his parlors from the Kerry Patch to more pretentious Union Boulevard. But, in 1895, Vondy soon decided Joe's side line was too suggestive of the position of the Browns, and turned the job over to Roger Connor, formerly a slugging first baseman under Jim Mutrie of the Giants but by this time pretty well washed up. Next came Arlie Latham, the third baseman of Comiskey's champion Browns and one of the first of the baseball clowns. Arlie also still did a little third basing. To this day ball players speak of giving a hot grounder "the Arlie

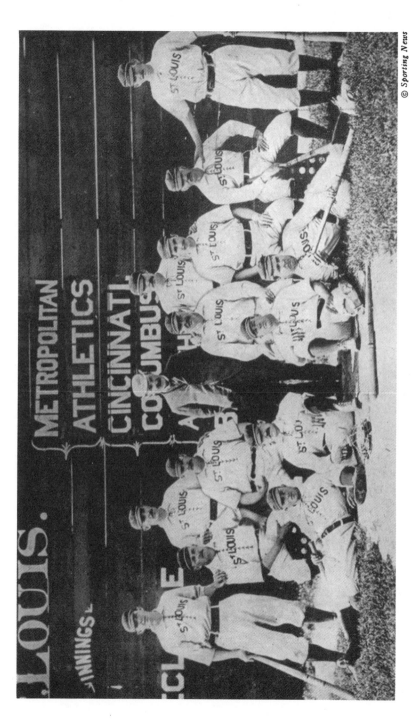

CHRIS VON DER AHE AND HIS BROWN VON DER BOYS

Charles Comiskey, Manager, with bat, extreme left.

"BUGS" RAYMOND
Managers' problem child.

ROGER BRESNAHAN
The Duke of Tralee.

Latham," which means letting the hard ones go by after a phantom try. Perhaps that was the Arlie of 1895.

Latham was quite a practical joker and he wasn't above playing his jokes on Der Poss Bresident, himself. One day Von Der Ahe heard a commotion in his outer office, and some one was speaking derogatory of the boss. Dashing to the door, Chris yelled: "Dot remark will cost you $50, Latams." Other players present hastened to explain that Arlie wasn't there.

"Vell, where the devil is he?" asked Chris. "If he isn't dhere, he should be dhere. So, he is up to one of his chokes, and the $50 fine stands anyway."

When Arlie heard of it, he rushed to the office to remonstrate; the argument grew so hot that Latham blurted out something else Chris didn't like, and der poss said: "Latams, dhat will cost you another $50."

"Look here, Boss," said Arlie, "that $50 wipes out the other fine. Now, if you give me $50 in cash that will make us all even, and there will be no hard feeling."

"Latams, you will drive me crazy yet," protested Chris.

In his younger days with the American Association Browns, Arlie was one of the great base-runners of baseball. The Chicago White Stockings had a kid outfielder named Billy Sunday who, the Windy City players insisted, could pick 'em up and lay 'em down faster than Arlie. With both clubs backing their speed-boys to the limit, the pair put on a foot-race on a Sunday morning at Lucas Park, Vandeventer and Case Avenues. Billy Sunday ran away from Arlie and the St. Louis players were broke until their next payday. Sunday, of course, became the famous evangelist; Arlie Latham at eighty-three still is in baseball as special cop in the Yankee Stadium press box in New York.

Latams, and his chokes, lasted only a few weeks in the Brown pilot's seat, and Monte Cross, later Connie Mack's shortstop on his early American League Athletic champions, was No. 4 on the 1895 list, followed by Harry Diddlebock, a former sports editor of the Philadelphia *Inquirer* and one of Chris's eastern drinking companions. Von Der Ahe's club treasurer and inside man was Stewart B. Muckenfuss, and St. Louis writers of the period had a lot of fun in describing a double play of Diddlebock, Muckenfuss to Von Der Ahe.

The wind-up man in the managerial sextet was Tommy Dowd, the St. Louis center fielder, one of Holy Cross's early big leaguers, a player of some ability and somewhat of a playboy after dark. Yet, with each managerial change Von Der Ahe had remained hopeful his new appointee would be another Charley Comiskey. Under their six leaders of 1895, the Browns finished a snappy eleventh with a percentage of .298. Believe it or not, a Louisville club, owned by Barney Dreyfuss, later head man in Pittsburgh, managed to do worse—.267.

3

Baseball wasn't drawing National League customers to Sportsmans Park, so Von Der Ahe tried something else. Lieutenant Colonel Larry MacPhail, former Cincinnati and Brooklyn impresario, who introduced to the majors night ball, a yellow ball, fireworks, college bands, girl canaries, and a pipe organ, was a conservative compared to the mustachioed St. Louis German of the middle nineties. Chris put a chute-the-chutes in center field, night horse racing, boating, an all-girl cornet band, a wild west show and boxing. He called it "Coney Island of the West." A streetcar company, which had run a streetcar line to his Natural Bridge ball park, disappointed with the lean baseball fares, backed Chris in his extra activities.

The first year his Coney Island of the West was in operation, 1896, the Great Commoner, William Jennings Bryan, ran for the Presidency on his 16 to 1 slogan. The St. Louis Democrats booked the Boy Orator of the Platte at Von Der Ahe's baseball orchard, despite its beery smell. When the crowd collected, Chris charged for reserved seats, much to the indignation of the campaign manager, who had paid the baseball-beer garden man a sizable fee. Chris explained: "I forgot to put in a charge for the Silver Cornet Band, and the reserved seats make up for it. And, with Mr. Bryan liking silver so much, he'll like my Silver Band."

The Silver Cornet Band was made up of two dozen glamor girls of the nineties. They were the grandmas of the girl orchestras of today, wearing long striped skirts, wide white sailor hats and leg-of-mutton sleeves. And they played all the hot tunes then in vogue.

Oh yes, there still was a St. Louis National League club. That year, Chris had only two managers, Tommy Dowd, who finished the

1895 season, and Hugh Nichol. Again the 1896 Browns finished eleventh, once more beating out Louisville, and the $7,500 Von Der Ahe obtained from Cincinnati for The Breitenstein helped pay for his $15,000 chute-the-chutes.

Billy Hallman, former Philly second baseman, was manager in 1897, and Hal Lanigan, then a young squirt of a baseball writer with the *St. Louis Globe Democrat,* tells this story. Bills piled up, and to save expenses Vondy was living above his office at the ball park. He had just fired Hallman, and called up Hal to give him the story of his new managerial appointee. "And, by golly, this time I've got a goot one, chust like Charley Comiskey," he telephoned.

Fenske, the faithful groundkeeper, was making Chris's bed as Hal entered the room. A tub of beer bottles on ice was standing nearby.

"Excuse me, Mr. Von Der Ahe," said Fenske. "I think I have a good idea."

"Vhat ees it, Herman?" Chris asked.

"Why have a manager at all? The season is nearly over, and we can't get out of last place by winning all our games. We can save the manager's salary. Those guys we had, all of them, were no good. We can't win games with a manager; maybe we can win more games without."

"Herman, dhat is a damn good idea," said Vondy.

4

However, in the next year—1898, and it was to be Chris's last in baseball, he had one more manager, the famous umpire and fight referee, Tim Hurst, one of the great umpires of his day, a legendary character in American sport, and a man who bubbled with color, Irish wit and vinegar. Vondy also made a change in the president's office. To combat his increasing unpopularity, Der Poss Bresident stepped aside and made his man Friday, Stewart Muckenfuss, president of the club.

Dozens of stories have been written about Tim Hurst, the new manager, and one classic is repeated every time umpires get together. Some of the umpires, Hank O'Day, Jack Sheridan and others, were bemoaning their lot. "Umpiring is an unhappy job," said dour Hank; "We have no friends; we are pariahs." After listening to the moaning, Tim broke in: "But you can't beat the hours, men; you can't beat the hours."

Hurst's coming aroused some enthusiasm among St. Louis' faithful and tormented fans, and Tim had succeeded in landing a few new players: Pitchers Willie Sudhoff, Peter Daniel, Jimmy Callahan; catchers Joe Sugden and John Clements, infielders George Decker, Jack Crooks, Lave Cross, and outfielder Jake Stenzel. Callahan later became a famous outfielder and playing manager of the later-day Chicago White Sox; Clements was one of the game's few lefthanded catchers, but was pretty well washed up after a long career with Philadelphia. The same held true of Stenzel, once a great base stealer in the old Association. And Tim was a forceful, aggressive character; he knew baseball—had something on the ball! Yes, maybe he might prove "that goot one like Comiskey," who would lead the St. Louis club out of the Wilderness of the Second Division into the Promised Land.

Tim led them through one of baseball's worst fires, which wrecked Sportsmans Park, and left one hundred persons burned and blistered. The Browns had opened at home with Anson's Chicago club, April 16, and Hurst's team lost to that wily Old Fox of Pop's staff, Clark Griffith, by a 2 to 1 score.

The second game of the series was played on Saturday, April 16, with some 4,000 persons in the stands. In the second inning, a fire started under the grandstand. The players could see the fire under the stands; they ceased play, and with the umpires, Hank O'Day and McDonald, shouted warnings to the crowd. Being accustomed to the rowdy baseball conduct of the 90's, the crowd thought a fight of drunken spectators had stopped the game, and there were cries from the grandstand: "Play ball," and "Throw the fighters out." Then laps of flame reached into the stands, and in the ensuing panic, many persons were trampled and burned.

It took several hours for city firemen, with their old horse-drawn apparatus, to extinguish the flames. The entire grandstand and left field bleachers were burned to charred embers. The club's offices and Von Der Ahe's saloon also went up in smoke. Ticket sellers got out only half of their cash before they had to retreat before the hot and angry flames. Chris lost most of his personal effects, including the proud trophies of his old championship Browns, and that night his friends thought the man would go mad.

Anson, the Chicago manager, wanted to transfer the Sunday game to Chicago, but Hurst refused. All that night Hurst and his players helped workmen clear the field of burned timber and other debris. Building inspectors and fire marshals were more lenient, and Muckenfuss made prompt arrangements to put up 4,000 circus seats for the Sunday game. Drawn by curiosity and to see the wreck of Chris's place, a 7,000 crowd came out, 3,000 of them massed behind outfield ropes, and they saw the Browns, wearied by their arduous night's work, lose to Chicago by a score of 14 to 1.

Somehow that score was fitting for Chris Von Der Ahe's last season in the National League. It was the Spanish-American War year, and an off year in all baseball. It again was a season of frustration and disappointment in St. Louis. Many games were transferred to other cities while the stands were being rebuilt, and when the standing of the clubs was printed in early October the Browns again were at the foot of the 12-club ladder with the ignoble percentage of .260.

IV ⊗ THE SPIDERS COME TO TOWN

1

Not only did Chris Von Der Ahe exhaust the patience of his St. Louis public, but also of the National League. It had become fed up with his chute-the-chutes, girl silver trumpeters and Vondy's perpetual tailenders. It decided to take action after the 1898 season. Many lawsuits grew out of the April fire; St. Louis creditors besieged Von Der Ahe from every side, and with the strong support of the National League, they forced old Chris to the wall. His club was sold by court order, G. A. Gruner buying it in the east side of the old St. Louis courthouse for $33,000. Gruner quickly sold it at a $7,000 profit to Edward C. Becker, a St. Louis attorney, acting for the Robison brothers, Frank DeHaas and Matthew Stanley, owners of the Cleveland Spiders, and the National League.

The National League had decided on a sensational and interesting move, sensational especially to the famished and pennant-hungry St. Louis fans, the shift of Frank Robison and his colorful Spiders, the

Gas House Gang of the nineties—bag and baggage, from Cleveland to St. Louis. Frank DeHaas Robison had been a traction magnate in Fort Wayne, Ind. He and his brother also once had a controlling interest in the Cleveland traction field. Frank had plenty of money and was a free spender. During his more opulent days, he drew $100 cash each day and contrived to spend it before the sun arose the next morning.

His Cleveland Spiders, managed by Oliver Patrick Tebeau, had been a powerful aggressive club all through the nineties. Tebeau was a former sand-lotter from St. Louis' own tough Goose Hill district. His Spiders won no pennants, but they were always up there. When the National League played a split season in 1892, Cleveland won the first half, and then lost to Boston, winner of the second half in the play-offs. Twice the Spiders finished second to the great Baltimore Orioles, defeated them in one Temple Cup series, and lost in another. It was a rowdy ball club, even tougher and rougher than the Orioles, constantly fighting with umpires, rival players and spectators.

In 1896, the entire Cleveland club was arrested for precipitating a riot in Louisville, after the Spiders had quarreled with the umpires over a decision. The next day Captain Pat Tebeau, Jimmy McAleer, Jesse Burkett and Ed McLean were all fined in court and the National League fined Tebeau $200. He was to be suspended until he paid it, but Pat never paid. His boss, Frank Robison, as truculent as was Tebeau, got out an injunction restraining National League umpires from interfering with Tebeau playing first base. The old league backed down.

Robison had spent a lot of money giving Cleveland the best club he could put on the field. He felt that Cleveland, then still a moderately sized city on Lake Erie, hadn't appreciated his efforts or supported his club as well as the Spiders warranted. With the exception of Chicago, St. Louis was the nation's foremost city west of the Alleghanies, a wide open, sports-loving town. Back in the Association days, it had royally supported Von Der Ahe's Browns. It was an especially good Sunday town, and when Von Der Ahe's National League club had shown the slightest signs of arousing itself, the fans came out in droves. Often these St. Louis fans were crass and crude, careless, abusive and explosive in their language to the players on the field, but they were the breed which would take a fighting ball club like the transplanted Spiders to their hearts.

The Robisons still owned the franchise in Cleveland; Commissioner Judge Landis and present-day fans would view it as syndicate ball at its worst. They practically switched around the two teams, sending Lave Cross, Joe Sugden, Joe Quinn, Tommy Dowd and others of the 1898 Browns to Cleveland, where they became the most dejected tailender of major league history, winning only 20 games and losing 134 for an 1899 percentage of .130.

On the other hand, Pat Tebeau's 1898 Cleveland team was moved practically intact to St. Louis. The immortal Cy Young headed the pitching staff; he had won 30 or more victories in three seasons for Cleveland and was to close his memorable major league career twelve years later with the majestic total of 511 victories. Other pitchers brought from Cleveland were the big righthander, Jack Powell; Frank Wilson and George Cuppy. Rowdy Jack O'Connor, from the same Goose Hill section as Tebeau; Lou Criger, Young's favorite battery mate; and Ossie Schreckenghost, later Rube Waddell's colorful backstop in Philadelphia, came along as catchers. Tebeau, Clarence "Cupid" Childs, Ed McLean and Rhody Wallace were the new St. Louis infield, and Jesse Burkett, Emmett Heidrick and Harry Blake made up a slashing, strong-fielding outfield.

Later in the season, Lave Cross, who managed Cleveland for Robison in the first half of the season, was brought back to St. Louis, while among the interesting youngsters reared by Tebeau that year were a wild young pitcher, Mike Donlin, and a lively infield colt, Freddy Parent. Donlin, a daredevil spirit, was wild in more ways than his control; any minute he was ready for a fight on or off the field. After the turn of the century, he became a favorite at New York's Polo Grounds, where as Turkey Mike he strutted in the Giant outfield and was McGraw's hardest hitter on his New York champions of 1904 and 1905. Parent, too, did well later on, playing shortstop for the Red Sox American League champions of 1903 and 1904.

2

St. Louis fans were in the seventh heaven. At last, the Mound City again was to have a ball team worthy of the city and its traditions. Every one was pleased but Von Der Ahe and Muckenfuss, who claimed the National League had stolen their ball club. Muckenfuss wrote stinging letters to the league, and Vondy filed a $50,000 damage suit against Becker and Frank Robison. And the first time Pittsburgh came to town, he brought action against Frank Balliet, the Pirate secretary, for $25,000. He intended to collect $25,000 from each of the other eleven National League clubs, who were part of what he termed the conspiracy to steal his club.

At the start, Ed Becker, because of his local connections, was spokesman for Robison, and Ed and Von Der Ahe proceeded to get into a hot newspaper feud. When the season opened Becker said that he "didn't want Von Der Ahe hanging around the park." That brought a stinging reply from Chris. Later Becker had a pass issued to Mr. and Mrs. Von Der Ahe. "I now want Chris to come out," he said. "He'll serve as a good advertisement for the St. Louis club —what it was before—and after." That was rubbing salt into Chris's open wounds.

In order to checkmate Von Der Ahe's legal moves, the National League expelled the old St. Louis club from the league, and issued the franchise to a newly formed corporation, the American Baseball and Exhibition Co., of which Frank DeHaas Robison was president. And here's one which will knock Blake Harper, the master showman of the present day Cardinals' concession business, for a loop. The new owners made an announcement: "No beer waiters, peanut venders or score card boys will annoy patrons during games. Boys may sell score cards only before games, none after."

An indication of how well St. Louis received its transplanted Spiders was the opening game of the 1899 season. It drew a crowd estimated at 18,000, the greatest which had seen a St. Louis ball game up to that time. It was a beastly day, too, and we read: "A cold windstorm handicapped the players and chilled the spectators." The old wooden stands at what still was called Sportsmans Park were filled to overflowing, and thousands ringed the field in the outfield. The Mayor, with the good old St. Louis name of Ziegenhein, threw out the first ball. Those fans were given quite a treat. The St. Louis club, the erstwhile Cleveland Spiders, defeated what was left of the 1898 Browns, now wearing Cleveland uniforms, by a score of 10 to 1. *Sporting News* called the Cleveland team "the Exiles." The great Cy Young held the Exiles to six hits, while St. Louis made 13 off Willie Sudhoff, the former Brown hurler. The

24

St. Louis batting order on that happy day was Burkett, left field; Childs, second base; McLean, shortstop; Wallace, third base; Heidrick, center field; Tebeau, first base; O'Connor, catcher; Blake, right field; Young, pitcher.

Playing for Cleveland were such St. Louis discards as Lave Cross, Dowd, Quinn and Sudhoff. "It surely is great trying to score a run on that infield," said Tommy Dowd, speaking of the new St. Louis inner works. "You get on first and Tebeau gives you the shoulder; you pass second and Childs gives you the hip. Shortstop Big Ed McLean tries to trip you if he thinks the umpire isn't looking and they've even got that mild Wallace giving you his spikes. And, at the plate, O'Connor will do anything short of murder to keep you from scoring."

Wallace and Heidrick were the two Beau Brummels of the team. When other players went around in caps and were careless about their clothes, Rhody and Emmett patronized the best tailors in St. Louis.

The town went wild about this new ball club and for weeks was absolutely pennant zany. The Robison-Tebeau team won its first seven games, and as late as May 14, the St. Louis letter in Philadelphia's *Sporting Life*, a baseball weekly of the time, carried the head: "Everybody Sure of Pennant." However, after holding the lead from April 15 to May 22, the St. Louis club lost the top perch to Brooklyn on the 23rd. After that the bubble burst, for a month later Tebeau's team was in sixth place; it even dropped as low as seventh in August, but staggered home fifth.

Of course, the umpires took an awful beating from the transplanted Spiders and their new St. Louis partisans. The week the club slipped out of the lead in May, the following appears in the St. Louis letter to *Sporting News:* "The umpiring was unsatisfactory at all stages. Burns' judgment on strikes and balls was frequently questioned and Smith's base decisions were excepted to so often that the spectators tired of his yellow work. The result was that the players kicked and the patrons guyed. Think of it requiring two hours and 15 minutes to play six innings in one of the games! What better proof of the inefficiency of the umpires!"

The "inefficiency" of Hank O'Day, as honest as the day is long and one of the really great National League umpires, was so marked one day that a bitter, resentful St. Louis crowd chased him into the clubhouse. One man in the crowd appeared with a rope, and it was necessary for the police with drawn revolvers to rescue O'Day from the angry fans.

3

It was during that first Robison season that the term, Cardinals, was born. As with most baseball nicknames, there is a little doubt as to the derivation of the new nickname for the St. Louis Nationals. The club still was the Browns in the St. Louis newspapers when the 1899 season started. Possibly wishing to get away from the Von Der Ahe influence, Robison changed the stockings and trimmings of the uniforms to a vivid red. For years his Cleveland team had been garbed in blue. A woman fan supposedly exclaimed: "Oh, what a lovely shade of cardinal!" However, Willie McHale, young writer on the *St. Louis Republic,* generally is credited with being the first to call the team "the Cardinals" in print. There already was a Cincinnati Red team in the league, and another red-stockinged outfit had to be something different. It was to become one of the most famous nicknames in all baseball—in all the world.

After the 1943 World's Series, in which the Yankees took the measure of the Cardinals, four games to one, the result of the series was broadcast to our armed forces in all corners of the world. The German radio picked up the broadcast and Goebels' propaganda department tried to put it to good use. "There are fresh atrocities in the United States," Goebels' mouthpiece said. "The Yankees, not content with their pious interference all over the world, now are beating up their own Cardinals in St. Louis."

Even so, the new name did not click immediately with all the fans; all through 1899, *Sporting News,* the baseball bible, referred to the St. Louis club as the Perfectos.

In the winter of 1899-1900, the National League reduced its unwieldy 12-club league to an eight-club circuit, the same teams which now are in the league. The Cleveland, Louisville, Baltimore and Washington clubs were lopped off. Manager Ned Hanlon and some of the great players of the Baltimore Orioles, Willie Keeler, Joe Kelley, Hugh Jennings and Dan McGann, already had gone to Brooklyn the year before, and the Dodgers won the 1899 pennant. However, enough good players had been left in Baltimore to finish fourth under John McGraw, the scrappy third base playing manager. In the final liquidation of the Baltimore club, McGraw, Wilbert Robinson, the colorful Oriole catcher, and Billy Keister, a young second baseman, also were ordered to report to Brooklyn. McGraw and Robbie, then inveterate cronies, ran a café and bowling alleys, the Diamond in Baltimore; they refused to go, and for quite a time were 1900 holdouts. So was young Keister.

Frank Robison then thought he saw a chance for another ten-strike; he figured if he could get the aggressive McGraw, the hardworking affable Robinson and Billy Keister for the Cardinals, the trio might mean the pennant for St. Louis. He procured permission from the Brooklyn club to dicker with the players, but the season was several weeks gone before he could induce McGraw, Robbie and Keister to come to St. Louis.

When they eventually arrived, Robison gave them a real hero's welcome; they were met at the station by a band, taken to what then passed for a night club and with the popping of champagne corks the three agreed to play with the Cardinals—Brooklyn and Baltimore getting $15,000 for the players. All signed satisfactory contracts, with McGraw signing for $100 a game, then a lot of money. He also insisted on a contract with no reserve clause in it.

Frank Robison had had his eyes on McGraw as a possible Cardinal manager, but the bright little ex-Oriole took some of the joy out of the club owner's party, when after a handshake to seal the pact, he said: "I'll sign with you for only one season, Frank; I'll give you the best I have while I am here, but I will be in St. Louis only for the 1900 season."

"But why, Mac?" Robison asked. "You'll like it here; it's a great town; they'll like your style of play; they will be in back of you just as they were in Baltimore."

"I am sorry, Frank, but I can play with you for only one season," McGraw insisted.

Even then McGraw knew that the new American League, in its swaddling clothes and located only in western cities, had ideas of spreading to the east. It was run by the former Cincinnati baseball writer, Ban Johnson, with Von Der Ahe's former manager, Charley Comiskey, who had the Chicago franchise, serving as Ban's aggressive lieutenant. Robison was to know plenty about these gentlemen and their plans later on, but for the moment his concern was to get the Cardinals somewhere in the 1900 race. But again, it was a disappointing year. Despite the fact that McGraw hit .337 and stole 28 bases in 98 games, his heart never was much in his work. Some said he was more interested in the horses which ran across the street. He even had himself tossed out of games so that he could attend the Fair Ground races. The Redbirds again had to be satisfied with a fifth place finish. In 1899, in a 12-club league, fifth wasn't so bad, but in the new eight club circuit, it again meant the second division.

In fact, in mid-August, the club bogged down so badly that it slipped into seventh place. Tebeau, who had been a fighting successful manager for Robison in Cleveland, just couldn't put the job over in his own home town. It was another illustration of the old Biblical adage: "A prophet is not without honor save in his own country." Robison quarreled with Tebeau and Pat quarreled with his players. Tebeau resigned during the August slump, and Robison sent for McGraw. "I want you to take over, John," he said. "I need a fellow like you running the club."

"I am sorry, Frank, but I can't take it," McGraw replied.

So, Robison made Louis Heilbronner, the chief of his concessions, manager for the balance of the season, with McGraw and Outfielder Patsy Donovan agreeing to help Louie pick his pitchers. It was a move which smacked more of Von Der Ahe than the more baseball-minded Frank Robison. It was a close second to the naming of Harry Diddlebock as Cardinal chief five years before. Louie was scarcely five feet tall, a round little fellow, who could no more command the respect of those ex-Spiders than a fly could win the affections of a real spider.

The players then sat on benches placed out on the field, and as little Louie went through the motions of managing the club, pencil and score card in hand, the Cardinals gradually edged up on him until Louie would be pushed ker-plunk right off the bench. If that wasn't sport enough, big Jack Powell, the pitcher, once threatened to lock him in the club safe, and that young barbarian, Mike Donlin, once picked him up by the feet and dunked him head first into a rain barrel near the bench. But, somehow, during Louie's two months in charge, the club moved up two pegs.

There were a few interesting developments. With the acquisition of McGraw for third base, the brilliant young third baseman,

Rhoderick (Bobbie) Wallace, was shifted to shortstop, where he was to acquire even greater fame. Patsy Donovan, who had succeeded Connie Mack to the management of the Pirates in 1897, was purchased from Pittsburgh for $1,000; First Baseman Dan McGann came from Brooklyn and Pitcher Gus Weyhing from Philadelphia, and the prankish Donlin, because of his hitting, was converted into an outfielder.

And the particularly bright spot in the team's play was the hitting of Jesse Burkett, called the Crab. He batted .402, but was beaten out by Ed Delehanty, Philadelphia slugger, who hit .408. It made Burkett the first major leaguer to bat .400 or better three times, as Jesse had hit .423 and .410 for Cleveland in 1895 and 1896, respectively. Only two other players were to collect three .400 batting averages, the immortal Ty Cobb and Rogers Hornsby, a later day hit-churning Cardinal.

V ☯ WAR FLAMES LICK ST. LOUIS

I

THE AMERICAN LEAGUE, which McGraw saw coming in 1900, moved east as a full-fledged major in 1901, putting second clubs in Boston and Philadelphia and taking up the vacated National League territory in Washington and Baltimore. Players jumped right and left, with Ban Johnson, Comiskey, Clark Griffith, Connie Mack and Jimmy McAleer raiding the National League of many of its stars. All clubs were hit hard, and while the Cardinals lost heavily, they were not dented as badly as some of their fellow clubs. McGraw went to Baltimore as manager of the new American League Orioles and took with him Wilbert Robinson, the catcher, and young Mike Donlin. The famous battery of Cy Young and Lou Criger, after only two seasons in St. Louis, jumped to the new Boston Americans, as did George Cuppy, another Cardinal first line pitcher. Lave Cross became Connie Mack's captain and third baseman on the modern Athletics.

Robison matched some of the American League offers and managed to retain enough players to make a creditable showing in the weakened National League of 1901. Under Patsy Donovan, promoted to the management, the Cardinals finished fourth with a percentage of .543; thirteen years would elapse before the Redbirds again would see the first division. To replace Young and Cuppy on the pitching staff, the club regained old Theo Breitenstein and signed such other newcomers as Bob Wicker, Mike O'Neill and Stanley Yerkes. With the departure of Criger and Robinson, the catching department was shot and Donovan engaged a batch of catchers, Al Nichols, John Ryan, Bill "Pop" Schriver and Mike Hayden. Dick Padden joined the club as a second baseman, and Otto "Oom Paul" Krueger, a chunky dwarf, was McGraw's successor at third base.

In addition to a fourth place finish, the Cardinals for the first time in their history had the distinction of having the National League batting champion. Though Jesse Burkett dropped 20 points, from his .402 of 1900 to .382, his average was good enough to top the league. It was Jesse's third batting crown, as he had won two earlier ones with the Spiders.

2

The thunderclouds of the American League war, which already had vexed Frank Robison sorely, broke in their full intensity in 1902. Ban Johnson decided to invade St. Louis, switching the Milwaukee club to the Mound City to complete the four present western clubs —Chicago, Cleveland, Detroit and St. Louis. The newcomers resurrected the old St. Louis nickname, the Browns, took over the old Sportsmans Park used by Von Der Ahe's American Association club at Grand Avenue and Dodier, and put Jimmy McAleer, former crack center fielder for Robison in Cleveland, in command of the Browns. McAleer had done considerable under-cover work for Johnson and Comiskey the year before in raiding National League teams.

Jimmy was supplied with a roll of bills fat enough to stuff the throat of an ox, and now pulled a raid on the Cardinals which made those of the previous year look like a peanut stand robbery. McAleer practically stripped the Redbirds of their remaining stars. He lured Pitchers Jack Powell, Charley Harper and Willie Sudhoff, Infielders Rhody Wallace and Dick Padden and Outfielders Jesse Burkett and Emmett Heidrick to the new St. Louis American League club.

Cardinal First Baseman Dan McGann also took a leap which landed him with McGraw's Baltimore team. With the aid of players who had jumped from other National clubs, McAleer put together a strong aggregation and finished second to Connie Mack's Athletics, one of the two modern Brown teams to finish that high in four decades.

As for the Cardinals, it was the start of another dizzy dip to the nadirlands of the National League. The Birds had lost five regulars and three starting pitchers and slumped to sixth. Robison, heartbroken at what he considered the disloyalty of his players, many of whom he had befriended in times of need, worked like a beaver with his manager, Patsy Donovan, to repair the damage. They did some counter-raiding, and joined in the scramble for minor league players. No reserve clauses were respected—either in the majors or minors, and players went to the highest bidders. A varied assortment of Cardinal pitchers came and went, Clarence Currie, Aleck Pearson, Jimmy Hackett and Chappy McFarland. Bill Hazleton went to first base, and other newcomers were Infielders John Farrell, Fred Hartman, Otto Williams and Red Calhoon, Catchers Jack O'Neill and A. C. Weaver and Outfielders Homer Smoot and George Barclay.

Smoot and Barclay became pretty fair National League journeymen outfielders. Catcher Jack O'Neill was the brother of Pitcher Mike O'Neill, procured by Patsy Donovan the year before. They made up a Cardinal brother battery, which anteceded that of the Coopers—Morton and Walker—by four decades. They were older members of the famous O'Neill clan of the Pennsylvania mining town of Minooka. Steve, the most famous, now is manager of the Detroit Tigers, after a noteworthy catching career with the Indians, Red Sox and Yankees. A fourth brother, Joe—the youngest—played shortstop for Washington until poor health cut short his career.

Donovan's club plunged back into the cellar in 1903, with a drop in percentage from .418 in 1902 to .314. The club won only 43 games and lost 93. Even so, Patsy brought up a few pretty good players that year, Pitcher Mordecai "Miner" Brown, from the Indiana mining town of Nyesville, and a pair of promising infielders, florid-faced Jimmy Burke, one of St. Louis' own sand-lotters, and Dave Brain. Both Burke and Brain became regular big league third basemen.

Whenever things go badly for a man in baseball, he is likely to become panic-stricken, and make any kind of a bad deal in an effort to change the bad luck of his club. He thinks if he can only give his fans a few new faces, it will help. And he often is blinded by a name. With that thought in mind, Robison followed his tailend 1903 season with the worst deal ever made by the Cardinal ball club. To get Jack Taylor, a veteran pitcher from the Chicago Cubs, Frank gave up pitchers Mordecai Brown and Bob Wicker and Catcher Jack O'Neill. Taylor had been a strong pitcher with Chicago, but was a flop in St. Louis, and was sold back to the Cubs in 1906.

Wicker was an able pitcher, a winner in Chicago, but Mordecai Brown was one of the real nuggets of the game. With two fingers gone from his right hand, the result of a threshing machine accident, "Brownie" obtained an amazing amount of stuff on the ball with the use of the remaining three fingers. Donovan used him only in spots and in relief in 1903; in Chicago, the "Miner" developed fast, became the head of the great Cub pitching staff of Brown, Ed Reulbach, Orville Overall and Jack Pfiester, and Christy Mathewson's only serious rival for the No. 1 pitcher of the National League. Had the Cardinals retained the great Brown as an anchor man for their staff—as he was in Chicago—the Redbirds could have avoided some of the wretched clubs which followed.

3

Robison handed Patsy Donovan the pink slip after three years at the helm. Pat had bad luck all during his managerial career; he knew baseball and had unquestionable talent for leadership, handling the Pirates, Dodgers and Red Sox in addition to the Cardinals. But for the American League raids, he might have had a winner— even a champion—in St. Louis. Later in Boston, he put together a strong Red Sox club, including that famous outfield trio of Duffy Lewis, Tris Speaker and Harry Hooper, but was released just as this young club was ready to win pennants and world's championships under Jake Stahl and Bill Carrigan.

Patsy's 1904 successor on the Cardinals was Charles "Kid" Nichols, who, like Jack Taylor, had been a pitching great, but now also was at the twilight of his great career. The Kid is one of the twelve major league pitchers who have won 300 or more games.

Nichols was an early baseball gentleman, perhaps too much so for the still rough-and-tumble baseball played in the National League. He was the exact opposite of such an early predecessor as Pat Tebeau. Ban Johnson was waging a fight to keep rowdyism out of his new American League, but the umpire-baiters and the roughnecks still were riding high in the National League.

Nichols' first year was quite a success as he advanced the Cardinals from eighth to fifth, jacking up the percentage to .487. Among his player acquisitions were Pitchers Joe Corbett, a brother of Gentleman Jim, and Jim McGinley; Catchers Mike Grady, Dave Zearfoss and Larry McLean; Infielders Jake Beckley, Danny Shay and Simon Burch, and Outfielder Spike Shannon. Beckley, a steady .300-hitting first baseman, came from Cincinnati; he was one of the last of the mustachioed players in the majors, the others being Monte Cross, the former Redbird pilot, then Athletic shortstop, and Silent John Titus, right fielder for the Phillies. Shannon was a dashing truculent player and brought $10,000 when sold four years later to the Giants.

McLean, though a good catcher and hard hitter, was one of baseball's colorful playboys, a problem child for any manager who tried to make him go to bed before midnight. One of his St. Louis escapades was to dive into the goldfish pool in front of the Buckingham Hotel, now the Kingsway, in his street clothes. He didn't last long with Nichols, but did well later on in Cincinnati and New York, only to succumb eventually to a violent death. What a battery partner he would have made in St. Louis to "Bugs" Raymond, who was soon to join the pitching staff!

Speaking of that 1904 Cardinal club, Ed Wray, veteran sports editor of the *St. Louis Post-Dispatch,* remarked: "I don't know whether they stuck to it all season, but down at the Houston training camp everybody was trying to pitch the spitball. Elmer Stricklett had made a success with the delivery in Brooklyn, as did Jack Chesbro with Pittsburgh and the Yankees. I never saw so much spray go through the air as when the Kid's pitchers warmed up."

Nichols couldn't follow up on the promise shown by the club in 1904, and 1905 saw the Redbirds riding the chutes again. They slipped back to sixth, with Jimmy Burke, the home-bred, supplanting Nichols in August. The Kid was released to the Phillies. Infielder

Arthur Hoelskoetter came up that season to plague telegraph operators and proofreaders, and Josh Clarke, a brother of Fred Clarke, the dynamic Pirate manager, did a hitch in the outfield, but Josh had neither skill, nor the élan, of his famous baseball brother.

In 1906, Frank DeHaas Robison began to lose interest in his baseball enterprise. His former robust health was failing, and financial burdens also were taking their toll. He retired as Redbird president in December. Those who knew him intimately said he suffered as much from a broken heart as from physical ailments. Frank never got over the desertion of his crack Cardinal stars of 1900 and 1901, most of them his former Cleveland Spiders, to the American League, and in his later years the former gay frolicsome spirit was a disappointed, disillusioned man.

Though still retaining a financial interest in the Cardinals, he returned to Cleveland, where he bade farewell to this world, September 25, 1908. He died of apoplexy at the age of 54.

VI ⊖ BROTHER STANLEY
TAKES OVER

1

WITH THE RESIGNATION of Frank DeHaas Robison as president, his brother Stanley became the Cardinal executive. Matthew Stanley Robison was associated with Frank in Cleveland, and accompanied him to St. Louis, but had remained more or less in the background. Frank was the more forceful figure.

One of Stanley's most amusing experiences happened when he represented the Cardinals at a National League annual meeting at the old Waldorf-Astoria in New York shortly after he became the St. Louis club's president. The session was held a fortnight before the Christmas holidays and there was considerable demand for parlors. The league held an afternoon meeting and then recessed to meet again at night. The hotel management, however, gave the league a smaller room for its night session. After the club owners had convened for half an hour, Stanley hadn't appeared, so Harry

Pulliam, the league president, sent the secretary, John Heydler, on a one-man hunt for the missing Robison.

John found him in the big parlor where the afternoon meeting had been held—all alone, and puffing on a big black cigar.

"A lady just came in and asked me whether the Browning Club meets here," Stanley said to Heydler. "I told her I didn't even know they had named a club after him."

Stanley was thinking of Pete Browning, the old Louisville slugger.

In Frank's last year as president, his manager was John J. McCloskey, known to all baseball as Honest John, and Stanley continued him in office in 1907 and 1908. McCloskey was one of the great characters of the game, a kindly, lovable chap, who was an institution all by himself. A bat-boy for Louisville in 1876, the National League's maiden year, Honest John personally organized ten minor leagues, managed or owned clubs in 47 towns, and developed many stars for the big league market. When he died in 1940, Taylor Spink got up a fund to erect a fitting monument over his grave to which most of baseball contributed.

Managing the Cardinals was not one of Honest John's major accomplishments. It was going back to the dire years of Von Der Ahe as the Redbirds skidded from bad to worse; the man of many leagues started with a seventh placer, following it with two tailenders, as the club lost 98, 101 and 105 games, respectively, in 1906, 1907 and 1908. However, McCloskey had little money to work with, and Cardinal finances were so low that in two winters Stanley Robison, returning to an old Chris custom, slept over the clubhouse.

Yet, in those years, McCloskey brought in some interesting—even great players: Pitchers Charles "Babe" Adams, Eddie Karger, Fred Beebe, Arthur "Bugs" Raymond, Art Fromme, Stoney McGlynn and Johnny Lush, First Baseman Ed Konetchy, Shortstop Eddie Holly, Second Baseman Chappie Charles, Third Baseman Bobbie Byrne, and Catcher-Outfielder Red Jack Murray. Most of them were to show at their best with other clubs.

The Cardinals had the same bad luck with Babe Adams in 1906, as they had three years before with Mordecai Brown. Maybe Honest John didn't recognize Adams' latent genius, or he wasn't ripe for major league picking. Anyway, Babe was shunted back to the minors to reappear two years later with Pittsburgh, where almost single-

35

handed he pitched the Pirates into the 1909 World's Championship, and remained a Pittsburgh pitching ace for fifteen years.

Konetchy, a big Bohemian, who had worked in a candy factory in his home town, LaCrosse, Wis., was called the Bohemian Chocolate Dropper. He swung a mean wagon tongue at the plate. Byrne was a peppery product of the St. Louis sandlots, fast as a flash, and a dynamic, colorful little personality. He still makes St. Louis his home, and has two sons, both former minor league players, Captain Bobbie Byrne and First Lieut. Bernie Byrne, who are famous war birds. Young Bob had six Messerschmitts to his credit and Bernie, who started later, had bagged three at the time of writing.

Second Baseman Chappie Charles was a Pennsylvania Dutchman, who came from Phillipsburg, N. J., across the Delaware River from the Pennsylvania Dutch town of Easton, Pa. His name really was Charles Ashenbach. One day, when the Cardinals were playing at the Polo Grounds, New York, a delegation from Easton came to the big town to see him play. The leader ran down to the rail in front of the boxes, and yelled: "Vhat's all dhis Charles business? We don't know Chappie Charles; we know Charley Ashenbach. Vhat would your papa say? Don't you like his name?"

2

Bugs Raymond was a character like Rube Waddell, Connie Mack's great Athletic lefthander; his antics, eccentricities and weaknesses have become part of the legend of baseball. Bugs, a really great spitball pitcher, had an unquenchable thirst, and some of his wiles to wet his parched whistle are classics, especially after John McGraw, his later day manager, employed a keeper for him. However, McCloskey got much more work out of Raymond than did McGraw, simply by letting Bugs enjoy himself between his turns on the mound. In 1908, Raymond's last season in St. Louis, he pitched 365 innings, second only to Mathewson's 416, and with a feeble .318-percentage tailender, Raymond won 15 games and lost 25.

In that same season, the year of the great three-cornered race between the Cubs, Giants and Pirates, McCloskey told Raymond he wanted him to pitch a certain game against Chance's great Chicago machine. The St. Louis players drifted into the clubhouse on the particular day, one at a time—all but Bugs. The Cardinals went through batting practice, and fielding practice—and still no Raymond. McCloskey yelled: "This time I've had enough. I'll shoot him; I'll fine him $500; I'll suspend him for the balance of the season."

A boy from the Cardinal office told McCloskey that he was wanted on the telephone by a person who said it was "business—important business."

"I hope it's somebody else in the league," said Mac, leaving the bench. "Maybe, they'll want to buy Raymond. If they do, I'll sell him for 50 cents."

When McCloskey answered the phone, it was Bugs. "I'm sorry, boss, I can't pitch today; I got an awful toothache," he pleaded. ·

"Toothache, me eye," bellowed Honest John into the mouthpiece. "I don't care what you got. This game is starting in twenty minutes, and I want you over here ready to pitch."

Five minutes before game time, Raymond, a little bleary-eyed, arrived, and said: "Gimme a ball."

"Just a minute, Arthur, me boy, can you do it?" asked Mc-Closkey, his sympathetic Irish nature getting the better of him.

"Sure, the toothache's gone and I'm all right."

"Who's your battery, Mr. McCloskey?" asked Bill Klem, the umpire.

"It's Raymond and Bliss for me," said John.

Without warming up, Bugs went safely through the first inning, and went on to defeat the great Cubs, 3 to 1.

Perhaps the classic of all Raymond stories came after he went to New York. He had been cutting his usual capers, and after losing a game in Cincinnati, he got on the train with his usual half bun. In his younger days, McGraw used to love horseplay and frequently scuffled with his players, Dummy Taylor, the deaf and dumb New York pitcher, being one of his favorite "razzling partners."

Sore as a boil, McGraw jumped on Raymond as he came into the car, and forced him on the floor between two Pullman seats. As McGraw bounced Bugs' head up and down on the floor, the big spitballer laughed hilariously. Then McGraw started to recite all his complaints.

It suddenly dawned on Bugs that this was no friendly scuffle. "Say, is this on the level?" he asked. "Let me up, McGraw, and I'll punch the tar out of you."

VII ❂ THE DUKE OF TRALEE

THEY WERE SAYING in St. Louis that John McCloskey finished last in 1908 with the best pitching staff in the league. That was an exaggeration, of course, but there have been many worse staffs than Bugs Raymond, Art Fromme, Fred Beebe, Johnny Lush, Grant "Stony" McGlynn, Ed Karger and Irving Higginbotham. Robison was getting desperate; McCloskey was bringing him nothing but tailenders. He threw himself on the mercy of the league, and asked its help in finding him a manager. McGraw, the Giant manager, heard of it; he knew his star catcher, Roger Patrick Bresnahan, had managerial ambitions, and he told Robison he might have Roger for a price. First he suggested that Stanley talk to the fiery Irish-born catcher. It was while the Giants were playing their last 1908 series in St. Louis, and it was thought to be a smart thing to keep any hint of a New York-St. Louis deal away from the St. Louis and Gotham sports writers. The precautions to keep the conference secret would have done credit to a Hollywood scenario writer. Maybe Bresnahan thought it up; at that time he used to be employed during the off-season as a house dick in a hotel in his home town, Toledo.

"Take a room at the Marquette Hotel (it now is the Milnar) and register as John Doaks," McGraw instructed Stanley Robison. "Leave your door unlocked. Bresnahan will inquire from the clerk for Doaks' room. He will come right up, and enter the door without knocking."

They gave Stanley a room on the third floor. To make it still more mysterious, Roger took the elevator to the fourth, walked down to the third, and entered Robison's room.

Bresnahan was more than willing to accept the management, but wanted a $10,000 salary, a lot of money in those days for a poor club, promises of new players and a free rein. Robison promised everything; the main thing, however, was to arrange a deal with McGraw, which wasn't completed until the baseball meetings of the following winter.

The New Yorker drove a rather hard bargain. He took Red Jack Murray, the club's fine young outfielder, and the erratic Bugs

Raymond, who had it in him to become a 25-game winner on a contender. The St. Louis club also had to provide a catcher to replace Bresnahan, so Pitchers Art Fromme and Eddie Karger were sent to Cincinnati in exchange for Catcher George "Admiral" Schlei, who was turned over to New York. The tailenders almost wrecked their fine pitching staff to get the scrappy catcher-manager from Manhattan.

Bresnahan was a great catcher, one of the greatest of all time. Roger was really an all-around player, who could have starred in any position. Born in Tralee, Ireland, he pitched for the Washington National League club of the nineties at the age of seventeen. Later he played second base and the outfield for McGraw's American League club in Baltimore in 1901 and 1902. Going to the Giants with McGraw during the American League war, he divided his early years in New York between the outfield and the catcher's box. He was so fast on the bases that in the 1905 Giant-Athletic World's Series, in which Roger did all of New York's catching, Bresnahan was the Giant lead-off man.

He was only 29 when he came to St. Louis, still at the top of his game. He had caught 139 games for McGraw in 1908 and hit .283. He was as truculent and as much of a battler with umpires and rival players as was his energetic New York chief. But Roger also was smart and crafty; he and Johnny Kling of the Cubs were considered the great baseball brains behind the plate. As when the Spiders came to St. Louis, Mound City fans again were lifted into the clouds. Maybe Roger Bresnahan, picturesquely called the Duke, or the Duke of Tralee, would be "the goot one like Comiskey," who would lead the St. Louis club out of the baseball wilderness.

2

There were no rich dividends in the first year of the Duke's leadership. He raised the Cardinals only one notch out of the cellar. He battled the umpires even more furiously on his own than when he was McGraw's fighting lieutenant in New York. He ran into one suspension after another, as the then youthful John Heydler succeeded Harry Pulliam, a midseason suicide, to the National League presidency. From his great work in New York the previous season, Bresnahan took part in only 69 games in 1909 and hit .244.

With Raymond, Fromme and Karger gone in the deals to get the Duke, the pitching staff was inexperienced and weak. Some felt that if the crafty Roger had spent more time with his kid pitchers behind the plate and less time battling umpires, the Cardinals would have fared better.

However, two young pitchers showed great promise, Harry "Slim" Sallee, a long stringbean of a lefthander from Higginsport, Ohio, and Bob Harmon, a stocky righthander from Liberal, Mo. Slim Sallee came to St. Louis in midseason of McCloskey's last year, and Bresnahan procured Harmon in June, 1909 from the Shreveport, La. club of the Texas League. Both were destined to become great National League pitchers, though Sallee was to add a few extra gray hairs to the pates of his managers, especially in his more frolicsome days as a youngster in St. Louis.

As lefthanded as Rube Waddell, Slim wasn't as colorful as the Rube, but he had many of Waddell's foibles. Where Rube was partial to the old horse-drawn fire engines, Sallee's favorite vehicles were milk wagons and farmer's wagons. Now a bartender in Cincinnati, Sallee used to have a farm near Higginsport, where he once wore a Sheriff's star, and he still liked to be around cow-juice and fresh vegetables. He still liked to keep farmer's hours, but instead of going to bed and arising at sunbreak, now he stayed up for St. Louis' sunrises. He helped milkmen deliver their morning milk, or he met farmers coming in from St. Louis County and rode with them to old Produce Row. Sometimes Harry got a little confused in his deliveries and left a head of cabbage or a bunch of carrots on a doorstep instead of a bottle of milk. However, he was a likable, willing chap, and like Waddell he usually delivered when he was in the ball game. Until he was sold to the Giants in 1916, he was St. Louis' best pitcher.

Sallee pitched what is termed a cross-fire ball. He started it well to the left of the mound; with his long reach and scarecrow build, he whizzed it across the letters of his opponents from all sorts of impossible angles. "It's like the first baseman pitching to you," batsmen of his day used to say.

In his first season in St. Louis, Bresnahan released Higginbotham to the Cubs, and acquired another pitcher named Higgins in his stead, also twirlers Grover Lowdermilk and Lester Bachman. Charley Ashenbach was released to the Reds on waivers, and in August,

Roger traded peppery Bobbie Byrne, the home town favorite, to Pittsburgh for an even smaller third baseman, Jap Barbeau, and Allen Storke, a first baseman and all-around infielder. It was a good break for Byrne, as he played in the Pirate-Detroit World's Series of that year. Roger also had one of the five Delehantys—Joe, perhaps the weakest hitter of the tribe—as part time outfielder. George "Rube" Ellis and Louis "Steve" Evans, later left and right fielders of the Cardinals, came up from Los Angeles and Montreal, respectively. Steve, one of the delightful screwballs of baseball, also had played a little for McGraw's Giants; he died within the past year.

A light-hearted cheerful fellow, Evans was accused by some of his managers of not taking his baseball seriously enough. But, he believed in extracting every bit of fun there was in the game. Patrolling his right field beat at old League Park on a hot St. Louis summer day, he played his position rather deeply so that he could stand in the shade of the grandstand. Several fly balls—Texas Leaguers, fell between him and the infield. The crowd rode him unmercifully. So, when the Cardinals again took the field, Evans marched out to his position carrying a Japanese paper parasol. He had it slung over his right shoulder, but dignified Hank O'Day wouldn't let the game proceed until Steve put it down. "Well, you try playing right field in that sun without an umbrella; see how you would like it," Evans protested.

3

At the end of the 1909 season, Bresnahan made a deal which was to have an important bearing on his own career, as well as that of the little infielder he procured from the Cincinnati club to plug his hole at second base. He sacrificed one of his remaining first line pitchers, Fred Beebe, St. Louis' No. 1 winner in 1909, and Storke, the infielder he had procured from Pittsburgh in the Byrne deal, to Clark Griffith, manager of the Reds, for Griff's midget second sacker, Miller Huggins; Rebel Oakes, a pretty fair country center fielder; and Frank Corridon, once a pretty good pitcher with the Phillies. A bad arm and a batting slump kept Huggins on the side lines during the better part of the 1909 season, and he played in only 46 games. What's more he had played for his home town team since 1904, and was anxious to get away.

As readers of Frank Graham's book, "The New York Yankees,"

well know, Huggins was to become one of the famous characters of baseball. At that time, he was a pesky little fellow, weighing only 140 pounds, but as game as they came, taking the spikes of such strong and husky base-runners as Frank Chance, Fred Clarke and Larry Doyle without yielding an inch. Miller was only a fair hitter, but one of the toughest lead-off men in the two leagues. He had an unerring eye at bat, and scored 100 or more runs three times, when that used to be considered an accomplishment.

Bresnahan had another seventh-placer in 1910, but it was a more respectable one, as he boosted the 1909 percentage of .355 to .412. Roger felt he was getting results. He added Rube Geyer, Bill Steele and Louis Lowdermilk, pitching youngsters to his staff, and took on a pair of old-timers, Vic Willis from Pittsburgh and the aforementioned Corridon. Arnold Hauser, a likely shortstop from Dubuque, was teamed up with the veteran, Huggins, and the pair made a good double-play combination.

Roger's Cardinal team suddenly found itself in 1911, and for two-thirds of the season St. Louis was in its worst pennant frenzy since 1899, the year Frank Robison's transplanted Spiders threatened to tear apart the old 12-club league. For a good part of the campaign, the National League staged a great five-cornered race between the Giants, the eventual champion; the Cubs, still possessing some of their old spark; the Phillies, kept up by the brilliant pitching freshman, Alexander; the resuscitated Cardinals; and Fred Clarke's always dangerous Pittsburgh team. An indication of the closeness of the race was the standing on July 6, immediately after the Fourth of July holiday games: New York, .627; Philadelphia, .612; Chicago, .612; St. Louis, .577; Pittsburgh, .561. The Cardinals reached the halfway mark only three games out of the lead.

Bresnahan was playing a line-up of Huggins, second base; Hauser, shortstop; Ellis, left field; Konetchy, first base; Evans, right field; Mowrey, third base; Oakes, center field; Bresnahan and Bliss, catchers; Sallee, Harmon, Geyer, Golden, Steele, Hearne, Dale, Grover Lowdermilk and Louie Lowdermilk. The Lowdermilks originally came into the league as Laudermilk; Grover was a hefty righthander, and Louie a lanky lefthander, even slimmer than Slim Sallee. St. Louisans generally admit that was the best Cardinal team until Rogers Hornsby won St. Louis' first National League pennant fifteen years later.

Little Huggins was an inspired player that year, enjoying one of his greatest seasons. An item from Cincinnati in the June 29, 1911 edition of *Sporting News* should prove interesting, especially in view of later-day happenings. Clark Griffith, winding up his three-unhappy-year sojourn as Cincinnati manager, was being grilled to a crisp for having traded Hug down the river to St. Louis.

The piece was headed: "May Cost Griff His Job," and ran as follows: "Cincinnati fans are so touchy over 'The Trades of Griffith,' particularly the deal which sent Miller Huggins to the Cardinals, that they never will forgive Griffith for it. Some of them think the proper way to punish the 'Old Fox' would be to secure the return of Huggins and make him manager in place of the man who traded him away.

"That may never happen; Huggins may not get Griffith's job literally, but indirectly he will have a lot to do with Griffith and Cincinnati parting company, for the trading off of little Miller is one of the things treasured up for an accounting."

Griff may well smile at that article today; there was an accounting. The Old Fox was fired from his Cincinnati job, though he was ready to go, and it proved a kick upstairs. He won fame and fortune as manager, part owner and later as president of the Washington club, and baseball fates playing queer pranks as they are wont to do, seven years later little Hug led New York's American League club against the Old Fox's Senators. And six years after that, Griffith blocked the efforts of the little man he had "traded off" to match the Comiskey and McGraw record of four straight pennant winners, when his 1924 Washington club, led by the then boy manager, Bucky Harris, won the Senators' first championship after a bitter race with Huggins' Yankees.

Returning to the Cardinals' pennant fight of 1911, the Redbirds didn't have the drive to stay in the grueling day-to-day, hand-to-hand fighting with the other contending clubs. By August 1, the Cards had slipped to fifth with a percentage of .550, but still were in the race. On that date a *Sporting News* column asks St. Louis not to expect too much and quotes Bresnahan as saying "this may not be a Cardinal year after all." Roger Patrick further said he had pointed out before that his pitching strength consisted largely of two pitchers, Sallee and Harmon, and that he didn't have the hit power of some of the other contenders. The prediction was borne out, and late in the season the club skidded fast. Eventually, after the season of high hopes and big expectations, the Cardinals finished fifth with only one more victory than defeats for a percentage of .503.

In July, the club was caught in a railroad wreck at Bridgeport, Conn., while traveling between New York and Boston. While some of the players were forcibly thrown to the floor of their car, none was injured, outside of a few skinned knees and elbows. Oddly enough, the club never was the same after that wreck. The start of that train ride marked the high tide of the Duke of Tralee's reign as Cardinal manager.

4

Despite the late season slump, 1911 was a bonanza year for the Redbirds. The Cardinals drew handsomely at home, also on the road. Bresnahan's club did especially well in New York, Roger's old stamping ground. The Redbirds, enjoying the best financial year in their history, made $165,000, wiped out a lot of old debts, had money for new players and looked forward to a bright future.

And the Cardinals came up with another pair of likely youngsters, Ivy Wingo, a red-headed catcher from Georgia, and Lee Magee, a combination first baseman-second baseman-outfielder. Lee was of Cincinnati German stock, born into the world as Leopold Hoernschmeyer, and eventually he left baseball under a cloud. He was a blond, clean-cut, handsome youth, with the speed of a deer. At one stage of his career, they called him "the coming Ty Cobb of the National League." He never was quite that good, and a broken leg after he later joined the Yankees also hindered his career.

Eddie Konetchy, the La Crosse Chocolate Dropper, had enjoyed a fine season and wanted a substantial raise for 1912. Bresnahan invited him to St. Louis to talk over terms. About 9 A.M., Roger telephoned Sid Keener, then a young baseball writer on the *St. Louis Times,* that if he came over to the Planters' Hotel Bresnahan would have a story for him.

"I found Roger and Koney seated in one of the side booths," said Sid. "It was early in the day, but they already had a number of beer bottles in front of them. Roger had nothing to announce, but said, 'stick around a bit.' I did for several hours; a lot of beer was consumed, but nothing happened. I went to the office, and came back around noon. They still were beering up, but still there was no story. Again I returned the office, and was back at the Planters' at 5 o'clock. By that time you couldn't see the table for empties. 'Well, Sid,' Roger said, 'Ed was a little stubborn; he needed lots of convincing, but he has just signed a new contract.' "

A manager then needed not only to outsmart and outtalk his players, but to outdrink them.

Pat Monahan, present Cardinal scout and former minor league pitcher, tells another one on the Redbird thirst of that period. As a kid, Pat fooled around both St. Louis ball parks, chased balls and ran errands for the players. In the clubhouse in deep center field, there was a loose board, which could be shoved back. There also was a can, lined with pitch on the inside, hanging on the fence. Maybe, it was a bird bath. Pitchers knocked out of the box, warm-up battery men, or players making some excuse to go to the clubhouse between innings, pushed back the loose board, and handed the can to young Patrick on the outside. He had it filled with suds at a nearby saloon, and slipped it back into the park. Well, when the temperature in St. Louis' outfield reaches 110, one couldn't blame the thirsty ball hawks.

Many of the St. Louis players then lived at Mother Doran's boarding house on Grand Avenue, between Hebert and Sullivan, near both St. Louis ball parks. Mother Doran was a kindly understanding soul, and frequently it was necessary for her to put her "baseball boys" to bed.

VIII ⊝ LADY BEE AND LITTLE HUG

I

STANLEY ROBISON didn't live to see the Cardinals make their pennant fight of 1911. He died while the club was in training, March 24, at the home of his sister-in-law, Mrs. Frank DeHaas Robison, in Cleveland. Stanley was only 54.

The baseball property was inherited by Mrs. Helene Hathaway Robison Britton, niece of Stanley, and daughter of Frank DeHaas. She was a striking looking woman, a real beauty, with plenty of style, snap and sparkle. She was a militant votes-for-women disciple, and she plunged actively into the affairs of the St. Louis ball club, though a friend of the family, E. A. Steininger, succeeded the deceased Robison as president. However, the Cards went under petticoat rule, as Mrs. B., as the league called her, was the real head and made all important decisions. Sid Keener called her Lady Bee. She lived on Lindell `Boulevard, then known as Millionaires' Row, where she was a charming hostess and great entertainer.

Mrs. Britton, sometimes accompanied by male associates, sometimes alone, represented her club at all National League meetings in New York for the next six years. Dressed in the height of fashion, she didn't miss a league session in the years the club was hers. Though far from a prude, she had a salutary effect on some of the boisterous boys who then made up the National League's family of club owners. Always she sat in front in the council room, and when a picture of the club owners was taken Lady Bee was in the front row. Usually that old walrus, the late Garry Herrmann, a wily old bachelor from Cincinnati, contrived to sit next to the attractive brunette from St. Louis when the club owners posed for the league photograph.

Mrs. Britton's husband, Schuyler Britton, whom she later made president of the club and then divorced, had been in the printing business in Cleveland. Schuyler, called "Skipper" Britton, was president of the Cardinals from 1913 to 1916; like his father-in-law, Frank Robison, he loved a good time and was a free spender.

Lady Bee, who was raised in an atmosphere of baseball, was thrilled at the fight the Cardinals made in 1911, and was pleased as punch with the club's financial statement. She rewarded Bresnahan's good work by giving the former Giant a five-year baseball contract at $10,000 a year; then Roger signed another civil contract whereby he was to receive 10 per cent of any profits.

The 1912 season started with optimism rampant, but it was to be a sorry flop, one of the most distressing in the story of the Cardinals. The high hopes built up by the brave fight of 1911 quickly crashed. The best thing the club did all season was to win three of its first four games. The Cards suffered a bad break when Bresnahan cracked one of his knee-caps in April, which was followed by an attack of pneumonia in May. He played in only 48 games, catching in only twenty of them. The left side of the infield was a sieve when Mike Mowrey, the third baseman, carried his holdout into the playing season and Shortstop Hauser was out for weeks because of the illness and eventual death of his mother. By May 6, the Cardinals had won only five games and lost thirteen, and plopped into the cellar. They never were in the race, but managed to limp in ahead of weak Brooklyn and Boston teams.

Court wrangles vexed the woman club owner and there was a battle on as to who should be executor of the estate. In midseason, *Sporting News* said: "The court recognized that Frederick N. Albercrombie must be recognized as legal executor of the estate.

"In the meantime the estate left by Stanley Robison is being drained of resources; resources that should go toward building up a ball team and a decent plant find their way into the pockets of the lawyers.

"Despite everything, Mrs. Britton has been at her post of duty, on the firing line, encouraging by word, if not by deed, her athletes. Some game spirit that, when so many troubles beset at home. Mrs. Britton may be only a weak woman, but she is doing more than many a strong man would think of doing."

There also were some unpleasant repercussions from the insinuations made by Horace Fogel, president of the Philadelphia club, that the National League race of 1912 was "crooked," that the umpires unduly favored the Giants and that Bresnahan played his weakest St. Louis club against the Giants, bossed by his old manager, McGraw. Fogel, a former Philadelphia baseball writer, had no money of his own, and was a sort of stooge-president for Charley Murphy, head of the Cubs, who had supplied the Philadelphia purchase money and controlled both clubs. The Cubs were in the 1912 race; the Phillies were not.

Fogel frequently was in his cups, when he was likely to make tactless remarks. However, Tom Lynch, the National League executive, and most of his club owners took the charges seriously. The National League's annual meeting at the Waldorf-Astoria in December, 1912 convened as a court, with Julius Fleischmann, a former Cincinnati Mayor, serving as presiding judge. Fogel was found guilty of five of the seven charges brought against him, and was "barred forever from the councils of the National League." Bresnahan was fully acquitted of having favored the Giants, but it left talk. St.

Louis always has been intensely anti-New York in its baseball rooting, and some Mound City fans sided with Fogel.

2

There were some tiffs and recriminations during the season between Lady Bee and the Duke of Tralee. Bresnahan, reared by McGraw in a tough baseball school, wasn't particular about his language. He talked to Lady Bee Britton as he would have talked to Frank DeHaas or Stanley Robison. As she criticized, Roger blustered. "He was like a bull in a china shop," recalls Ed Wray.

The breakup came after the Cardinals' sixth place finish. Maybe Mrs. Britton erred in calling Roger to account; anyway, the big Toledo Irishman raged all over her living room. Mrs. Britton was livid; no man could talk to her like that.

During the season, James C. Jones, the club attorney, had succeeded Steininger to the club presidency. Mrs. Britton called him on the telephone early next morning.

"I want you to release Roger Bresnahan," she said. "He is not the type of man I want for manager."

"But, we can't do that; he's signed for four more seasons," replied the president-attorney.

"I do not care if we have to buy up his contract—if we have to pay him in full for four years; I do not want him running my club any longer."

The firing of Bresnahan wasn't so easy. He was released on October 22, 1912, but Roger, at the age of 33, still was considered a great catcher, and the Cubs, Phillies, Pirates and Dodgers all refused to grant waivers on him. Roger also insisted that the St. Louis club live up to the full terms of his side contract; the controversy even reached the National League meeting the following winter. It wasn't completely settled until June, 1913. Charles P. Taft, acting for the Cubs, assumed Bresnahan's five-year player contract, and the St. Louis club settled with him for $20,000. Roger later succeeded Hank O'Day, the umpire, to the management of the Cubs.

48

Lady Bee's candidate to succeed the fiery Roger was that mite from Cincinnati, Miller Huggins. Hug got off to a poor start in his first season in command, the club again slipping back to the old McCloskey slot at the bottom of the list. Bresnahan left with bitter charges and insinuations that the little guy had undermined him with Mrs. Britton and had carried tales after school. It was refuted by Miller's friends, both on the club, and outside. They pointed out it took no undermining to get the Duke out after his explosions with Lady Bee.

Those who didn't like Miller said he was too small to enforce discipline; some of his players needed an occasional sock on the chin to be made to behave and give their best. Bresnahan could do it; Hug couldn't. It was the same story when Huggins later went to New York to take command of the Babe Ruth Yankee Circus. Many St. Louisans were saying Mrs. Britton had been hasty in getting rid of the aggressive and dominant Bresnahan. They said getting rid of dynamic Roger and putting the little shrimp in charge was "just like a woman."

The Cardinal players split more or less 50-50 on the controversy; some supported little Hug; others still were loyal to the departed Duke of Tralee. Big Konetchy, who hit .314 in his last year under Bresnahan, fell to .276. Bob Harmon, however, was the Redbird who took the real 1913 nose-dive; from 23 victories in 1911 and 18 in 1912, he plummeted to a record of eight victories and 21 defeats. Slim Sallee, despite his occasional lapses, was Hug's big comfort in the box; the lean left-hander brought in 19 victories for the tailender. Poll Perritt, who had come up the fall before, showed promise, but his 1913 record was six wins against 14 defeats.

4

A rather amusing follow-up to the regular season was the fight which broke up the 1913 Cardinal-Brown City Series. Such series, spring and fall, used to be St. Louis fixtures. With the Browns, managed by Branch Rickey, leading three games to two, the two clubs met in a double-header, October 13. In the first game, Derrill Pratt, playing first base for Rickey, insisted a ball which Hildebrand, the American League umpire, ruled fair had hit him in the eye and was a foul ball. While he was arguing with the umpire, the Cardinal players, seated on a bench on the field, took him for a merry ride. One Redbird especially called Del something which seared his Alabama ears. Pratt, a former All-America back with the University of Alabama, stormed over to the leering Redbirds and knocked utility infielder Zinn Beck off the bench with a hard right to the button. Other players tore the irate Dixie boy away. They said Del didn't get his man either, as another Cardinal had called him the name which had aroused his ire.

Pratt was tossed out of the game, which the Cardinals won, 5-2, tying up the series at three-all. When the clubs prepared to start the second game, Pratt tried to resume at first base for the Browns. Rickey claimed Hildebrand had promised him that Del could play the second game.

Hug ran out and yelled: "He can't play! He can't play! He's out for the day."

"Judas Priest, will you close your trap, you little runt," said Mr. Rickey.

The arbiters, Hildebrand and Brennan went into a huddle, and decided Pratt couldn't play, but as Rickey and his players continued their arguing the umpires walked to their dressing room. Eventually the game started without them, with Crossin on first base for the Browns. Later the umps reappeared and took over the ball game. So much time had been lost in jawing at each other and arguing with the umpires that the game had to be called after five innings with the score 1 to 1.

Pratt's knockout punch and the attending arguments resulted in so much bad feeling between the rival clubs and players and the fans, that the series was not completed. Interesting for Cardinal fans is that Buzzy Wares, the popular and able coach of the last three Redbird championship teams, played second base for the Browns in that series.

Catching for the Cardinals in most of the City series was a husky six foot, 200 pound catcher from San Antonio, Frank Snyder, who next to Rogers Hornsby was destined to become the greatest player developed by Huggins in St. Louis. The Cardinals had acquired him late in 1912 from Flint, Mich. through a former part-time scout, Jack Burke. Snyder was farmed to Springfield, O. most of the 1913 season, but came back to the Birds in the fall. Frank was big, strong and raw-boned, a horse for work, who soon was catching 140 games a season for the Redbirds; he threw like a shot and became one of the hardest-hitting catchers in baseball.

Huggins, and his great scout, Bob Connery—a native St. Louisan —brought in several other good prospects that year. George Whitted, who was equally at home at second or third base or the outfield, was picked up during the season from Jacksonville in the Sally League, and Ted Cather, another outfielder, was drafted from Toronto. A tall likely-looking hurler, Bill Doak, who was to win fame in St. Louis and Brooklyn with his spitball and slow drop, was acquired from Akron, while Hug took on Charley O'Leary, the former shortstop of the Detroit American League champions of 1907-08-09. Miller made Charley, a sweet character now deceased, his pal, lieutenant and confidant. "Charley me boy," as he was affectionately called, later accompanied Huggins to New York as coach and shared in six rich Yankee World's Series.

5

If the flop back into the callar wasn't enough for Mrs. Britton in her third year as a club owner, she suffered the same experience as did her father, Frank Robison, in 1901, and found herself in the middle of a new baseball war. St. Louis had been no baseball gold mine, with the town scarcely able to support two major league clubs, but a new independent league, the Federal, calling itself a third major, entered the field in 1914 and its glib-tongued president, Jim Gilmore, talked two wealthy St. Louisans, Otto Stifel, a brewer, and Phil Decatesby Ball, an artificial ice plant manufacturer, into backing a third club in the Mound City. They called their team the Sloufeds, engaged Mordecai "Three-Fingered" Brown, the old Cub pitching ace, as manager, and threw their hats into the St. Louis baseball arena at the old circus grounds, Handlan's Park, centrally located at Grand and Laclede Avenues.

Brown lured a few big leaguers to his fold, Otey Crandall and Grover Hartley, a former Giant battery, though Otey jumped the Cardinals, Outfielder Ward Miller from the Cubs, and Pitchers Bob Groom and Dave Davenport from Washington and Cincinnati, respectively. In addition to Crandall, Outfielders Rebel Oakes and Steve Evans jumped the Cardinals to take bigger money from Gilmore promoters.

Things looked rather bleak for the Cards when the 1914 season opened, but before it closed the Redbirds had made the amazing leap from last place to third, the highest position of any St. Louis National League team since the 1876 club finished second. For weeks the club was in the thick of the race; it made a tidy profit; Lady Bee again was happy, and Miller Huggins was considered almost as much of a miracle man as George Stallings, who won the pennant and World Championship with his upstart Boston Braves.

Mr. and Mrs. Britton, accompanied by their mite manager, had gone to the December annual meeting of the league in New York the previous winter, and Hug pulled off one of the biggest National League deals up to that time. Barney Dreyfuss's Pittsburgh club had finished fourth the year before, which was low for Barney; in thirteen previous seasons he had four winners, four runners-up and four show teams. He looked around for players to bolster his club for 1914, and thought the tailend Cardinals were the answer to his prayer. The St. Louis players he eyed avidly were First Baseman Ed Konetchy, Third Baseman Mike Mowrey, and Pitcher Bob Harmon.

"Sure, I'll trade with you," said Miller, "but what have you to offer?"

Barney was liberal, and let Huggins mention the players he wanted. Miller named a list of players, and Dreyfuss talked them over with his manager, Fred Clarke. They gave the little shrimp five for three—Second Baseman Jack Dots Miller, Right Fielder Chief Owen Wilson, Shortstop Art Butler, Pitcher Hank Robinson, a lefthander, and Cozy Dolan, a third baseman-outfielder, for the St. Louis trio—Konetchy, Harmon and Mowrey.

Dreyfuss rubbed his hands in glee, when the deal was completed. He was happy. "This is all I need to beat McGraw in 1914," he said. McGraw's Giants had enjoyed a pennant monopoly in 1911, '12 and '13.

They weren't so happy about the deal back in St. Louis. Some thought Huggins and the Brittons had traded away "their ball club" for some cast-offs Dreyfuss and Clarke were getting ready to junk. "What can I lose?" Miller told the doubters. "We're last; we had to make changes; and we can move in only one direction— up."

And up Miller went! He moved Dots Miller to first base, played Butler at shortstop and put the newcomers, Wilson and Dolan, in the outfield, working them with Lee Magee and Walton Cruise. Early in the season, he traded his two young outfielders, George Whitted and Ted Cather, to the Braves for Hub Purdue, a veteran pitcher, called the Gallatin Squash. It wasn't one of Hug's best deals; Whitted became a star with Boston and the Phillies, while the Squash soon faded from the big league picture.

The 1914 Cards started a little slowly, and by the start of May, they had won seven games and lost eleven. The Pirates, in the meantime, with their new players, looked as though they would crack the old league wide apart, winning fifteen out of seventeen. The Cardinals still were sixth on June 1, but a month later they had nudged their way into third place. No one then was paying much attention to Boston, Pittsburgh long since had fallen behind, and the Giants seemingly were the club to beat.

On August 26, the Redbirds met McGraw's New Yorkers at League Park before a remarkable midweek crowd of 27,000—7,000 in the grandstand, 10,000 in the packed bleachers, and another 10,000 behind outfield ropes. And glory be, the Cards took the first game, 1 to 0, as Bill Doak won a twirling duel from Al Demaree and Rube Marquard. Huggins scored St. Louis' only run on a walk, steal, sacrifice, and squeeze play. The victory put the Redbirds within a fraction of a game of first place; success in the second game would put the Cardinals on top, but Christy Mathewson spoiled St. Louis' fun by pitching a 4 to 0 shutout. It was a real Matty game, he gave up only two hits, didn't walk a man, or strike out a single Cardinal. He let the men behind him take care of the putouts.

The fast-coming Braves followed New York into St. Louis. They were on their amazing climb from cellar rags in July to World's Series riches in October, and knocked off the Birds in three games out of four. A week later, they passed the Giants in a Labor Day series in Boston and went on to win, New York winding up second and St. Louis third. As for poor Dreyfuss, after his club's fine start, the Pirates crashed to seventh, and to rub salt in Barney's wounds, two of the Cardinal acquisitions in the big "Three for Five" deal, Konetchy and Mowrey, jumped to the Federal League in the following winter.

Huggins pulled a play in that exciting National League race that managers still warn young pitchers about today. Maybe it wasn't simon pure sportsmanship, but every game counted and Hug couldn't be too particular. He won this one with his wits. It was in the seventh inning of a game at old League Park; the score was tied and St. Louis had a runner on third base with two out. Huggins, coaching at third base, suddenly yelled at Ed Appleton, the kid Dodger pitcher, "Hey, bub, let me see that ball."

The startled stripling tossed the ball over to the coaching box; Huggins stepped aside, let the ball roll into foul territory, while the winning Cardinal run pranced in from third base. Of course, Uncle Robbie, the Brooklyn manager, was wild, but the umpires could do nothing about it. They hadn't called time, and Appleton was under no obligation to throw the ball to a coach.

6

As was the case in 1912, the 1915 Cardinals failed to follow up their fine work of the preceding season. Another dark horse, Pat Moran's Phillies, shot up from sixth to win the pennant, while Hug's Redbirds found the first division atmosphere too rarefied and floundered back to the second division hole vacated by the Quakers.

The season started with more Cardinal desertions to the Federal League. Lee Magee, who had been one of the live wires of the 1914 third place finish and was a warm favorite with Lady Bee, jumped to the Brooklyn Federal League club, where he became manager. Mrs. B. couldn't match the handsome salary which the rich bakers Ward offered Magee.

The young battery, Poll Perritt and Ivy Wingo, also signed Fed contracts. However, the Cards traded Poll Perritt to New York for Bob Bescher, the old speedboy, who had lost much of the lightning in his feet, and Wingo to Cincinnati for the Cuban catcher, Miguel Gonzales. The Giants and Reds then succeeded in winning Poll and Ivy back for the National League. Gonzales, the Cardinals' present-day popular coach, was then a fine-throwing young catcher, serving his first of four engagements with the St. Louis club. Mike then fitted his own much quoted description of a rookie player who was a little weak at the plate: "Good field; no hit."

IX ⊖ A STAR IS BORN

I

EVEN IF THE CARDINALS finished sixth in 1915, it was an eventful year in the club's history. On September 10, the name, Hornsby, appeared for the first time in a St. Louis box-score. There was no undue excitement at old League Park, and a line in a St. Louis newspaper read: "A 19-year-old Texas kid, Rogers Hornsby, dug up by Bob Connery in the Class D Western Association, finished the game for the Cardinals at shortstop."

That kid was due to go high in baseball—to the very zenith. He was to make diamond history wherever he went and before he was to leave St. Louis in the most criticized deal in the city's baseball annals, he was to lead the National League six times in batting, three times with averages over .400, reach the batting peak for any player in this century, win St. Louis' first National League pennant and the city's first world's championship in thirty-eight years. With the possible exception of Hans Wagner and Napoleon Lajoie, who hit against a deader ball, he was the greatest righthanded hitter in baseball history. Along with Honus and King Larry, Grover Cleveland Alexander, one of Hornsby's pitchers on the Cardinal World's Champions of 1926, and a few other baseball immortals, his name has been preserved for posterity with a tablet at the Hall of Fame at Baseball's National Museum at Cooperstown, N. Y.

Perhaps it is well to let Bob Connery, Hornsby's discoverer, tell of how he roped the young Texan. Bob, in his way, was almost as famous as Huggins, and the pair worked wonders with the little cash they had at their disposal.

"The Brittons were fine people," began Bob, at his present St. Paul home. "It was a pleasure to work for them, but they were rather short on the bank-roll. As a result, I usually stayed away

55

from the larger leagues and tried to find talent in the smaller circuits which were passed up by scouts from more opulent clubs. As a matter of fact, I wasn't on a scouting trip when I first saw Rog; I more or less bumped right into him.

"The Cardinals trained at Hot Wells, Texas in the spring of 1915, and when we broke camp, Huggins put me in charge of our second team. One of our stops was Denison, Texas, and there I found Hornsby playing shortstop. Contrary to reports, I wasn't so much impressed with his hitting. What I saw was a loose gangling kid, with a good pair of hands, a strong arm, and a world of pep and life on the field. I think I noted then that he was a personality, as I found myself unconsciously attracted to him. So I made it a point to talk to him before we left town. I wanted to get a line on just what kind of a boy he was. I was pleased with the little chat; I remember his eyes were clear as crystal, and that he was all baseball. Those eyes always retained that clarity, and had much to do with his later wonderful batting record.

"I kept the youngster in mind, and returned to Denison shortly after the Western Association season opened. I followed the club for about a week and then bought Hornsby for the Cardinals. I've got to be perfectly honest. I didn't recognize his budding genius, and then figured him far from being ready for the big leagues. He was just a good prospect, a lad who had a chance."

Connery set back the Britton bank-roll by only $500 to bring young Rogers into the corral. The Cardinals were going nowhere fast in the fall of 1915, so Huggins brought in some of the youngsters purchased by Connery for September trials—among them Hornsby. He was a chatterer, full of pep, was in every play and showed promise at bat. In 18 games, he hit .246, good for a kid jumping from a class D league, but no indication of the hitting ability he was to show later.

Shortly before the season's end, Hornsby, never lost for words, asked the mite Cardinal manager: "Mr. Huggins, what do you think of me?"

Huggins replied: "I like your hustle, but you're young, and I think I'll have to put you out on a farm."

"You needn't do that," said Rog, "I can go to my father's farm."

Huggins laughed; he meant farming Rogers to a minor league club, but the boy took his "being sent to pasture" quite literally.

When the young Texan left St. Louis in the fall, he weighed 155 pounds; when Huggins, Connery and the St. Louis writers reached the 1916 training camp, they had the surprise of their lives. The Texas calf had grown into a young bull, boosting his weight to 180 pounds. During the winter, he drank gallons of milk and ate pounds of steak. Had Rogers been battling for the hit crown the last two seasons, he would have his troubles with his red meat coupons. He always was famous as a steak eater, and in his years as batting champion a steak at dinner was as regular a part of his daily diet as his morning cup of coffee. In other words: "A steak a day kept Joe Jinx away."

The previous fall, young Hornsby was more or less of a choke and crouch hitter; at the 1916 training camp Connery had Rog change his batting stance.

"I think we can get more power into your swing, young fellow, if we stand you further back of the plate," said Bob. "I want you to get the full power of that heft you picked up last winter into your swing."

He stood Hornsby quite a distance back of the plate, and asked: "How does it feel, Rog?"

"Well, I'm pretty far away from the ball," the young hitter replied.

"Keep at it a while; you'll like it better," said Connery.

Hornsby did; it was from that position that he later leveled off at a pitched ball; it became one of the most famous and unusual stances in baseball. No other top ranking star ever stood so far away from the plate.

2

Hornsby did not start the 1916 season as a St. Louis regular, but he got past the early spring pruning as an extra infielder. The club had picked up Roy Corhan from the San Francisco club to play shortstop. Corhan was one of the great young shortstops in baseball with the White Sox in 1911, when Russell Ford, the Yankee emery ball pitcher, nearly killed him with a pitched ball. Neither Corhan nor Ford were the same players after that. Corhan had slipped back to the minors, and Huggins was bringing him back for another fling at the big leagues. Again the unlucky Roy ran into difficulties, and Hug was forced to put his young Texas spare tire in the game. It was to be many years before aging legs were again to put him on the bench. Hornsby finished the 1916 season, in which he played 139 games, with an average of .313.

Connery dug up more finds for the Cardinals; other players he purchased on the so-called Britton "shoe string" were Lee Meadows and Jake Geyer, pitchers; Bruno Betzel and Zinn Beck, who became regular infielders; and Mule Watson, Tommy Long and Walton Cruise, outfielders. Along with Hornsby, Bob probably didn't pay more than $10,000 for the lot of them.

The purchase of Meadows, the spectacled hurler, who was acquired from the Durham, N. C. club for the munificent sum of $500 is a story in itself. William Baker, Phillie owner, later peddled "Specs" Meadows to Barney Dreyfuss of the Pirates for $50,000 in players and cash, and Meadows was worth it, helping Pittsburgh to its flags of 1925 and 1927.

The Cardinals were in Philadelphia in midseason of 1916 when Huggins received a wire from Connery: "Have just purchased Pitcher Lee Meadows for $500. He wears glasses, but you can't fire me."

Little Hug indignantly showed the telegram to Sid Keener, and some of the other St. Louis writers. He was frantic at Connery's extravagance and foolishness. "Can you imagine that Irish so and so!" he exclaimed. "Buying me a pitcher with glasses. He must be getting soft in the head. I hate to think what McGraw, George Stallings, Pat Moran, Joe Tinker and some of those other tough managers will do to a pitcher with glasses. Why, they may kill the guy, and I'll be held for murder."

No one killed Meadows, and Lee won as many as 22 games a season. He did so well on the mound that he broke down the belief that it would be suicide for a player, especially a pitcher, to wear glasses in major league competition. Today a scout doesn't hesitate a moment in recommending a "goggle-eye" if the young pitcher has other necessary qualifications.

Apart from the fine promise of young Hornsby, the season of 1916 was another drab one for the Cardinals. The club tied with the Cincinnati Reds for last place.

Huggins also played his last ball that season, except for an occasional pinch-hitting or utility chore. Sid Keener once asked Miller when he would stop taking the spikes of rival base-runners on his

ROGERS HORNSBY
Seven-time National League Batting Champion.

MILLER HUGGINS, MITE MANAGER

well-hacked shanks and manage the Cardinals from the relative cool of the bench. "I'll tell you when I will quit, Sid," he replied; "when my public tells me I no longer am filling the bill."

The fans booed Miller when he failed to come up with several ground balls in a tight game that season. He invited Keener to have dinner with him. "You asked me some time ago, when I would call it a career as a player," he said. "Well, my public gave you the answer this afternoon. You've seen the last of Miller Huggins as this club's second baseman."

3

The club finally parted company with the frolicsome southpaw, Slim Sallee. Harry had had several new escapades, and had his run-ins with Huggins. He cut loose the traces while the Cardinals were in New York, which was to be Temptation Town for other famous later day Redbird players. The Sheriff left the club for his farm in Higginsport; among his other complaints was that he didn't like the bed they gave him in New York.

While he was under indefinite suspension, Mrs. Britton, who had succeeded her husband to the presidency of the club, sold Sallee to the Giants for $12,000. It was freely hinted that the Giants tampered with him, and John K. Tener, then the league president, said: "No other deal like that will be sanctioned while I am in office." "Sal" went on to help McGraw compile his remarkable 26-game winning streak in August and September, 1916, though the Higginsport Sheriff was in the box for New York when the Braves finally checked the Giants' great run of victories.

Late in the 1916 season, Mrs. Britton called Huggins and her legal adviser, James C. Jones, to her home on Lindell Boulevard. She had been having domestic trouble; World War I was in its third year; war clouds were hovering in the American sky; and her Cardinal tailender again was playing to empty benches. She didn't mince her words and greeted them with: "Gentlemen, I want to get out of baseball. I guess I have had enough. I want you to be the first to know it, in case you should be interested in buying the club yourselves."

Huggins said: "I'll get a buyer, or take it on a verbal option."

He immediately got busy on the idea. Miller and Connery went to Hug's home town, Cincinnati, and interested the wealthy Fleischmann yeast family in backing them. Both Julius and Max Fleischmann were at various times minority stockholders in the Reds. Julius was the same man who had sat as presiding judge at Horace Fogel's trial; he was quite fond of Huggins, and regarded Miller as "his boy." For his summer recreation, Fleischmann used to run a crack semi-pro club in the Catskill Mountains in New York, a place which still is called "Fleischmann's." It was in this Catskill resort town that Miller got his baseball start under the name of Proctor; he used it as a stepping-stone to St. Paul and the majors. Fleischmann agreed to back Huggins, and Hug was all ready to present his proposition when he read in the newspapers that the Cardinals had been sold to a stock company of St. Louis fans and enthusiasts organized by Barrister Jones.

Unbeknown to Huggins, while he was working on the idea of financing the purchase of the club in Cincinnati, Jones had similar notions in St. Louis. It was a sore disappointment to Hug and was responsible, in good measure, for his severing relations with the St. Louis club a year later.

X ⊖ SEVEN NAMES IN A HAT

I

THE PRICE FOR WHICH Mrs. BRITTON agreed to sell her property, including the real estate at old League Park, to the syndicate of St. Louis baseball enthusiasts was $375,000. Of this amount, $25,000 was to go to the law firm of Jones and Hocker, their cut for putting over the deal. There was so much difficulty later on in scraping up the dollars to pay off Lady Bee that Jones knocked off the lawyers' commission. Despite that difficulty, it was one of the big bargains of baseball. Four years later, the real estate, some 20 acres in the valuable northwestern section of St. Louis, brought $200,000, and the club turned down offers of better than a quarter of a million dollars for one player, Rogers Hornsby, from the New York and Chicago clubs.

Jones recruited most of St. Louis' better-known businessmen in his stockholders' army; a man could buy stock anywhere from fifty dollars' worth to $10,000. The latter amount was the maximum. One of the small stockholders was Sam Breadon, a prosperous automobile dealer, but that's a chapter in itself. The whole thing was advanced as a sort of civic duty. W. E. Bilheimer, a St. Louis insurance man, introduced the idea of the Knot Hole Gang. With each fifty dollars' worth of stock went one Knot Hole ticket, good for one kid during the season. An entire section of the bleachers was to be set aside for these young Knot Holers. Figures on juvenile delinquency were quoted in the stock-selling campaign. One bought two shares of stock, and kept a St. Louis boy off the streets—or out of the Juvenile Court. If you didn't know a deserving boy, the Y.M.C.A., or some kindred organization, would find one for you. Though changed from the original plan, the Knot Hole Gang has been a St. Louis baseball institution ever since.

Early in 1917, Jones was well pleased with the way the stock-selling campaign was going. He assembled seven of St. Louis' sports editors and baseball writers in his office.

"Gentlemen," he said, "our campaign has progressed splendidly. We have the club; we have a good manager (Miller Huggins was still with the club); we have our Knot Hole Gang, but I need a man to run all of this as club president. Now you boys have been around; you know baseball and you know St. Louis conditions. I want your suggestions as to a man who might meet the requirements. Would you be so kind as to write a name on a slip of paper and drop it into my hat as I pass it around the room."

When Barrister Jones took out the bits of paper, there was only one name on the seven slips—Branch Rickey, then the business manager of the St. Louis Browns. Jones immediately offered Branch the presidency.

A former catcher-outfielder for the Browns and New York Yankees, Rickey managed the St. Louis Americans in 1913-14-15. At the expiration of the Federal League war, Phil Ball, owner of the Sloufeds, combined the club with the Browns, moved to Sportsmans Park, and put Fielder Jones, his Federal League manager, in command of the merged teams. Ball wanted to get rid of Rickey at first, but Branch had a holdover contract with the Browns, and Ban Johnson and other American Leaguers told Phil that Branch was a smart baseball man and a valuable asset to his organization. Besides, Rickey, a former baseball coach at Michigan, had brought George Sisler, Michigan's great pitching and first base star, to the Browns in 1915, and with the aid of Johnson, had fought to hold the player against the claim of Barney Dreyfuss of Pittsburgh before the old National Commission. So Ball put Rickey in charge of the club's business office, but Branch, a Y.M.C.A. man and Sunday School teacher, never was happy under the blustering Ball with his high voltage adjectives.

Rickey asked Ball's permission to accept Jones's offer, but Phil said, "No." Branch claimed he had an agreement with Ball that permitted him to change his job if a better one presented itself; Ball thought otherwise; the case eventually reached the courts, and each party accused the other of bandying with the truth. Eventually it was settled, but with ill feeling on Ball's part, and Branch Rickey duly began his long career with the Cardinals and the National League. It was a historic moment, for no man in baseball in the last quarter of a century, with the possible exception of Judge Landis and Babe Ruth, has left so deep an impress on the game as Branch Rickey.

Judge Landis's appointment in 1920 served as a pillar on which to rebuild the public's confidence after the Black Sox scandal. The Chicago jurist's honesty, integrity, fearlessness and firm-handed administration was a pretty good guarantee that chances for a repetition of such an offense would be reduced to the minimum in a game where the human equation is such a factor. Babe Ruth's home-run hitting ability and colorful personality gave us a new game, made it possible for one player to draw a greater salary than that paid to the President of the United States, and raised the pay checks of players all along the line. But Rickey devised a method whereby the poorer clubs could cope on equal terms with the more opulent ones, even set a pace which the well-to-do Giant, Cub, Pirate and Dodger clubs have found difficult to follow.

A genius in his line, he is the man who made possible the later-day success of the Cardinals, their National League pennants and World's Championships, getting the players from the original source of supply—the nation's sand-lots, and developing them under capable supervision on the parent team's plentiful farms, or minor league clubs of various classification. In fact, the greatest tribute to the man's genius is that as early as 1931, the richest and most powerful club in baseball, the New York Yankees, which used to go into the open market for finished ball players with the late Colonel Ruppert's fat bank-roll, patterned a farm system after that built up by Rickey and his erstwhile St. Louis chief, Breadon, and now develop their own players almost from the cradle.

2

Hal Lanigan, a member of the *St. Louis Times'* sports staff in 1905, when Rickey was a catching rookie, must have looked into a crystal ball at the Browns' training camp at Dallas, as he sensed something of the man's future. He sent the following paragraph to his newspaper: "A nice-appearing broad-shouldered little gent named Branch Rickey looks fairly good in the workouts. He's a candidate for a catcher's job. He doesn't—and won't play Sunday ball, nor does he cuss. Just the same, he appears popular with one and all. We cannot at this early date forecast just how good a catcher Rickey will become, but we venture this prophecy: He's smart and some day may be running his own club."

Rickey was smart, eventually he had his own club, in fact had many clubs, but before he got there he had many vicissitudes. He never had a silver spoon in his mouth until he earned the silver. He was a poor farm kid, born on a farm near Lucasville, Ohio, December 20, 1881. When he had completed the little neighborhood brick school, he landed his first job at teaching in another country school for $35 a month. Out of this scant pay, he bought a bicycle to pedal the eighteen miles between the Rickey farm and the school, bought books on Latin, rhetoric and higher mathematics, and saved $76 toward his college education.

Two educators, J. H. Finney of Lucasville and Frank Appel of Wheelersburg, O., took a shine to the ambitious boy, loaned him additional books and coached him so that he had enough credits to enter Ohio Wesleyan after two years of teaching. Around that time Branch took a West Point examination and passed it. He didn't seek the appointment, but took the examination as a brain test.

After getting his degree from Ohio Wesleyan, he taught again— first in Alleghany College, then in Delaware College, both in his native Ohio. And somewhere between studying and teaching, this bundle of energy found time to play summer baseball and fall football, getting as high as $150 a game for playing the backfield for the strong Shelby, O. professional football club. A broken leg closed his gridiron career in 1902.

His leg healed by the following spring and he started the 1903 season as catcher for the Lamar, Wyoming team. Rickey went up quickly that season; by July he was with Dallas in the Texas League, and a month later Branch had the first taste of the majors when he was purchased by the Cincinnati Reds.

Rickey's middle name is Wesley; he had a strong Methodist upbringing and his refusal to play Sunday ball, a moot matter throughout his career, early brought him into conflict with Joe Kelley, one of the tough old Orioles, who then was managing the Reds.

The Reds then had only one mask and chest protector for their catching department; Heinie Peitz, the same Heinie of Von Der Ahe's "Pretzel Battery" of the early 90's, kept the protector in his locker, and Rickey stowed away the mask. After the Saturday game, Branch handed Peitz the mask, saying: "You better put this away, Heinie; I won't be here tomorrow."

Kelley's locker was only a few feet away; he overheard the remark and barked: "What do you mean; you won't be here tomorrow?"

"Didn't the Dallas club advise you that I don't play Sunday baseball when you purchased me?" asked Branch in surprise.

"Why don't you want to play on Sunday?" stormed Joe. "This is a Sunday town; that's when the dough comes in to pay you fellows."

"I am sorry, Mr. Kelley; but it's against my principles; it's the way I was brought up," said the young catcher.

"The other fellows aren't too good to play on Sunday, so there'll be no exception in your case. You'll catch whenever I call on you, or you can get whatever money is coming to you from Garry Herrmann."

Herrmann was the same Cincinnati club president who used to like to sit next to the comely Lady Bee in the National League club photographs. An utter materialist, who even during national prohibition never went on the road unless a barrel of beer, great chains of sausages and crocks of dill pickles were delivered to his hotel room, Herrmann had a greater understanding of the young catcher's problem than Kelley, the fiery New England Irishman.

"Garry wanted to know what was behind my release," said Rickey, discussing the incident many years later. "I was a little touchy about the matter, but finally I told him. He paid me twice what I thought I had coming to me and was so fine and sympathetic with my point of view that a friendship grew out of that meeting which lasted until Herrmann's death."

When Rickey became president of the Brooklyn club late in 1942, *The Sporting News* reprinted an interview with Rickey, the St. Louis Brown manager, from their issue of January 1, 1914, with Hunt Stromberg, the famous Hollywood producer, then a young writer with *The Sporting News*, on the subject of religion and Sunday baseball.

Mr. Stromberg introduced Branch with a paragraph which might be typical of the Rickey of today: "Offhand, he swung in his chair uneasily, peered beyond the edge of the foolscap, blinked and frowned—he didn't say a word. Ten minutes later, Mr. Rickey asked if we were in the habit of exploding bombs while a natty detail of police patrolled the beat along the busy thoroughfares of St. Louis."

In 1914, when Stromberg fired his list of questions at Rickey, there were only three Sunday towns in the majors—St. Louis, Chicago and Cincinnati; yet thirty years later, with Sunday baseball in every major league town and most of those in the minors, Rickey still would answer the same way. The future movie impresario's questions and Rickey's answers follow:

Q. What has religion to do with baseball?

Rickey: It has no more to do with baseball than it has with any other legitimate pursuit.

Q. Do you contend that it is better for a player to attend church once a week and pay proper respect to his religion in order to get on in baseball?

Rickey: Doubtless every man ought to pay proper respect to his religion if he has one. Going to church once a week has no connection whatever with the playing ability of any man.

Q. You do not play ball or don your uniform on Sundays. Would you censure any one of your men should he feel about the Sabbath in the same manner as yourself?

Rickey: The St. Louis American League Club signs the players to their contracts. Beyond a doubt, both parties would observe their contract.

Q. Would you permit him to remain away from the park on Sunday?

Rickey: Answered as above.

Q. Just for the sake of argument, suppose every man on the team would decline to play Sunday ball. What would be your policy if this were the case?

Rickey: Again answered as above.

Rickey's answers to Stromberg's last three questions might well come under Branch's well-known double talk of 1944. Years later, as he reread the 1914 interview, Rickey enjoyed a real laugh in retrospect as he surveyed his adroit answers to Hunt's questions.

3

After the Sunday ball squabble with Joe Kelley, Rickey's contract reverted to Dallas, but he reached the Browns in 1905 via the Chicago White Sox. Comiskey purchased him on a tip from the veteran organizer, Ted Sullivan, but traded him to St. Louis for Frank Roth, an older and more experienced catcher. Rickey had a pretty fair year with the Browns in 1906, hitting .280 in 64 games, when the club traded him to New York, then called the Highlanders, for Joe Yeager, an infielder-catcher. Clark Griffith, the New York manager, recognized Branch as a smart player, but Rickey's health started to crack that season, and his 1907 records are skeletons which still rattle in the Rickey closet. He hit only .182, was last among catchers with an average of .882 and last among outfielders with .846.

He quit the Highlanders that fall to take a law course at the University of Michigan, and the following spring was appointed coach of Michigan's baseball squad. He crammed a three-year law course into two years, and remained baseball coach until 1911. Then, his health broke completely from a combination of study and overwork, and his physicians ordered him to go west. He went out to Boise City, Idaho, bought himself a broad-rimmed western hat, and hung out a law shingle. It looked as though baseball had seen the last of Branch Rickey.

Branch might have become another Senator Borah if Colonel Bob Hedges, former owner of the Browns, hadn't called him to Salt Lake City for a chat in 1913. Out of the talk came an invitation to return to the Browns, first as an assistant to Hedges in the front office and later as successor to George Stovall as manager. In his two complete seasons at the helm, his 1914 and 1915 Browns finished fifth and sixth, respectively. He quickly got the reputation for being a theorist, who liked to try things out on his baseball chessboard. Fritzie Maisel, Yankee third baseman of 1915, who stole 83 bases that season, had a good day at the expense of Rickey's catchers.

"When Rickey came out to coach at third base, I tried to ride him," related Maisel, "and asked why he didn't go back of the plate himself, and see what he could do about stopping me. So he said: 'Judas Priest, Fritzie, will you shut your mouth? I am suffering enough!' How are you gonna come back at a guy who won't say anything worse than Judas Priest when he's mad?"

Jack Kieran, of "Information Please," always referred to Branch as the non-alcoholic Rickey in his New York sports column; Branch still is that way. He didn't drink as a player or manager, and still is a teetotaler; he even took the prohibition side during the great national experiment. He didn't smoke as a younger man, but now does a lot of his double talking with a cigar in his mouth. He didn't visit the ball park on Sunday; Burt Shotton was his Sunday manager on the Browns, also later on the Cardinals.

He is crafty, even brilliant, and like a crack bridge, chess or checker player, usually thinks two or three moves ahead. And, he knew ball players! Branch Rickey isn't loved by every one in baseball. But the author heard one man, who isn't listed among Rickey's admirers, comment: "I know no one else who can look at a group of kid ball players, after they have played a year in class C or D ball, and say: 'This fellow will be ready in three years; this one will take longer, but eventually will be a greater player; this one will move faster at the start but he never will get past Rochester or Columbus.' And, ninety-five times out of a hundred, Rickey will be correct."

Rickey loves to talk, teach, orate and has addressed many audiences, especially in Y.M.C.A., Boy Scout and church circles. He has four college degrees, a Bachelor of Literature and Bachelor of Arts from

Ohio Wesleyan, a Doctor of Jurisprudence from Michigan and a Doctor of Law from McKendrick College, Illinois. Despite some of his convictions, he never was a "holier than thou"; he enjoys a good laugh and is a solid substantial citizen. When he left St. Louis late in 1942, he was Colonel Branch Rickey, military aide to Governor Forrest Donnell, and was boosted by friends for the Republican Senatorial nomination from Missouri.

This is the man to whom those enthusiastic stockholders turned over their property in the winter of 1916-17. He was a natural-born organizer, promoter, trader, lawyer. For a quarter of a century, that selection spelled better baseball for St. Louis—pennant-winning baseball later on, while it enriched Rickey, the poor farm boy, by well over $1,000,000.

4

Branch's first year in the president's chair was crowned with success. The Huggins clubs in St. Louis went up and down like an old-fashioned razzle dazzle. This one shot up again from a tie for the cellar in 1916 to third place in 1917, the Birds trailing only the Giants and Phillies at the finish. The kid, Hornsby, now 21, served notice to the pitchers that he was going to be awfully tough, hitting .327, second only to the batting champion, Eddie Roush of the Reds, who led Rogers by 14 points.

In association with Huggins, Rickey pulled off several smart deals before and during the 1917 season. Branch acquired Third Baseman Doug Baird from the Pirates in a midseason swap for Pitcher Bill Steele, and the next few seasons Rickey was bandying Baird, the St. Charles, Missouri boy, back and forth like a shuttlecock.

The 1917 St. Louis third placer was an almost entirely different club from the "show team" three years before. Gene Paulette, who had been a Giant utility player, pushed Miller off first base; Betzel and Miller played second; Hornsby, shortstop, and Fred Miller and Baird, third base. Hug worked Tommy Long, Walton Cruise, Jack Smith, Jimmy Smythe and Bob Bescher in the outfield, and gave the box-score boys a lot of trouble with two Smiths and a Smythe. Snyder and Gonzales were the catchers, and Meadows, Ames, Doak, Packard and Goodwin were the pitching leaders. Huggins got a lot of good pitching out of Leon "Kalamity" Ames, then thirty-three, after the redhead had been passed up by the Giants and Reds. Ames won 15 and lost ten; Meadows almost duplicated this record with 15 and nine, and Bill Doak, worked harder than any of the others, had the odd record of 16 victories and 20 defeats.

Rickey, the new club president, got some of the credit for the spectacular one-year rise, but most of it went to Huggins. Again he was something of a miracle man, for third place then was a lower heaven for St. Louis fans. But the little Miller wasn't happy; he still was hurt over the manner in which he had lost his chance to buy the club the winter before.

In the meantime, Ban Johnson, who never liked the idea of the National League putting anything over on him or his club owners, planned to get even with the Cardinals for grabbing Rickey from his St. Louis club. He planned to snatch the successful midget pilot of the Redbirds for his own league. Ban recommended Hug to Col. Jake Ruppert, Yankee president, at a time when Lieutenant Colonel T. L. Huston, Ruppert's former baseball partner, was in France with the A.E.F. Johnson was most intimate with St. Louisan Taylor Spink, publisher of *The Sporting News,* and had him act as his emissary with Huggins. Miller wasn't so sure it wasn't a trick, but he agreed to accompany Spink to the New York games of the 1917 Giant-White Sox World's Series, when Taylor almost had to deliver him at Ruppert's office. And then Miller nearly lost the job by calling on the well-dressed, fastidious Ruppert wearing a cap. When Ban asked Ruppert what he thought of Huggins, Jake replied: "Does he always wear a cap?," but eventually Miller got the New York job at double his St. Louis salary over the protests of Huston, who wanted Wilbert Robinson—and again the St. Louis Cardinals were without a manager.

Discussing Huggins' five-year reign as Redbird manager, his old crony and associate, Bob Connery, remarked: "They were really five happy eventful years; we had our worries, yes, but funny things were happening to the club and in the front office all the time. We were younger then, could take it, and the laughs eased a lot of tough situations. Hug could stand his grief better then than in his later years in New York. We were together in both places, and those five years with the Cardinals were happier than any five years in New York, even when Huggins was winning pennants."

Rickey's choice as successor to Huggins as Cardinal manager was the late Jack Hendricks, who had acquired distinction as a minor league pilot in Indianapolis and Denver. Later Jack managed the Cincinnati Reds with some success, but in 1918, the second year of America's entry into World War I, the Cardinals rode Von Der Ahe's chutes from third place down to the cellar again.

Rickey made a few more deals, and even Bobbie Wallace, who came to the club from the old Cleveland Spiders in 1899, finished his great career with the Cardinals, playing in his twenty-fifth major league season. However, it was a war season, much like those of 1943 and 1944, especially the latter, when ball players went into the Services in droves. Managers played kids and old-timers, whomever they could get to fill out a line-up. Even so, Rickey managed to come up with a group of promising kids, Willie Sherdel, a young lefthander from Milwaukee, and Cliff Heathcote, fleet-footed outfielder from Penn State. Austin McHenry, a hard-hitting outfielder, was acquired from the Reds, sent to Milwaukee, and then was regained in a subsequent swap. And the nineteen-year-old former St. Louis score card boy, banjo-playing Charley Grimm, later famous first base-playing manager of the Cubs, got into 50 games at first base and hit .220. It was a season of low batting averages, and even the great Hornsby was down to a rating of .281 against the dead pumpkin used for a ball in that war year.

The War Department closed up baseball on Labor Day, 1918, with its Work or Fight order. Rickey entered the Army, and always a man to advance quickly, he soon wore the gold oak leaves of a Major in the new Chemical Warfare Service on his broad shoulders. Hendricks exchanged his Cardinal uniform for the khaki of a Knights of Columbus war worker and was overseas with the K. of C.'s when the Kaiser tossed in the sponge and took it on the lam.

6

Following the Armistice of November 11, 1918, baseball came back with a big bang, but the bang was only a mild pop in St. Louis. Hendricks was not re-engaged, and the new president, Major

Rickey, assumed the double role of president-manager. Branch never got over his itch to manage a club. His 1919 Cardinals finished seventh.

Again he went into the baseball trading marts and came up with a batch of new players. He regained the services of two of his old Brown favorites, Outfielder Burt Shotton and Shortstop Johnny Lavan, from the Washington Americans. Shotton later managed the Phillies, on Rickey's recommendation, and held high posts in the Cardinal organization, manager of Syracuse, Rochester and Columbus. *The Sporting News* picked him as the minor league manager of the year in 1941 for his great work with the latter club. When Sam Breadon notified Rickey in 1941 that Branch's contract would not be renewed after December 31, 1942, Shotton, always Rickey's man, accepted a coaching job with the Cleveland Indians. Doc Lavan, a graduate of Michigan, had done well in the medical profession, and now holds the rank of Commander in the Navy.

At the January, 1919 baseball meetings in New York, Rickey pulled off a big deal with the Phillies, obtaining Third Baseman Milton Stock, Catcher Bill "Pickles" Dillhoefer and Pitchers Frank "Dixie" Davis for Pitcher Gene Packard, and Infielders John "Stuffy" Stewart and Doug Baird. Dillhoefer and a pitcher, Mike Prendergast, had figured in one of baseball's biggest all-time deals the preceding winter when the Cubs gave up $70,000 and the two players to William F. Baker, the former Philadelphia president, for the great Phillie battery, Grover Cleveland Alexander and Bill Kille-fer, both of whom were later to land with the Cards.

Dillhoefer, a promising catcher, died three years later of pneumonia at St. John's Hospital, St. Louis. In the spring of 1919, Rickey obtained another fine catcher, Vern Clemons, from Louisville, giving up Davis, the newly acquired pitcher. Branch had had Clemons a while on the Browns, and Vern had improved steadily. In July, Rickey regained Baird in another deal with Philadelphia, when he sent the spectacled hurler, Lee Meadows, and First Baseman Pau-lette to Baker's club for the much-traded Doug and two pitchers, Elmer Jacobs and Frank Woodward.

The famous Rickey notebook, in which the names of many great players of the future were noted, already was a fixture. They used to laugh a lot about that notebook; writers, ball players, even rival managers have imitated Branch Wesley turning over the leaves of his notebook, saying: "Oh yes, when he was seven years old, he was playing with the Rinky Dinks in Squashtown. He didn't move in so well for fly balls to his left, so I had him shift to catching." Yet, that notebook gave St. Louis fans $100,000 ball players for the price of a railroad ticket.

The late Charley Barrett, one of baseball's ablest scouts, moved over from the Browns to the Cardinals with Rickey. Charley, too, could sense baseball talent in its most embryonic stage.

With Clemons and Dillhoefer in his catching department, Rickey felt safe in trading the club's ace catcher, Frank Snyder, to the Giants for Pitcher Ferdie Schupp and a big chunk of badly needed New York cash. The new New York owners, Stoneham, McGraw and McQuade, were spending money like sailors on a spree, and the cash which accompanied Schupp was badly needed.

Schupp, a lefthander, came out of a Sunday School League in Louisville. In his first season in professional ball, with Decatur in the Three-I League, the boy pitched 365 innings in 51 games and had so much stuff he found it difficult to find a catcher who could hold him. Pat Monahan, the Cardinal scout and then a fellow Decatur pitcher, roomed with him and taught Ferdie how to hold his feet in their hotel bedroom.

With the Giants, "Schuppie" spent several years as a relief pitcher and gave Heywood Broun, then baseball writer on the *New York Tribune,* a chance for one of his immortal lines. With the Giants behind, McGraw would send in a pinch-hitter for his starting pitcher in the fifth or sixth inning. Rube Schauer then would pitch until it again became the pitcher's turn to bat. Another pinch-hitter was called from the bench to hit for Rube, and Schupp wound up the game on the mound. So Broun wrote: "At the Polo Grounds, it never Schauers but it Schupps."

Ferdie found himself in midseason of 1916, and compiled the remarkable earned run record of .090 earned runs per game, the best in major league baseball; he did well in 1917, when he won 21 games for McGraw and a World's Series shutout. Ferdie then went to war, and when he got back his stuff was gone. However, Rickey thought he had a real prize, and tried to nurture the lefthander back to winning form. He even put on his old catcher's glove, worked with

Ferdie, tried psychology on him, but all to no avail. Schupp closed the 1919 season with five victories and nine defeats, had a fair season in 1920, and then faded from the big league picture.

XI ⊘ FROM POPCORN STAND
TO RICHES

I

IF RICKEY POSSESSES ELEMENTS of baseball genius, another go-getter entered the Cardinal picture about the same time, first in a minor role, but by the early winter of 1919-20 as Branch's superior, succeeding the Ohio catcher-teacher-lawyer to the Cardinal presidency. The man was Sam Breadon, with no more of a silver spoon in his mouth in infancy than Rickey, and as much of a character in his way as the present Brooklyn club president. They call him Singing Sam and Lucky Sam, and he doesn't deny the latter implication. "Sure, I've had my share of good breaks in life," said Sam. "Everybody's got to get them to succeed, but you've got to keep on pitching even when the score goes against you. That's the test." Not only is Breadon lucky, but he has been a strong executive and for twenty-three years served as Rickey's balance wheel.

Breadon met his tests at several important stages in his life. He was born in Greenwich Village in New York's old Ninth Ward, July 26, 1879, of North of Ireland stock. When he used to dive off the West Side docks into the Hudson River and play ball on the streets of downtown Manhattan, St. Louis was as far away as Madagascar or Tasmania. In four decades in St. Louis, he never has lost his New York accent.

After a grade school education, he obtained a job as a New York bank clerk and by the time he was twenty-three in 1902 he was doing quite smartly, earning a monthly stipend of $125. A year later, a New York pal, Gus Halsey, went out to St. Louis to start a garage and automobile agency with his brother, Oscar, who was salesman for the concern. The automobile industry then was in its infancy, but the Greenwich Village bank clerk, perhaps using his Irish psychic sense, envisaged, in some degree, the automobile business of the future. It was the business for a young ambitious fellow with ideas. Despite Mother Breadon's pleadings—and tears—Sam went west to take a job with the Halseys at $75 a month, $50 less than his bank pay.

Sam always had a gift of gab, and talked convincingly. He thought he would like to have an automobile business of his own, and broached the subject to several of his customers. His ideas on being his own boss got back to the Halsey brothers, who said politely: "Here's your hat, Sam; let us not detain you."

For some time thereafter Breadon wasn't Lucky Sam. His little bank-roll dwindled rapidly; the suit he brought from New York was wearing thin in the seat, and at one stage his budget for food was fifteen cents a day. But the young New Yorker never ran out of ideas. It was 1903 and St. Louis was staging its big World's Fair dedication parade. Breadon talked himself into credit with a confectionery company for thirty cases of Honey Boy popcorn, each case containing a hundred packages. Two elderly ladies erected a grandstand in front of their property at Lindell Boulevard and Sarah Street, and they permitted Sam to store his popcorn under their stand. Then he hired a dozen boys to pass through the stands, selling Honey Boy. One vender didn't return for two hours, but when he did get back, his basket was empty. The parade was late—and long; the day was cold, and the spectators became hungrier and hungrier. When the happy day was over, Breadon's net profits were $35 and he blew himself to a real steak.

With this little nest egg, things soon started to improve. He made $200 selling a second-hand car and later in 1903 entered into an automobile agency partnership with Marion Lambert, member of a well known St. Louis family. They called their business "The Western Automobile Co." and were among the first to handle Ford cars in St. Louis. The World's Fair of 1904 gave the automobile business a tremendous impetus, especially in the St. Louis district, and the young men made $20,000 that year.

LUCKY SAM BREADON

BRANCH (THE BRAIN) RICKEY

If Breadon hadn't gone into the automobile game, it is unlikely that he would have become interested in baseball as a club owner. He liked the game, though he never saw a big league contest until he came to St. Louis. He was a man who could take his baseball or leave it alone. The Cardinal stock-selling campaign of 1917 probably would have created only a ripple of interest with Sam if it hadn't been for Fuzzy Anderson, an automobile associate, a former bosom pal, and a fan of the rabid, dyed-in-the-wool species. Fuzzy went whole-heartedly into the idea of the St. Louis fans owning their own club, and to please Anderson, Breadon purchased four shares of stock for $200. Later Attorney Jones gave a dinner to the new stockholders at the Mercantile Club. Huggins and the Cardinal players were in attendance, and one of the inducements was to have the stockholders meet their players. The oratory must have been high-powered, for before the hard-headed Scotch-Irishman from Greenwich Village left the dinner he had subscribed to $1800 more of stock, increasing his holdings to $2,000.

In the meantime the nation had plunged into the first World War, and though the 1917 Cardinals finished third, it was a poor season in the club's ledger. As the war wore on, the public's mind was on cracking the Hindenburg line—and only incidentally on baseball. By the start of the 1918 season, the new city-wide stockholders' ownership had paid Mrs. Britton $180,000, but notes were due for the remaining $170,000, and there were other unpaid bills.

Sam received a telephone message from the Cardinal office to attend an urgent meeting of the stockholders. Would he please attend? "Not me," replied Breadon; "I'm not sending my good money after bad."

But his pal, Fuzzy Anderson, changed his mind. He called on Singing Sam, and asked that he attend the meeting as a personal favor. "I'm in this thing too deeply to let go, Sam," said Fuzzy. "I'm hooked for $16,000, and I've got to see it through."

So Breadon accompanied Anderson to the meeting. Though there were several hundred stockholders, most of them had Breadon's idea of not sending good money after bad, as only eight men put in an appearance. It was a rather dispirited group. Not only did they owe

Lady Bee money, but they needed money for immediate operations.

They were getting nowhere fast when Sam spoke up: "I'll advance the club $5,000 on a loan, if the rest of you gentlemen will do the same." A sum of $15,000 was raised at the meeting, and the Cards were carried over another emergency.

Ev ..tually Breadon loaned the club $18,000 and he still had his $2,000 of stock. He now was in the same boat as Fuzzy Anderson; he was hooked so deeply he had to hold on, and on the strength of his loans he was made a director.

Breadon picked up more stock; he is blunt and several times talked cold turkey at directors' meetings. Apparently he impressed Attorney Jones, who served as Chairman of the Board and a sort of liaison officer between Mrs. Britton, who was still owed a lot of money, and the fan owners, for in December, 1919, Jones called on Sam at his automobile office, and asked: "How would you like to take over the presidency of the Cardinals, Mr. Breadon?"

Sam gave it a moment of thought. "There are twenty-five directors on the club," he said. "That's entirely too many. They get together; everybody chews the fat, and they get nowhere. Reduce your directors to five, and I will accept."

Breadon and the other directors compromised; the board was reduced to seven and Sam was duly elected president in January, 1920. He now is the oldest National League president in years of service, and vice president of the league. When Breadon was elected to the presidency, Rickey remained as manager and was elected vice president.

3

"Once I was elected president, I really became vitally interested in the club, and baseball in general," said Breadon. "Starting with little, I had done pretty well in business, and I felt good business sense also could be used to advantage in baseball. I started to think up ways of making the Cardinals a winner, not only on the field, but in the box-office. And the first thing I decided to do was to get the Cardinals out of their old ramshackle wooden stands at League Park. Our grandstand, seating only about 7,000, was ready to fall down, and we had no money to fix it up. I recall Jim McKelvey, St. Louis Building Commissioner of the time, saying to me: 'Sam, I never sleep on Saturday night for fear that stand will collapse on Sunday when you get a double header crowd into it.'

"Looking back over the last quarter of a century, the two most important moves I made in changing the Cardinals from a chronic second division outfit to a winner was moving the club to Sportsmans Park, and the elevation of Hornsby to the management in 1925."

There was some precedent for two major league teams sharing the same park, for in New York the Yankees then were in their eighth year as tenants of the Giants at the Polo Grounds. However, it wasn't easy to move in on Phil Ball, the Brown owner at Sportsmans Park. Ball still was sore over the Rickey matter, and the attending court action. He was a wealthy man, and his club, then run by the capable Bob Quinn, had not become the financial drain it was in later years.

"I can pay you $20,000 to $25,000 rental when the Browns are on the road and the park is idle," argued Sam, "and we both can make money. We play a non-conflicting schedule anyway."

"I'm doing all right," said Ball. "Your park problem isn't my affair."

Breadon isn't the kind of man to take "No" for a final answer. He took an option on an old abandoned quarry in South St. Louis and ran advertisements: "Dump your dirt at the old quarry," while he spread word around that he intended to build a new ball park on the location. Maybe it was all bluff, or he would have had to go through with it had Ball remained obdurate, but after a month's negotiations Phil gave in and agreed to take Lucky Sam as a tenant. On June 1, 1920, the Cardinals returned to Sportsmans Park, where the St. Louis club played when it entered the National League as a charter member in 1876.

Oddly enough, the home plate, the playing field and the stands have been shifted completely around with the passing of the years. Originally, home plate was at Grand Avenue and Dodier, the southeast corner of the field. Then, when the American Association Browns used the field, home plate moved diagonally across the field to the extreme northwest corner of Spring and Sullivan Streets. Now home plate is at the southwest corner, Spring and Dodier.

Having moved into Sportsmans Park, Breadon next turned a shrewd piece of business in getting rid of the real estate on which

League Park was erected. As the old wooden stands were torn down, the city ran two streets through the property; the field was subdivided into building lots and several small houses went up. Then Breadon sold the entire plot to the Board of Education for $200,000, and Beaumont High School stands on the site where Young, McGraw, Bresnahan, Huggins and Hornsby played ball, Louie Heilbronner was dunked in the barrel, Gene Dale fell asleep in the bull pen and Pat Monahan chased the growler for thirsty Redbirds.

Enough acreage was left for another $75,000 windfall, paid by the Public Service Corporation for a loop for their street cars.

"What the $35 I made selling Honey Boy did for me personally, the money we made selling League Park did for the ball club," said Breadon. "It gave us money to clean up our debts, and something to work with. Without it, we never could have made our early purchases of minor league clubs."

4

One of Sam Breadon's early problems as president was Fuzzy Anderson, his old boon companion, and the man who talked the New Yorker into his first $200 investment. Just before assuming the presidency, Breadon had become the largest individual stockholder. Anderson held the second largest block of stock, so he wanted to be vice president.

"I don't think it would be fair to the other stockholders," said Sam. "Every one knows we've been friends for years, and they sort of look at our interests as one. So, it seems to me it would be unjust to the others if we held both the presidency and vice presidency."

Fuzzy didn't see it that way. "Either I am elected vice president or I'll sell my stock," he said.

Previously Anderson and Breadon had entered into an agreement whereby one or the other could buy his associate's stock at one and a half times its value, $150 for $100's worth of stock. So Breadon and Rickey took over Anderson's holdings, each taking half, with Breadon endorsing Branch's note for his bank loan. Rickey's stock, raised considerably in value, was later to go to Hornsby, and cause all the trouble in the league when Rogers left the Redbirds.

Even before buying out Fuzzy Anderson, Breadon had been buying stock all over town. "I learned early the idea of fan ownership of a ball club is the bunk," Sam says today in his characteristic language. "You wouldn't think of running the average business that way, and baseball isn't so different from most businesses. Every fellow who had a few shares of stock felt he should tell you how to run the team. I know, for at the start I did a lot of talking with my few shares. It was a case of too many cooks making a stew out of a ball club. I realized being president wasn't enough—to really run the club I had to own a majority of the stock."

Two years after his election to the presidency he had that control, and within three years he owned two-thirds of the stock. Now he owns between 75 and 76 per cent of the club's holdings. Some of the fan owners of the 1917-19 period felt the Cardinals had become a pretty good thing and held on. It has proved a tidy investment.

The club made Sam Breadon a rich man, and in 1936 his baseball interests became so vast that he gave up his automobile business to devote his full attention to the Redbirds and affiliated clubs. As for his former associate, Rickey, in a number of years he paid the highest income tax of any salaried man in baseball—more than Commissioner Landis.

If Rickey left his impress on baseball, so did Breadon. He started the practice of Sunday double headers in St. Louis. The practice was criticized and maligned; today it has swept through both major leagues and is an accepted thing throughout baseball.

"In the days of the automobile, movies and radio, I found we had to give the fans of Missouri and southern Illinois, to say nothing of our St. Louis fans, more than a two-hour show to bring them to the ball park on Sunday," said Sam. "We had to give them a full afternoon's entertainment."

Breadon also was the original plugger for night ball in the majors. In the summer of 1930, he gave a picnic to New York and St. Louis baseball writers at his farm in St. Louis County. Sam then said that night ball for the majors was inevitable. "It makes every day a Sunday," was his theme song.

A year later, he was a member of the major league rules committee, along with Judge Landis, the two league presidents—John Heydler and Will Harridge, also Connie Mack, Clark Griffith and the late Bill Veeck of the Cubs. There was a rule which said no ball game should start less than two hours before sundown. Breadon suggested the rule should be repealed, and after half an hour of argument, he won his point.

He gave some phony reason for doing away with it, but withheld the real one—to change the rules so night ball could be played in the majors.

He got permission from the National League in 1932 to play night ball in St. Louis, and went to Phil Ball with a proposition to install lights at Sportsmans Park at Breadon's expense, the Browns to pay half of it when they were ready for night ball. Ball turned it down, saying the American League was against night games.

As a result, Larry MacPhail, who formerly ran the Cardinal farm club in Columbus, O., was the first to put lights in a big league park—at Crosley Field, Cincinnati, in 1935. Breadon, the pioneer for major league night ball, didn't get his lights until 1940.

While Rickey was the club's ambassador to the Y.M.C.A. and the church element, Breadon was the mixer for the club. Sam didn't mind knocking off a few highballs to celebrate a Cardinal victory. He liked jovial, congenial people around him—also to sing, and in his earlier years as Cardinal president, he enjoyed having the baseball writing gang from his old home town gather for a sing. Rud Rennie of the *New York Herald Tribune* was one of his favorite singing companions.

Until the war moved the Cardinal training camp from sunny St. Petersburg to Cairo, Ill., Breadon, though in his early sixties, liked to put on a Cardinal uniform and work out with the so-called "12 o'clock infield." George P. Vierheller, director of St. Louis' world-famous zoo and Sam's friend of long standing, worked out with the same creaky infield combination. Vierheller is a great Cardinal fan, and even has some of his talented trick chimpanzees doing a baseball act in Redbird regalia. Any similarity to the play of the "12 o'clock infield" is purely coincidental.

XII ⊖ FARMER IN THE DELL

AS FAR BACK AS 1919, Rickey conceived the idea of a farm system. He racked his brain on how he could compete with the stronger clubs, especially the Giants, who under McGraw were going into the major and minor league marts with their big bank roll, and taking all the cream. By the time the Cardinals had access to the supply, there was little left but skim milk. It was bad enough during the Brush-Hemstead regime in New York, but after Stoneham, McGraw and McQuade came into possession of the New York franchise in January, 1919, the rubber band really came off the Giants' fat wad.

"Starting the Cardinal farm system was no sudden stroke of genius," says Rickey today. "It was a case of necessity being the mother of invention. We lived a precarious existence. We would trade one player for four, and then maybe sell one who developed for a little extra cash with which to buy a few minor leaguers others passed up.

"When the Cardinals were fighting for their very life in the National League, I found that we always were at a distinct disadvantage in trying to get players from the minor leagues. Other clubs would outbid us; they had the money and the superior scouting machinery. The Giants, who then had a lot of loose money, were the worst thorn in my side. We simply couldn't compete against McGraw. So, we had to take the leavings, or nothing at all."

Even that wasn't the worst of it. Charley Barrett, then pretty much the Cardinals' scouting department, or Rickey, through his contacts, might hear of a promising youngster in one of the lower minor leagues. So Branch would start dickering for the youth, or ask the club to name a price. Then came a procedure which really burned Rickey up: instead of the minor league club owner selling the player to St. Louis, he would wire the Giants, Yankees, Cubs or some other opulent club: "Rickey here. He likes Blong, our shortstop, so he must be good. Has offered $2,000. What do you offer?" Sometimes, without even looking at the player, the rival major league club came through with a $3,000 offer, and right under Branch's nose his discovery was sold to the wealthier club.

"That kind of thing drove me mad," said Branch. "I found we even were scouting players for other clubs to pick up.

"I pondered long on it, and finally concluded that if we were too poor to buy, we would have to raise our own."

And the players raised and developed by the Cardinals since then read like a World's Series Who's Who: Jim Bottomley, Tommy Thevenow, Chick Hafey, Taylor Douthit, Bill Hallahan, Charley Gelbert, Pepper Martin, Bill DeLancey, Rip Collins, Dizzy and Paul Dean, Tex Carleton, Joe Medwick, Terry Moore, Johnny Mize, Mickey Owen, Mort and Walker Cooper, Enos Slaughter, Stan Musial, Whitey Kurowski, Jimmy Brown, Marty Marion, Max Lanier, Howard Pollet, Ernie White, Harry Walker, Alpha Brazle and a host of others.

Another reason Rickey had to try to find a dependable place to send players was to prevent unscrupulous minor leaguers from double-crossing the Sunday School teacher by violating so-called "gentlemen's agreements."

"I always have retained many of my college contacts," said Rickey, "since my early baseball and football experience at Ohio Wesleyan and my later coaching post at Michigan. Frequently an old college friend tipped me off to a good prospect. I would quietly sign the player, and knowing he was not ready, send him to a minor league club under one of the gentlemen's agreements which then were quite in vogue in baseball. Too often the club owner to whom I sent the player forgot all about the agreement when the player developed and sold 'my find' to a rival club."

The extensive farm empire of the Cardinals had its start in 1919 when Rickey purchased 18 of the 100 shares in the Houston club of the Texas League. By making the Cardinals part owners of the Texas club, Branch felt he could safely send a player there and get him back when he wanted the man returned. Doak Roberts then was head of the Houston club, and worked harmoniously with Rickey. The Cardinals eventually raised their holdings in Houston to 75 per cent, and by 1925 took full control.

"Experience taught us that owning half of a minor league club, or even a majority of its stock, was unsatisfactory," said Branch. "There naturally are many deals between the parent club and the minor league team. When we purchased a player from the minor league associate, we always had to be mindful of the minority holdings in determining a price. We had to make it high enough to avoid criticism. Then, when we sold a player from St. Louis to the minor league team, we had to be equally careful not to make the price too stiff. Or, again, some one would feel that he was getting hurt. The solution, of course, was to own the minor league club outright."

Shortly after going into the Texas League, the Cardinals acquired Fort Smith, Ark., of the old Western Association. Through his faithful scout, Charley Barrett, Rickey first purchased a half ownership, but eventually took over the remaining 50 per cent of the club's stock. Fort Smith was owned by the colorful Blake Harper, now a prominent member of the Cardinal family and head of the concessions department for both St. Louis clubs. Blake is a character and his cubby-hole of an office under the Sportsmans Park stands, with its private telephone system reaching all over the park, showers and rathskeller, also is an institution. He served in the Navy before and during World War I, was a Navy lightweight champion, Sheriff and Tax Collector for Sebastian County, Ark., a wholesale grocer and minor league club owner. As an imaginative, high-powered concessions man, Harper is a true Cardinal—he leads the league. It was just faint praise to be told that he was "the Harry Stevens of the Mississippi." Blake would have beamed more if told that the Stevens boys, successors to the immortal Harry, are "the Blake Harpers of the Hudson."

Fort Smith was only a class C team, but a lot of famous Cardinals, Martin, Hafey, Thevenow and Douthit among them, got their start in the Arkansas town or played there early in their minor league careers.

2

In December, 1920, Sam Breadon attended the annual convention of the minor leagues in Kansas City. It was in the early years of prohibition, and though the Muehlebachs, then owner of the Kansas City Blues, had ceased manufacturing beer for commercial purposes, George Muehlebach was too good a host not to brew several barrels for the city's baseball visitors. Sam found a congenial beer-drinking companion in Ernie Landgraf, a former silversmith, then owner of the Syracuse club of the International League, and before the night was over Ernie had sold the St. Louisan half of his club. It was the first time that the Cardinals acquired a farm as high as class AA, right under the major leagues in playing strength. Though wishing to expand into the higher minors, Rickey opposed going into partnership with Landgraf, and two years later, the Cardinals bought out the silversmith. Later, in 1927, the Cardinals transferred their International League franchise to Rochester, where the Red Wings, under Cardinal ownership, developed into one of the great minor league clubs of the country, winning championships in 1928-29-30-31 and 1940.

Following the acquisition of Fort Smith, Houston and Syracuse, the Cardinal empire took in Sioux City, Joplin, Mo. and Springfield, Ill. A second-class AA club was procured when the Cardinals acquired Columbus in the American Association in 1931, and the Breadon-Rickey organization won representation in the third class AA circuit, the Pacific Coast League, in 1936, with the purchase of the Sacramento club. The Columbus Red Birds have been either champions or hot contenders ever since the Cardinal ownership took over, and Pepper Martin led Sacramento to its only championship in 1942 with an amazing finish against Phil Wrigley's Los Angeles club. Because of the difficulty of providing three Class AA leagues with capable players under war conditions, Breadon gave up the Sacramento club in February, 1944.

Rickey even went so far as to back entire leagues, and at one time he controlled the entire player supply in the Nebraska State and Arkansas-Missouri League. But this was too much for Judge Landis, opposed to Rickey's idea from the start, and the Cardinals were limited to one club in each of these leagues, Farmer Branch finding big league sponsors for the other teams.

Arthur Feltzner, of the St. Louis organization, has a room in the Cardinal offices in which he has numerous blackboards, on which he lists all the clubs and players in the Redbird organization. As soon as a player is shifted, he is rubbed off one slate and placed on another.

In 1940, shortly before the nation started to feel the effects of World War II, Arthur had 33 slates in his office, with some 600 players listed. Here was the Cardinal empire in its greatest glory:

Class	Team	League
Major	St. Louis	National
AA	Rochester	International
AA	Columbus	American Assoc.
AA	Sacramento	Pacific Coast
A-1	Houston	Texas
B	Asheville, N. C.	Piedmont
B	Columbus, Ga.	South Atlantic
B	Decatur, Ill.	I.-I.-I.
B	Mobile, Ala.	South Eastern
C	Jacksonville, Tex.	East Texas
C	Pine Bluff, Ark.	Cotton States
C	Portsmouth, O.	Middle Atlantic
C	Springfield, Mo.	Western Assoc.
D	Albany, Ga.	Georgia-Florida
D	Albuquerque, N. M.	Arizona-Texas
D	Cambridge, Md.	Eastern Shore
D	Caruthersville, Mo.	N. E. Arkansas
D	Daytona Beach, Fla.	Florida State
D	Duluth, Minn.	Northern
D	Fostoria, O.	Ohio State
D	Gastonia, N. C.	North Carolina State
D	Grand Island, Neb.	Nebraska State
D	Greensburg, Pa.	Penna. State Assoc.
D	Johnson City, Tenn.	Appalachian
D	Kinston, N. C.	Coastal Plain
D	Martinsville, Va.	Bi-State
D	Midland, Tex.	West Tex.-New Mex.
D	Monett, Mo.	Arkansas-Missouri
D	New Iberia, La.	Evangeline
D	Paducah, Ky.	Kitty
D	Taft, Tex.	Texas Valley
D	Union Springs, Ala.	Alabama-Fla.
D	Williamson, W. Va.	Mountain States

"Of these 32 minor league teams, we owned the clubs outright in Rochester, Columbus, O., Sacramento, Asheville, Columbus, Ga., Decatur, Portsmouth, Springfield, Mo., Albany, Ga., Gastonia, Grand Island, Taft, Greensburg, Johnson City and Monett," explained Feltzner. "We worked with the others under optional agreements.

"There were 20 Class D clubs in the United States in 1940 and the Cardinals had a team in each of them. One actually had to go out of the country to find a class D league in Organized Baseball in which we weren't represented; that was the Canadian Colliery League, which operated in New Brunswick."

Even though the war sharply reduced its minor league operations, the St. Louis club has around $2,000,000 invested in its farm system. "During their years of Cardinal ownership, we have erected new up-to-date ball parks in Rochester, Columbus and Houston at a cost of $1,500,000, and spent $50,000 in improving the park at Sacramento," said Breadon. "We have invested another $100,000 in lighting equipment in our lesser parks. Yet, a bad year can almost engulf you. We still operated most of our minor league clubs in 1942, the first year of our entry in the war, and lost $240,000 in minor league operations, which does not include $120,000 spent on our scouting system, or Branch Rickey's salary that year. Fortunately, the Cardinals won the pennant in a close race and had a spendid year in 1942, and we were able to show a small profit despite the heavy drain of our minor league clubs."

The Cardinal farm teams are run on sound business lines, and in normal times the higher clubs, such as Rochester, Columbus and Houston, frequently make tidy profits. Breadon doesn't expect to make money on the lower clubs, though if the patronage gets too poor, the Cardinals pack up and move elsewhere. The Class D clubs are the proving ground for the youngsters, who are picked up in the numerous tryout camps, which during the summer months are conducted in all sections of the country and are run by Eddie Dyer, present head of the minor league chain, and his able assistants, Joe Mathes, Pop Kelchner, Tony Kaufmann, Walter Shannon and Joe McDermott.

The career of Marty Marion, great shortstop of the parent St. Louis club, is a splendid illustration of the Cardinal farm system in actual operation. A Georgia high school player, Marion visited a Redbird tryout camp at Rome, Ga. in 1935. He immediately made the grade and was signed to a Huntington, W. Va. contract for 1936. One season in Huntington and three in Rochester polished him for the big leagues, and in 1943 he was the National League's shortstop in the annual All-Star game and St. Louis' outstanding player in the fall World's Series.

With the exception of such war replacements as Debs Garms and Frank Demaree, or players acquired in trade such as Danny Litwhiler and Harry Gumbert, it has been years since the Cardinals have gone outside of their organization for players. If money now is lost on the farm organization, such money is chargeable to the amounts that formerly would be spent for buying new players in the open market.

3

Breadon and Rickey, before Branch left the Cardinal organization, frequently have been criticized—by the fans in St. Louis and elsewhere, for seeming lack of baseball sentiment in selling crack stars to rival clubs: Hornsby and Johnny Mize to the Giants; Dizzy Dean, Rip Collins and Tex Carleton to the Cubs; Curt Davis, Joe Medwick and Mickey Owen to Brooklyn; Chick Hafey and Jim Bottomley to the Reds, etc. Yet, the policy of the club in that respect has been sound and good business. It disposes of stars while they still have considerable sales or trading value to make room for the budding stars from the lower leagues who are struggling to find an outlet at the top.

Even so, the Cardinals rarely are weakened; a Hafey goes from left field, and they have a Medwick. Medwick is sold, and the farm system has a Musial to replace him; in center field the line runs unbroken from Taylor Douthit, to Pepper Martin, to Terry Moore, to Harry Walker. Injuries and accidents cut down such fine shortstops as Tommy Thevenow and Charley Gelbert, but the St. Louis farms soon reared a Marion. First Baseman Bottomley went when he was a fading star, because Rip Collins was ready to take over. Collins was traded to the Cubs while he still had a lot of good baseball left, because Mize was itching to fire his big blunderbuss at big league fences. Later the Cardinals could sell Mize to the Giants because Ray Sanders was in the background. Bill DeLancey, a great young catcher, had his career cut short by illness. but the club came up with Mickey Owen and Walker Cooper.

Even so, youngsters often matured so rapidly the Cardinals could not absorb them as they became ripe for big league picking. Major league rosters permit only 25 men on a club, during the better part of the championship season. The top farm clubs frequently have sold crack stars to other major league clubs at fancy prices, Pitcher Bill Lee and Catcher Ken O'Dea (the latter now is with the Cardinals) to the Cubs; Pitchers Bob Klinger, Hank Gornicki and Preacher Rowe and Outfielder Johnny Rizzo to the Pirates, and Outfielder Hershel Martin to the Phillies.

4

Farmer Rickey's path was no bed of roses and his farm system was fought during the better part of his tenure as General Manager of the Cardinals. His most bitter opponent was Commissioner Landis, who as far back as the early twenties, battled Rickey's idea of chain farms with all the might of his powerful office. Year after year—in his annual meeting with the major league club owners, the Commissioner lashed out at Rickey's idea, the one which, according to Branch, made it possible for the under dog to live.

Landis, an individualist, felt that minor league baseball should belong to the town publisher, undertaker, wholesale grocer or the type of men who formerly owned minor league clubs prior to World War I. He felt Breadon and Rickey, with their great supply of players, were strangling such independent minor league clubs which still were trying to go it alone and had only a limited field and resources from which to obtain their players.

There is no doubt that the Commissioner's thought of home ownership for all baseball, major and minor, is desirable, but not always feasible. Minor league baseball always was a heavy gamble. In the nineties and first decade of this century, it was almost the sole summer recreation in the small city; today—speaking of normal times—the minor league club must compete with the automobile, radio, movies, beaches, night clubs.

Rickey feels that his idea of having major league clubs own, back or sponsor minor league clubs, along with night baseball, is all that saved minor league baseball in the United States. And there are many who agree with him.

Landis, at various times, tried without success to get baseball legislation to scotch Rickey's system of wholesale farms. However, he awaited his opportunity and cracked down hard on Rickey and the Cardinals in March, 1938, in the famous "Cedar Rapids case." Landis made free agents of some eighty Cardinal farm-hands, including Pete Reiser, who two years later—at the age of twenty-two, won the National League batting championship while playing with the Brooklyn Dodgers. He fined Cedar Rapids, also the Cardinals' Sacramento club for so-called "wash-sales," and hauled Rickey over the hot coals.

In his findings, Landis asserted working agreements were being perverted "into arrangements for complete control of the lower-classification club through secret understandings" and that the Cardinal associated clubs were violating orders "that no club should contract away its right and obligation to get competitive playing strength as needed and wherever obtainable" and circumventing the rule against one club having a working agreement with more than one organization in a league.

During the past winter, Clark Griffith of Washington, with the active support of William Bramham, head of the minor leagues, again sought to curb major league clubs with big farm organizations, especially the Cardinals, New York Yankees and to a lesser degree Rickey's Brooklyn club. Landis allegedly was sympathetic with Griff's platform. Jack Zeller of Detroit offered another plan to curtail baseball farming.

Rickey, the small town farm boy, who revolutionized baseball, doesn't take Landis's antagonism or criticism of his methods sitting down.

"Tell me just one constructive thing that Judge Landis ever has done for baseball," Rickey says almost defiantly. "Of course, he has honesty and integrity, and has been a strong administrator. But, during his long term in office, he has done nothing to extend baseball, nor has he ever shown any real understanding of the difficulties of baseball operation, especially how they have been affected by changed conditions. He has made no move to build up the baseball structure where it is so badly in need of reinforcement—in the colleges and high schools."

For years, Rickey has lectured and talked on baseball to high schools and colleges. An old college player, he has felt keenly the decline of baseball as a major college sport, and its suspension by many high schools. Even New York's High School of Commerce, for whose nine Lou Gehrig first swung his big bludgeon, has dropped baseball. It was players of this type who first got into Branch's famous notebook; such stars-to-be as Joe Medwick, Stan Musial, Max Lanier, Marty Marion and Pete Reiser were signed to contracts in the St. Louis organization when they were high school boys.

5

Rickey has lived to see his farm idea, once ridiculed, scorned, criticized and fought, adopted throughout the entire major leagues. Even if Clark Griffith and Jack Zeller of Detroit would curb and limit the number of farms, no club is so poor today that it doesn't have its own small farm system. A club without minor league affiliations found the cards stacked against it as badly as did Rickey when he tried to compete against the rich New York, Chicago and Pittsburgh clubs as an independent operator a quarter of a century ago.

No club owner in baseball ever spent greater sums for players than the rich New York brewer, Colonel Ruppert; at first a critic of the farm idea, Ruppert became a firm convert, and said, "That man, Rickey, has the right idea. No minor league club will hold me up again for an exorbitant figure." At the time of his death in 1939, Ruppert had the next greatest farm system to the Cardinals. As with the Cardinals, the great players of the Yankee champions of 1941-42-43 are home grown, and with the exception of Joe DiMaggio—a real bargain—the wealthy Yankees have made no important purchase outside of their organization in the last decade.

The multimillionaire Red Sox owner, Tom Yawkey, also decided Rickey had the right answer for building up a present-day championship team after spending well over $1,000,000 for such ready-made stars as Jimmy Foxx, Lefty Grove, Joe Cronin, Rube Walberg, Roger Cramer, Wesley and Rick Ferrell and a host of others. Failing to "buy a pennant," Tom turned to a farm system, and was on his way to a first placer with such home-developed stars as Ted Williams, Johnny Pesky, Bobby Doerr, Tony Lupien, Charley Wagner, etc., when the war broke up his team.

And perhaps the travesty of fate is that the Giants, the club which Rickey first tried to circumvent with his crude efforts in the early twenties, was at the foot of the National League in 1943, while the Redbirds were on top. The once formidable New York club was among the last to take up the farm club idea on a big scale.

Furthermore, Rickey's former executives and farm heads in the Cardinal system now hold prominent positions throughout baseball. Warren Giles, the former Cardinal head in Syracuse and Rochester, now is the live-wire General Manager of the Cincinnati club, and one of the best minds in baseball. Rickey first was drawn to Giles when the latter was business manager and part owner of the Joplin club in 1925. Rickey had placed his California collegian, Taylor Douthit, with Joplin, subject to recall by a certain date. Through a slip-up in the Cardinal office, the date passed without Douthit's recall. Taylor was a hot prospect, and Giles could have sold him to half a dozen clubs for a big price. Instead he called up Rickey, explained the office slip-up, and later was rewarded with a high executive position in the Cardinal organization.

Bill DeWitt, General Manager of the Browns, originally was Rickey's office boy on the 1916 Browns, and shifted with the boss to the Cardinals the following year, becoming in turn Rickey's stenographer, treasurer of the Cardinals and vice president of the many Cardinal farm clubs, until he went to the St. Louis Americans in his present post in 1936.

The dynamic Lieutenant Colonel MacPhail, Rickey's colorful predecessor as president of the Brooklyn club, was the Cardinal executive in Columbus, Ohio, while George Trautman, president of the American Association, served the Redbird organization in the same capacity. So did Don Beach, who headed Columbus, Rochester and other Cardinal branch farms. Don, a classmate and fraternity brother of Rickey at Ohio Wesleyan, is back with his old pal in Brooklyn. Ed Staples, assistant to the president of the Dodgers, formerly served the Cardinals as publicity man and secretary of the club. Bob Rice, former director of the Redbird minor league properties in Columbus, Albany, Ga., and Asheville, now is head of the Pittsburgh club's farm system, succeeding the late Joe Schultz, a former Cardinal player and minor league executive.

Eddie Dyer, who now heads the Cardinals' minor league chain, came into the St. Louis organization as one of Rickey's notebook players from Rice Institute in 1922, and moved on to his present job after a successful career as manager of the Columbus, Ohio club. Sam Breadon was breaking in his nephew, Lieutenant William Walsingham, as Rickey's successor when the young man entered the Navy in 1942. Bill served his apprenticeship as Rickey's secretary, even chauffeuring Farmer Branch from farm to farm, and was one of the early heads of the Cardinal Knot Hole Gang.

XIII ⊖ REDBIRDS GET SOCK APPEAL

I

IN THE YEARS immediately after Breadon took over the presidency, the club won no pennants, but Cardinal fortunes distinctly were on the upgrade. St. Louis National clubs began to have color other than the vivid shades in their stockings, and grabbed more of the national spotlight. They ceased to be door mats and had a lot of batting power. If they didn't lead in club batting, they were right up there. Hornsby, of course, carried the big shillelagh, but there were other lads on the club who spoke with authority at the plate. And ever since Abner Doubleday thought up baseball, the team with a substantial batting average has enjoyed sock appeal at the gate. Business at home perked up, and the Redbirds suddenly found themselves quite a drawing card on the road —especially in New York. During the Giants' pennant monopoly of 1921-22-23-24, the Cardinals kicked up more of a commotion in McGraw's Polo Grounds home run orchard than any other competitor.

The season of 1920, the first in which Breadon and Branch looked after St. Louis' destinies, was fair, though the finish wasn't so hot. While the last day of the season saw St. Louis tied with the Cubs for fifth, for a good part of the campaign the Redbirds held their heads well above water. After a rocky start, the club landed in third place June 15, held the spot for a month, and it wasn't until late July that the Cardinals started to backtrack into the second division. The clubs which took heaviest toll on Rickey's Redbirds were Uncle Robbie's champion Dodgers, who beat them 14 times, and the third place Reds, who slammed them for 13 defeats. Even so, the finish saw the Cardinals with only four more defeats than victories.

After threatening for several years, Rogers Hornsby went over the top for his first of seven batting championships with an average of .370. Milt Stock, the former Philly third baseman, hit a satisfactory .319, while Jacques Fournier, a picturesque French Canadian with a home run bat, belted the ball for .306. Rickey obtained Jack from Los Angeles; prior to that Fournier had played with the White Sox, and in the war season of 1918 he was a war replacement for Wally Pipp on the Yankees. There was plenty of life in a clubhouse whenever Jack was around; he never was lost for words. Frenchy and the fiery Texan, Hornsby, mixed it up in the clubhouse one day, but that merely added to the season's merriment.

An even more important player acquisition was Pitcher Jesse Haines, a sturdy righthander, who came from Kansas City. Cincinnati foolishly had turned him back to the minors a year before. Jesse, who could mix a real hook with a crackling fast ball, lasted with the Cardinals nearly two decades, long enough to acquire the nickname, "Pop." And the Cardinals switch players around as boys used to swap baseball picture cards.

Rickey added Clarence Heinie Mueller, nicknamed "Rockhead" by his mates, to his outfield. Heinie was a St. Louis sand-lotter, who was fast, could hit, loved to play ball, but frequently forgot his instructions from the bench to the plate. Branch started the former Red Sox infielder, Hal Janvrin, at shortstop, but soon switched to Dr. Johnny Lavan, his old favorite, who had played for him on the Browns.

The club easily led the National League at bat, hitting .289, 12 points better than the champion Dodgers, who were second. Pitching held back Rickey's sluggers. Outside of Bill Doak, who won 20 games and lost 12, the club had no real winner. Schupp, in his last year to show major league class, won 16 and lost 13, but was far down in earned runs. Little Sherdel started to come, with 11 victories and ten defeats, while the newcomer, Haines, worked like a stevedore, was credited with 13 wins against 20 defeats. Jakey May, the pint-sized lefthander, Goodwin, Jacobs and North helped round out the staff.

The season saw the Giants make their first attempt to buy Rogers Hornsby, the Cardinals' star, for a fabulous figure. Charley Stoneham, the Giant president, invited the non-alcoholic Rickey to meet him, John McGraw and Judge McQuade at a restaurant at 110th Street and Broadway, Manhattan, to talk "important business." Rickey attended with Oscar Cooper, a banker friend, who was just a bystander.

"I'll give you $300,000 for Hornsby," said Stoneham, "and I'll throw in another $50,000 if he wins the pennant for us."

"But you can't do that," said Branch.

"Why not, Major?" demanded the New York broker.

"Because I still have a lot of games to play with the New York club. It wouldn't be right if it was to our advantage to have you win."

McGraw agreed.

"Well, the $300,000 offer still stands," said Stoneham.

Rickey telephoned it to James C. Jones, who was still chairman of the board, and with the new president, Breadon, they decided to turn it down.

2

The season of 1921 was one of those years where everything happened. The club started off by losing seven of its first eight games, but put on one of those late summer and fall drives which since then have become famous in Redbird history. As late as middle August, the club was fifth with one more victory than defeats, but by winning 32 games out of their last 44, they managed to finish a strong third, seven games behind the champion Giants and two behind the second place Pirates.

The season started with Branch Rickey's noble experiment of trying to make an outfielder out of one of baseball's greatest second basemen. At the Orange, Texas training camp, a former New York sand-lotter, George Toporcer, was a hitting fool. He was the first major league infielder to wear glasses, and now is head of the Red Sox farm system. He had come from Landgraf's Syracuse club, and nobody could get him out. In a Yankee-Cardinal exhibition game, Babe Ruth and Rogers Hornsby were the featured stars, but Toporcer stole the thunder with a home run and three singles in four times at bat. Specs hit all the way back into St. Louis.

"I've got to play this fellow somewhere," argued Rickey, "and he only plays the infield, with second base his best position. Hornsby can play anywhere, so he'll start the season in left field."

How far the Hornsby outfield experiment would have gone if it hadn't been for the Cardinals' dismal start, there is no telling. However, after six games, only one of which resulted in a St. Louis victory, Hornsby was back at second base as the Redbirds played a Sunday game at Sportsmans Park, and before the campaign was over Toporcer was back with Syracuse for more seasoning.

Undiscouraged by his turndown the previous year, Stoneham made another attempt to buy Hornsby. Frankie Frisch then was playing third base for New York, with Johnny Rawlings, a stop-gap infielder, at second base. Charley called up Sam Breadon on the long distance telephone.

"This is Charley Stoneham of the Giants," he said. "I'll pay you $250,000 and throw in four good ball players for Rogers Hornsby."

"He's not for sale," said Sam.

"Do you know how much $250,000 is?" asked the New Yorker.

"Yes, twice that is a half million dollars," replied Sam.

Stoneham hung up without saying "Good by."

It was the year after Babe Ruth amazed all baseball by hitting 54 homers in 1920; the public seemed to like it, and they hopped up the ball in both major leagues. And Rickey's Cardinals were the boss hitters of the two majors with a team average of .308. With Hornsby again leading his loop with a near-.400 rating, Branch had nine .300 hitters: Hornsby, .397; Mueller, .352; McHenry, .350; Fournier, .343; Jack Smith, .328; Mann, .328; Clemons, .319; Schultz, .309; Stock, .306.

Several new pitchers were added that season: Bill, also known as "Bull," Pertica, a big husky from Los Angeles; Roy Walker, one of the numerous Dixie Walkers in baseball, who had pitched for Cleveland and the Cubs; Jeff Pfeffer, the former Dodger ace; and Art Reinhart and Freddy Frankhouse, two promising youngsters. Rickey also took on Eddie Ainsmith, the former American League catcher who had caught Walter Johnson in Washington, Leslie Mann, former Brave and Cub outfielder, and Herb Hunter, who later led several baseball expeditions to Japan.

The 1922 season had its tragedies, but compared to earlier Cardinal years, it was a huge success. While the club couldn't follow up the brilliant fall drive of 1921, it was a pennant threat all through 1922, and eventually wound up in practically the same spot as the year before. The Redbirds again came home seven games behind the champion Giants, and were tied with Pittsburgh for third place, only one game behind the second place Reds. It almost needed the development of a photo finish plate to disentangle the Reds, Cardinals and Pirates on the last day of the season. Cincinnati had a percentage of .558 and St. Louis and Pittsburgh each had .552.

The Cardinals were close enough to the lead for Branch Rickey to file a vigorous protest with both Commissioner Landis and league president, John Heydler, when in early August the Giants acquired Pitcher Hugh McQuillan from the friendly Brave club for $100,000 and Pitcher Fred Toney. Rickey also asked the city's Chamber of Commerce and Rotary Club to follow up his protests. A few days before the Giants-McQuillan transaction, St. Louis was in a high dudgeon over a deal by the other New York club, the Yankees, which acquired the great third baseman, Joe Dugan, from the Boston Red Sox. This deal was made with the Browns in first place, but gave the Yankees the added strength to nose out the St. Louis Americans by a game. The two deals, coming together, had St. Louis fighting mad. "What chance have we ever to win a pennant in St. Louis if such conditions are permitted to go on?" asked Rickey. Chamber of Commerce protests usually are just so much hokum in baseball, but such a furore was raised over the McQuillan and Dugan transactions that Landis had a rule passed prohibiting any player deals, except for the waiver price, after June 15.

Death stalked through the Cardinal roost, as two Redbirds, who had become strong favorites, died within seven months of each other. Dillhoefer, the popular catcher, contracted pneumonia just as the club was leaving for its Orange, Texas training camp. Pickles breathed his last, February 23. Austin McHenry, the clubbing left fielder, complained of headaches, but stuck gamely to his post until midseason, even hitting .303 for 64 games before he could go no farther. It later was discovered that the boy was suffering from a brain tumor, which resulted in his untimely death in November.

The club had other bad breaks as Shortstop Lavan frequently was ill, and Outfielders Flack and Mueller were out with injuries. Flack was procured from the Cubs in a trade for Outfielder Cliff Heathcote during the Decoration Day holiday. The two players exchanged uniforms after the morning game; Flack played before luncheon for the Cubs and in the afternoon for the Redbirds.

After leading the league twice in team batting, the Redbirds lost first position to the Giants, 1922 World's Champions, but still were robust apple knockers with a tidy club average of .301. After missing the .400 class by three points in 1921, Hornsby went over by a point, winding up with the brilliant average of .401. The clouting Texan also established a new National League home run record of 42, though Hack Wilson of the Cubs left that total far behind with 56 eight years later. After shifting all around the St. Louis infield, Rogers located permanently at second base.

Jack Fournier, never too agile, started to slow up around first base, and in the late summer Rickey brought in that cheerful, sunny spirit, Jim Bottomley, for some years thereafter the club's regular first baseman. Bottomley had a way of wearing his cap on the right side of his head, and the fans soon learned to call him Sunny Jim. Destined to be one of the league's foremost hitters, he was one of the first fruits of Rickey's farm system. Hailing from Oglesby, Ill., where he still has a farm, Sunny Jim got his first baseball schooling with Mitchell in the Dakota League and was groomed for the majors with Houston in 1921 and Syracuse in 1922. He proved an apt pupil in the hitting grades, and broke in with an average of .327 for 37 games.

The 1922 pitching headliner was the Brooklyn cast-off, Jeff Pfeffer, who won 19 games and lost 12. So often a fading star will have one more good season with a change of scenery, and Big Jeff enjoyed such a year in St. Louis. Sherdel, the little lefthander, began to show more endurance and won 15 games, while losing 11. Haines was just fair, winning 11, while suffering nine setbacks. North had a 10-3 record. Rickey's big disappointment on the staff was lanky Bill Doak, whose record was 11 wins against 13 defeats, while in earned runs the spitballer dropped from the head of the class in 1921 to almost the foot with 5.50 earned runs per game. If Doak's slump did not lose the Cards the pennant, it surely cost them second place.

The Cardinals were directly concerned that season in one of the last scandals to hit baseball, as it was their duty to bring the offender to baseball justice. In New York, McGraw had a sturdy Alabama spitball pitcher, Shufflin' Phil Douglas, who had the thirst of Waddell and Raymond without some of the quaint eccentricities which made Rube and Bugs legendary figures in baseball. Douglas was one of the Giant pitching aces in McGraw's 1921 World's Series victory over the Yankees. Always a tough customer for his managers, Phil was particularly difficult in 1922, and McGraw engaged Jesse Burkett, the Cardinal slugger of the Frank Robison-Pat Tebeau period, as his keeper. Douglas had been having some trouble with his arm, and after he had escaped from Burkett, McGraw gave him a scathing dressing down in the clubhouse.

The Redbirds were running second at the time, and Douglas wrote to—of all people—the Y.M.C.A. man on the Cardinals, Les Mann, that if the Cardinals made it worth his while, Shufflin' Phil would shuffle off on a fishing trip when the St. Louis club next played the Giants. Mann handed the letter to Rickey, who sent it to Judge Landis. The Commissioner immediately took a train to Pittsburgh, where the Giants were playing, summoned McGraw and Douglas to a conference in his room, confronted the pitcher with the letter to Mann, and when Phil admitted writing it, Landis expelled him from Organized Baseball.

4

There was enthusiasm by the bales and good will by the bucketsful when the 1923 season got under way. Rickey was the last word in managers with the young automobile man, Breadon, and his associates. Branch hadn't won any pennant, but twice in a row he had finished seven games out of first place; his teams had played interesting ball; the Cardinal sluggers had given the Mississippi River town its share of diamond thrills; and Rickey was bringing in a fine crop of young players. Breadon decided to show his appreciation and confidence by signing Rickey to a five-year contract as manager on February 8. In fact, newspaper accounts of the time said Breadon wanted to sign the manager to a ten-year contract, but Branch decided that would be tying himself up for too long a period and compromised on the five-year document.

Yet, strange as it may seem, when Branch was signed at an enthusiastic meeting of the stockholders, he immediately proceeded

98

to pour cold water on the enthusiasm. In the issue of *The Sporting News,* which followed the signing of the five-year contract, we read: "Mr. Rickey removed all illusions by telling the men who put their money behind the club that it hasn't a chance to get much of anywhere unless pitchers, infielders, outfielders and maybe a catcher are developed—and note that he says 'developed,' indicating that he has abandoned all ideas of trades and purchases.

"Mr. Rickey's statement was that unless the developments were as indicated, the Cardinals' backers might as well look forward to a lean year in 1923, but hold on to hopes for 1924, when some of the prospects now a year or so away might naturally be expected to come through."

Coming from a man who had just managed two hot contenders, Breadon and the other stockholders merely grinned, and said: "He's cagey; he knows he has a good team, and just doesn't want to build our hopes too high, in case something goes wrong."

Well, a lot of things went wrong. Rickey did make a trade; with Bottomley showing signs of a coming star, Branch had no further need for Fournier, and sent him to Brooklyn for Uncle Robbie's center fielder of his 1916 and 1920 champions, Hi Myers, then pretty well along. The club also picked up Fred Toney from the Braves; the Man Mountain from Tennessee had figured in that McQuillan deal which had made Rickey see red the year before. The 1923 Cardinals got off to a poor start, but moved into third place on May 8. Rickey took the runner-up position five days later, and when he held it until near Decoration Day, the pennant bee again was buzzing. The town and the stockholders felt at last they had a pennant winner. But Pittsburgh and Brooklyn suddenly pushed ahead of the Redbirds, and in June St. Louis skidded to fifth. During the remainder of the season the Cardinals bobbed back and forth between fourth and fifth, eventually winding up in the top rung of the second division with 79 victories against 74 defeats, their .516 percentage being unusually high for a fifth placer.

The highlight of the season was the trouble between Rickey and his slugging second base star, Rogers Hornsby. After several sharp clashes during the season, the pair had a bitter verbal run-in on the Polo Grounds bench in the St. Louis club's last visit to New York, and when they reached the clubhouse the manager and the league's No. 1 batsman had it out with their fists. Coach Burt

Shotton and others rushed between the feudists before there was a decision.

Then, in September Rogers was fined $500 and suspended for the balance of the season for absenting himself from duty on the plea of continued illness when the club's physician, Dr. Robert F. Hyland, had declared that he was well enough to play. Hornsby was suffering from a skin irritation, which had broken out on his body.

However, Rickey was quoted as saying: "It is more a state of mind than anything else. Hornsby would play if outside influences did not have him hypnotized." With Christianly charity, Branch added that he "would overlook unprintable names which Hornsby called his manager."

In giving out the statement of Hornsby's late season fine and suspension, the club added a line: "Rogers Hornsby will not be sold or traded."

Between his illness and his troubles with Rickey, Hornsby played in only 106 games that season, hitting .384. There was some question as to whether he had played in sufficient games to be recognized as the official batting champion, but John Heydler ruled that he was the National League's first hitter.

Apart from troubles with Hornsby, Rickey had other difficulties; both of the veteran infielders, Milt Stock and Doc Lavan, slipped perceptibly. After their big season the year before, the veteran battery, Jeff Pfeffer and Eddie Ainsmith, became just ordinary workmen. Pfeffer dropped from 19 victories to eight and Ainsmith's batting average crumbled from .292 to .212. Doak's spitter also showed further disintegration and reports were that Bill wanted to get away from St. Louis.

Yet, the season wasn't entirely a flop for Rickey; he had his pleasant moments. His new farm system was beginning to show splendid results. Bottomley, the young first baseman, hit .371 in his first complete season, and was topped only by Hornsby. From the campus of Rickey's own Alma Mater, Ohio Wesleyan, came Howard Freigau, a promising infielder, who could play either shortstop or third base. For some years he was Branch's "boy" on the club. Howard apprenticed at the Syracuse farm, and played a few games for Rickey in 1922. Ray Blades, a speedy kid from Mt. Vernon, Ill., had taken his prep course in Houston and also played a little for Farmer Branch the season before. Fast, and a difficult man to pitch to, he was to go far in the Cardinal organization, even becoming one of Rickey's numerous managerial successors. Lester Bell, a hustling infielder from Harrisburg, Pa., joined up late in the 1923 season, and hit .371 in 15 games at shortstop. He had been polished up at Syracuse and Houston.

Harry McCurdy joined the catching staff and Eddie Dyer and John Stuart looked like the best of a slew of young pitchers. Dyer is the same chap who now heads the Cardinal farms. A sturdy left-hander, Dyer was a crack football and baseball star at Rice Institute, Texas, captaining a great Rice eleven in 1921. Eddie was fast and could hit, and doubled in the outfield. Stuart, a product of Ohio State, was one of the last big league hurlers to pitch and win a double header. He turned the trick against the Braves, July 10, winning by 11 to 1 and 6 to 3, but never followed up this early promise.

XIV ⊖ TROUBLE BREWS FOR BRANCH

I

IF THE CARDINALS' drop to fifth place in 1923 was a disillusionment, their further plump to sixth in 1924 was gall and wormwood for the St. Louis stockholders. It was the season Rickey thought might be "the year," but there the club was, back where it had been in the early days of the Breadon presidency. Men around the league were saying Branch knew ball players, but that in running a ball club he was "too much theory," with "not enough practical baseball." Singing Sam was anything but pleased and was thinking: "Maybe I was too enthusiastic with that five-year contract; but I'm lucky he didn't sign for ten years."

Except for Rogers Hornsby hitting .424, the highest average of this century in the two majors, and the bringing up of some additional promising farm hands, there were few bright spots in 1924, not even a brief incursion into the first division. While the club slipped back only one position, actually the 1924 club dropped 15 more games than the respectable .516-percentage fifth-place team of

1923. At no time during the 1924 season were the Redbirds ever in the race, and on only two days were they as high as fifth.

We read that Rickey was too quick in releasing experienced pitchers, without having the men to replace them. He released Pfeffer to Pittsburgh and North to Boston, and in May traded Bill Doak to Brooklyn for Leo Dickerman. Dickerman never was more than a mediocre pitcher, while Doak immediately regained stardom in Brooklyn. He finished with 13 victories and six defeats, and almost pitched the Dodgers into the pennant, his pitching highlighting a late season Brooklyn winning streak of 15 straight.

That weak pitching pulled the Cardinals down was indicated by the substantial team batting average of .290. The club scored plenty of runs, but the opposition tallied even more often. However, we also read: "Rickey had his full share of hard luck. Catcher Clemons had a season-long disability, a cartilage torn off his knee just as the season started. Jim Bottomley was put on the sidelines for a month by illness; Blades turned an ankle; Roscoe Holm, a promising catcher-outfielder, broke a bone in his foot and had to knock off the rest of the season; and even the great Hornsby, despite his brilliant hitting, did not escape; he was out with a dislocated thumb in May and a back ailment late in the season."

Even Hornsby's remarkable batting achievement was not properly rewarded, and the failure of the Rajah, as he was then called, to win the National League's most valuable player prize brought Breadon additional grief. Through his automobile connections, Breadon always has had a pretty good publicity sense. In 1923, he sold the National League on the idea of having a publicity bureau, something which up to that time never had been done in baseball. The following winter he put over another idea, the league officially naming its most valuable player and rewarding him with $1,000 in gold. Sam had won no pennants, but he felt he had the league's outstanding star and that some glory—and publicity, would come to St. Louis and the club by having Hornsby win this award.

The author was chairman of the first National League Most Valuable Player committee, and Dazzy Vance, a Brooklyn hurler, who had enjoyed a great season, winning 28 games and losing only six, was awarded the 1924 honor; Dazz defeated Hornsby by three votes.

When the vote was announced, Breadon was indignant; his own

pet measure had backed up on him. He called up the writer on the long distance telephone and asked: "What does one have to do in this league to win that prize? All Hornsby did was to hit higher than any man in the major leagues in 40 years and he loses out to a pitcher who was in less than 50 games. That isn't right."

It was explained to Sam that the committee chairman had nothing to do with the selection; his job was to count the ballots. However, there was a colored lad in the Cincinnati wood-pile. He was the late Jack Ryder, of the *Cincinnati Enquirer,* Redland's representative on the committee. Committeemen were instructed to vote for ten names; the first received 10 votes, the second nine, down to one vote for the tenth selectee. Ryder failed to name Hornsby on his ballot. His reason was that Hornsby was valuable to himself, but not to his team, and that his .424 average had failed to lift the Cardinals above sixth place. The argument was unsound and unfair; Rog had his faults, but he always was a hard aggressive player; if he fought for hits for himself, he also fought for victories for his team.

In this season, William Wrigley, Jr., the chewing gum millionaire, then the fan owner of the Cubs, tried to separate Hornsby from the Cardinal roster in a deal whereby Breadon could have written his own ticket.

The Cubs were playing a Sunday game in St. Louis and Bill Veeck, Wrigley's club president, called up Sam and asked whether he could meet Wrigley at the latter's apartment at the Chase Hotel.

"Mr. Breadon, I won't mince words," said Wrigley. "I've come here to buy Rogers Hornsby."

"We have no wish to sell Hornsby," Sam replied.

"But, you don't understand," continued Wrigley. "The price is no object. You name your price on Hornsby, and we will meet it."

Sam then related the telephone conversation with Charley Stoneham, when he told the New Yorker that he knew how much $250,000 was, that twice it was a half million.

"If that is the way you feel, I respect your views. But, if you ever change your mind, the offer remains open," concluded Wrigley.

2

Prior to the 1924 season, Rickey picked up another former Brown discard, Pitcher Allan Sothoron, and traded Third Baseman Stock to Brooklyn to get back the Cuban catcher, Miguel Gonzales. Since leaving St. Louis in 1918, Mike had played with the Reds, Giants and St. Paul. Brooklyn procured him from the latter club, so they could forward him to St. Louis. He was a member of the Giant World's Championship club of 1921, but as the former Cardinal, Frank Snyder, was McGraw's first string catcher, and Earl Smith his understudy, Mike's role on the New Yorks was largely that of bull pen catcher. He played in only 13 games that season, most of them at first base as a substitute for George Kelly. Commissioner Landis then had a rule that no eligible World's Series player could play in an exhibition game after October 31; today the rule is even more stringent. It barred Gonzales from playing in the Cuban Winter League, despite the fact that Miguel was manager of the famous Havana Reds. Mike worked out briskly at first base during the fielding practice, took part in batting practice, but as soon as the game started he confined himself to the coaching lines.

The author was on a vacation trip to the Cuban capital in the winter after the 1921 Series, when an indignant Havana sportsman said with much Latin vehemence: "John McGraw doesn't let Miguel play in summer; Judge Landis doesn't let him play in winter. So, when in the hell do they expect Gonzales to do his playing?"

Well, Branch Rickey found plenty of work for the Cuban Señor in 1924, catching Mike in 120 games.

Again the kids coming up from the new Cardinal farms brought some joy to Rickey and Breadon. Most of them were only names which appeared briefly in late season Cardinal box scores, but they were to write diamond history: Pitchers Charles Flint Rhem, Will Hallahan and Herman Bell; Outfielder Charles "Chick" Hafey; Infielder D'Arcy "Jake" Flowers; and Catcher-Outfielder Roscoe "Waddie" Holm.

Rhem came from Rhems, S. C., in the moonshine belt. His face was as tanned as the red soil of his native state; strong, sturdy and broad-shouldered, he broke in with a fast ball that snapped by hitters like Walter Johnson's early delivery. He spoke with such a pronounced Dixie drawl that his northern-born teammates had difficulty understanding him. Flint had the makings of a great pitcher, bordered on greatness for several seasons, and his adventures, though not always funny in the St. Louis front office, were among the most amusing in the Cardinal Cavalcade.

Hallahan, a city lad from Syracuse, came up as Wild Bill Hallahan, and it took some time before the stocky lion-hearted lefthander could tame his southpaw delivery, but eventually he became one of the Redbirds' best.

Chick Hafey, a tall gent from Berkeley, California, developed into one of the hardest righthanded hitters in the game. With the exception of Jimmy Foxx, no righthanded hitter of this generation drove a ball down the third base line with so much power. After four Hafey line drives whistled past his ears, Freddy Lindstrom, Giant third baseman of that period, remarked: "It sure will be difficult for third basemen to get insurance while that guy is in the league. He doesn't hit line drives; that's chain lightning that leaves his bat." As Cardinal Lee Meadows introduced spectacles to the pitching craft and Redbird George Toporcer to the infielders, Hafey, subject to sinus trouble, proved later that an outfielder is not unduly handicapped by wearing eyeglasses while on outfield patrol.

3

There seemed unusual interest in baseball in St. Louis when the 1925 season opened. A two-game early spring series between the Cardinals and Browns drew respective crowds of 20,000 and 22,000, and was considered an augury for a big year. Rickey even thought the worst might be over, and that his younger players would make their presence felt in his line-up. Yet, he was less than two months from the great crossroads of his career.

The head over a story discussing the 1925 prospects of the Redbirds gives this information: "Walter Mails' arm not yet in shape— Thevenow wonderful fielder; weak at bat—Bell a vastly improved batsman—Flint Rhem looks like a great strike-out pitcher."

Mails was the colorful Duster, who should have been on St. Louis' later day Gas House Gang. He called himself "The Great Mails." Duster previously had pitched for Brooklyn and Cleveland, and saved the 1920 pennant for the latter club by winning eight straight games after he joined the club in August and followed it up by pitching 16 scoreless innings in the World's Series with Brooklyn. The Cardinals obtained him from Oakland, but a lame arm retarded his 1925 efforts. At 47, Duster is a Sergeant in the Marine Corps. Thevenow, an agile Centralia, Ill. lad, had been out to pasture in Joplin and Syracuse.

Opening before a capacity crowd in Cincinnati, the Cardinals were shut out by Pete Donohue by a score of 4 to 0, no Redbird reaching third base. Perhaps that was an omen of what was to happen in the next few weeks. Rickey's line-up as he started his last season as active manager was: Flack, right field; Mueller, center field; Hornsby, second base; Bottomley, first base; Bell, third base; Schmidt, catcher; Thevenow, shortstop; Haines, pitcher. The catcher was Walter Schmidt, formerly of Pittsburgh, and a brother to the more famous Charley Schmidt, strong-man catcher of the Detroit Tiger champions of the Jennings-Cobb-Crawford period, 1907-8-9.

The Redbirds avenged that opening day shutout in Redland Field by knocking out Donohue a week later in the St. Louis inaugural, as the Cardinals drove out 14 hits to win, 12-3. It was the last time that Rickey's face was wreathed with smiles as he took off his uniform in the Cardinal clubhouse. No matter how Branch lined up his forces, the club went from bad to worse, and soon hit bottom. On May 23, a week before the big blowup, Rickey made one of his best deals, though it cost him some heart pangs to close it. He traded his fellow Ohio Wesleyan alumnus, Freigau, and Gonzales to the Cubs for Catcher Bob O'Farrell.

As the Decoration Day holiday rolled around, Sam Breadon's Irish dander rose with each additional defeat. It was a double holiday that year; the Cardinals were scheduled in Pittsburgh for two games on the thirtieth, a Saturday, and they were home with Cincinnati on Sunday, May 31. The club was in last place, and Breadon called up the downtown ticket office for a report on the advance sales for the May 31 game. There weren't any sales—or hardly any.

That was the final straw. Breadon took a night train for Pittsburgh, arriving the day before Decoration Day. There were reports on the team that the boss was "red-headed" and a big shake-up was in order. The reports were not unfounded.

Breadon is a man much to the point, who doesn't beat around

the bush. "Branch, I'm sorry to do this," he said to Rickey at the hotel, "but we can't go on this way any longer. I have decided we need a new manager on the field. We will be glad to keep you as vice president and business manager, where I think your talents are better fitted."

Rickey blinked. "You can't do this to me, Sam," he said. "You are ruining me."

"No, Branch, I am doing you the greatest favor one man ever has done to another."

"Who will be my successor?"

"I am offering the job to Rogers Hornsby."

"Why not Burt Shotton? He knows the players and he frequently has managed the club during my absence," inquired Rickey.

"No, Shotton has been too close to you," said Sam, seriously. "The fans know that, and I have decided on an entirely new set-up. If Hornsby won't take it, I'll go outside of the club. I hope you will stay with us, but if at the end of the season you wish to make a change, the club will not stand in your way."

Breadon then called on Hornsby, and said: "Rog, can you take over the management of the club in St. Louis on Sunday?"

Hornsby reacts quickly. "If that's what you want, I'll take it," he said. Star player managers then were all the rage; George Sisler, Hornsby's great hitting rival in St. Louis, was first base-manager of the Browns; Ty Cobb and Tris Speaker led the Tigers and Indians, respectively, from their center field outposts. Dave Bancroft ran the Braves from shortstop, while two second basemen, the veteran Eddie Collins and the boy wonder, Bucky Harris, were respective managers of the White Sox and Washington Senators. The Rajah was proud to enter that stellar society.

Rickey wasn't reconciled to the shift for some time. "If I can't be manager of the club, I don't want to hold any stock," he said.

"Well, that's up to you, Branch," Breadon said. He arranged for the transfer of Rickey's stock to Hornsby, endorsing the new manager's note. Rickey later admitted he acted hastily; even so he made a tidy profit. When Hornsby bought the stock, he paid $50,000 for $30,000 par value stock. Less than two years later, Rogers was paid $118,000 for it, with the Cardinals, the National League and the Giants putting up the money.

Despite the fact that there was no advance sale for the May 31 game, and the Cardinals dropped their Decoration Day double-header in Pittsburgh, the announcement that Hornsby was the new manager electrified the town, and a good crowd came out for the Sunday contest. Rajah got off on the right foot as commanding officer, as the Redbirds, with Rhem in the box, defeated Cincinnati, with Larry Benton and Jakey May, the former chubby Redbird, pitching, by a score of 5 to 2.

Reach's Baseball Guide tells us that "the 1925 Cardinals remained in last place almost to midseason, when under Hornsby's practical management, the club pulled itself together, became a harmonious and united aggregation and gradually climbed to the position to which its batting strength clearly entitled it."

The position to which Hornsby lifted the club was fourth place, the Cardinals winding up with 77 victories and 76 defeats for a .503 percentage. When Rog took over the club, May 31, it had won 14 games and lost 25 for a percentage of .359, so during Rogers' period at the helm, the team's record was 63 victories and 51 defeats for a percentage of .553.

It again was a strong hitting club—just missing .300—the .299 Cardinal club average was second only to that of the champion Pirates. Hornsby's new cares as manager did not slow down Rogers' mighty stick work; he hit .403 and crashed 39 homers in 138 games; it was his third .400 average, putting him in a class with only two other big league players, the old Cardinal, Jesse Burkett, and the immortal Ty Cobb. Jack Ryder was dropped from the National League's Most Valuable Player committee, and this time Hornsby won the prize with 73 votes out of a possible 80.

Sunny Jim Bottomley again finished second to Hornsby with .367, while Blades hit .341 and Hafey, .302. Blades, an intrepid, harum–scarum kid, was running constantly—on the bases and in the outfield, regardless of obstacles. He came up with a damaged ankle, but managed to take part in 122 games. Thevenow, after playing in the early weeks, had been sent to Syracuse for still more seasoning.

"I want Thevenow back," Rogers told Breadon.

"But we sent him out to gain more experience, so he can learn to hit," said Sam. "And Syracuse needs him."

"The hell with Syracuse," said the impetuous Texan. "He'll learn here just as quickly. I want him back."

So Thevenow was recalled. Jimmy Cooney, the other shortstop, was hurt a good part of the time; he is the son of James Cooney, Chicago National outfielder of the nineties and brother to Johnny Cooney, the player who never grows old. Heinie Mueller suffered with a broken bone in his foot. Reach's Guide tells us that pitching again was the millstone around the club's neck: "Apart from Sherdel and Reinhart, the staff proved weak, even after Hornsby succeeded Rickey, Dyer, Mails, Haines, Sothoron, Rhem and Dickerman all were disappointments."

Sherdel easily was tops with 15 wins and only six setbacks, while another lefthander, Reinhart, recalled from Syracuse, won 11 and lost five. Haines won 13 and lost 14, but despite a lot of strike-outs, Rhem could show only eight victories against 13 defeats. The Great Mails broke even in 14 games; Dyer won four and lost three; and Dickerman, the man from Brooklyn, won four and dropped 11. That dropped him plumb out of the league.

New players brought up that season were Taylor Douthit, destined to be a great center fielder, and Ralph Shinners, an outfielder for whom the Giants had paid a fancy price, but whose career was impaired when a pitched ball struck his skull with almost fatal consequences.

XV ☻ LIGHTNING STRIKES AT LAST

I

FROM THE TIME the Cardinals reported at Terrell Wells, outside of San Antonio, for the first stages of their 1926 training, there was one man who never had any doubt where the 1926 Cardinal club was headed. That was the fiery and aggressive Texan leader— Rogers Hornsby.

Shortly after the players reported, Rog called a meeting in the training camp clubhouse. "I want you fellows to listen to every word I am going to say. We are going to win this year's pennant. Don't go around telling every one we're going to win. But we are going to win just the same. If there's anybody here who doesn't believe we are going to win, there's a train leaving for the north tonight and our secretary, Clarence Lloyd, will have a ticket for him. I'll trade away any one who doesn't think we are going to win. If there's a man here who thinks we are a second division ball club, well, I just don't want him around."

Maybe Rogers never had read many books on psychology; as a player he wasn't much of a reader, preferring to save his eyes for opposing pitchers, but he surely gave those Cards the impression that the manager thought they were good, and that—at long last, a St. Louis club was going places.

There were a few changes on the club, though the most important did not materialize until the season was fairly well under way. In the winter, the Cardinals obtained Pitcher Howard Victor "Vic" Keen and an infielder, Michaels, from the Cubs for Shortstop Jimmy Cooney. It was a smart deal, as Keen won a lot of early season victories for the 1926 Redbirds at a time when they were badly needed. Hornsby also wanted a coach who fitted better into his scheme of things than Shotton, Rickey's old Sunday manager, and Breadon engaged Bill Killefer, Alexander's old battery-mate, who was released in 1925 as Cub manager. Shotton took charge of the farm club in Syracuse.

John McGraw of the Giants didn't intend to play the part of Santa Claus for the 1926 Cardinals, but he did the Breadon-Rickey-Hornsby combination a mighty good turn. On June 14, as the season for trades, other than waiver price transactions, drew to a close, he approached Breadon and Rickey and surprised them by saying: "I'd like to have Heinie Mueller, and if you want to do business I'll give you Billy Southworth."

The deal was made quicker than you can say Frank DeHaas Robison.

In New York, they still call this Southworth-Mueller swap "McGraw's worst deal." He had gone high to get Southworth from the Braves only a year and a half before, giving up Shortstop Dave Bancroft and Outfielder Casey Stengel to obtain Billy from Boston shortly after the 1923 World's Series. Stengel had won both of McGraw's victories in that Series with home runs, while in 1920 the Giants gave the Phillies $100,000, Art Fletcher and Wilbur Hubbell, a pitcher, for Bancroft.

Before going to the Braves, Billy had played good ball for the Cleveland Indians and Pittsburgh Pirates, yet somehow, he didn't seem to click on McGraw's club. For one thing Southworth had played right field during the greater part of his big league career, but with Pep Young a fixture in right field at the Polo Grounds, McGraw had endeavored to make a center fielder out of Billy. And neither Billy nor McGraw was satisfied with the conversion. Mueller, on the other hand, was best in center field; McGraw always had admired his speed, and thought if he did Heinie's thinking, he might utilize Mueller's foot-work. However, the St. Louis Dutchman was just an ordinary performer in New York, while Southworth, immediately catching Hornsby's pennant fervor, reached the heights with St. Louis that season, hitting .320, and doing a masterful job in right field.

Eight days after the Southworth deal, the club put over another master stroke—the acquisition of Grover Cleveland Alexander from the Cubs for the waiver price. Despite Hornsby's brave insistence at the training camp that his Redbirds would win, it is unlikely that pennant lightning would have struck in St. Louis that year if Aleck's famous thirst hadn't got him into early difficulties with his new Chicago manager, Joe McCarthy. The present Yankee skipper had just come up from Louisville and was piloting a big league club for the first time without having played an inning in the majors. Alexander had remarked contemptuously that he "wasn't being ordered around by a bush league manager." Joe had to act to preserve discipline on his club, and Alexander—to his own good fortune —was sold down the river to a potential champion.

Breadon was in the Cardinal office when the Alexander waiver request came through. Rickey was away, inspecting one of the farm teams, and the club was on the road. Sam wired Hornsby: "The Cubs have asked for waivers on Alexander. If you want him, I'll hold up waivers."

As Singing Sam now tells the story, Hornsby didn't reply, or at least not immediately, so he wired league president Heydler in New York: "The St. Louis club refuses to waive on Alexander." The Cardinals were fourth at the time, and four other clubs had a crack at Aleck before them, but they all waived, and the Cubs sold the great pitcher to St. Louis.

Phil Ball, the Brown owner, also did Breadon and the Cardinals an involuntary good turn that year. With a third place club in 1925, Ball thought that Sisler, his popular manager, had a potential winner. He double-decked his grandstand at Sportsmans Park at a cost of $600,000, increasing the park's seating capacity from 18,000 to 33,000, and Breadon, the tenant, was to reap the benefit of it.

2

The Cardinals opened at home that year before a fine enthusiastic, expectant crowd, and with Hornsby lashing out three hits and Rhem holding in the pinches, the Redbirds batted out a 7 to 6 victory over Pittsburgh. Hornsby and the Cardinals were presented with great horseshoes of flowers and the Redbirds received an award for having been voted "the most popular club of 1925," a recognition of the strong finish under Hornsby. Before some of the subsequent changes, the opening day line-up was: Blades, left field; Mueller, center field; Hornsby, second base; Bottomley, first base; Hafey, right field; Bell, third base; O'Farrell, catcher; Thevenow, shortstop; Rhem, pitcher.

The club did not follow up this opening victory with any spring fireworks, and for the first seven weeks it seemed that Hornsby had been looking at a Texas mirage when he indulged in his pennant chatter at Terrell Wells. The Redbirds were acting like just another St. Louis' chronic second division ball club. With New York and Brooklyn setting the early pace, the Cards were floundering in the second division muck in the spring months. In the club standing on April 29, they held the fifth spot; a week later, May 6, they were tied with Pittsburgh for sixth; on May 13, they slipped down to seventh, and on May 20, May 27 and June 3, they held desperately to fifth place.

In the meantime, Hornsby never lost his faith. He bellowed at some of his players, and encouraged others. Lester Bell had a poor spring at third base, and the crowd was on his neck. "Don't you mind; I'm still sticking with you," Rogers told the third baseman.

The club held for a while around the .500 mark, and then started moving up. The coming of Southworth and Alexander helped, while shortly before Billy joined the club, Rog had sent the brilliant youngster, Taylor Douthit, to center field. Taylor was a Bachelor of Science from the University of California, and he really could play that middle patch of the outfield. He was recommended to Rickey by that erudite scout, Prof. Charles Chapman of the University of California faculty, later with the Reds.

Alexander paid quick dividends. On June 27, when he pitched his first Sunday game in a Cardinal uniform in a double-header with his old club, the Cubs, the paid crowd was 37,718. Prior to that, the Cardinals never had played to more than 25,000 at home. Grover won his game, 3 to 2, in ten innings, after which Sheriff Blake blanked the Birds, 5 to 0.

3

As the clubs reached the Fourth of July half-mile post, the race was taking on a peculiar aspect. All the strength in the league apparently was concentrated in the west, as Cincinnati, Pittsburgh, Chicago, St. Louis and New York were contesting for first division berths, with the Giants being crowded out. Cincinnati took the lead in mid-May, and the Reds held it to the end of July. The Pirates, the 1925 World's Champions, showed flashes of their former strength, but there was internal dissension on the club, and the Reds, led by Jack Hendricks, St. Louis' 1918 manager, looked more and more like the team to beat. But no club was showing any great strength, or marked superiority over the field, and it was apparent a comparatively low percentage would win the championship.

After Cincinnati surrendered the lead in late July, the Pirates held it for a month, with the Cardinals gradually pulling up. Pittsburgh came to St. Louis for a long six-game series in late August, a series which many St. Louisans figure gave the Redbirds their first pennant. Hornsby's gamesters won four games, tied one, and lost one. On August 29, Alexander and Vic Aldridge battled to a 2-2 ten-inning tie before a rain-soaked Sunday crowd. On the next day, a Monday, 29,522 fans—the greatest midweek crowd in St. Louis baseball history up to that time—came out for a double-header. Ray Kremer, the Pirate ace, was victorious in the first tilt, a 3-0 shutout over Rhem and Herman Bell, but faithful Jesse Haines gave the

Cardinal fans some solace, winning the second game, 5 to 3, in a battle with Joe Bush, the former American Leaguer.

And then, thrill of thrills for St. Louis fandom, the Redbirds captured both ends of a second double-header, August 31, and finished the day in first place! No other St. Louis National team in history went into September leading the parade. In the opening game, Sherdel easily defeated Specs Meadows, the goggle-eyed pitcher Connery had dug up for the Birds a decade before, by a 6 to 1 score.

Hornsby was pretty well stumped for his second game pitcher. He looked over his bench, and gave a nod to Allan Sothoron, the former Brown, who had become a semi-coach. "You can do it, Allan; we're depending on you," he said. Jug-handle Johnny Morrison, with one of the widest curves in baseball, warmed up for the Pirates and some of the St. Louis fans groaned. But Sothoron pitched the classic of his lifetime, a three-hitter, and his 2 to 1 victory hoisted the Birds to the top of the roost. St. Louisans still speak of Sothoron's victory that day with awe.

Bill McKechnie, the Pirate skipper, sent back Kremer, his only victor, to try to save something out of the wreckage, but Art Reinhart took care of him in the sixth game, September 1, winning by a score of 5 to 2.

4

St. Louis was confronted with an odd September schedule; the exciting Pittsburgh series finished the Cardinals' home slate and throughout the month of September they now must do their pennant battling entirely on enemy territory. The schedule called for a series in every city on the circuit. It started with a double-header in Chicago. The first game was meat for Alexander. McCarthy's Cubs still were in the race, but Grover won a brilliant 2 to 0 duel from Charley Root, and Rhem followed with a 9 to 1 breeze over Sheriff Blake. The next stop was a three-day week-end series with Cincinnati, and 5,000 loyal Cardinal fans made the jaunt to the Ohio River town to lend encouragement to their favorites. They sat through two disappointing games, September 3 and 4, as Carl Mays turned back Haines, 4 to 2, and Pete Donohue pitched a 5 to 0 shutout against Sherdel. The second defeat knocked the Birds off the crest.

That didn't phase Hornsby, as a capacity 32,000 crowd was out for the Sunday game, September 5. He handed the ball to Alexander to warm up, saying: "You've got to bring this one in, Pete." Pete did, defeating the Cuban, Luque, 5 to 2, and St. Louis regained the lead by a hair, with Pittsburgh so close an army blanket could have covered the three teams. The Cardinals divided their Labor Day double-header in Pittsburgh, and finished the holiday in first place, the three leaders ranking: St. Louis, .584; Cincinnati, .579; Pittsburgh, .562. Sherdel's 8-0 shutout over Aldrich of the Pirates the next day, September 7, enabled the Redbirds to go east a game in front.

The first stop was Boston, where Dave Bancroft's seventh place Braves proved unexpectedly tough. They knocked out Alexander and Reinhart with an 18-hit blast in the first game, winning by 11 to 3. On September 11, the two teams divided a double-header; Haines won a 2 to 0 shutout, but Johnny Cooney, the lefthander, won the nightcap game, 4 to 3, from Rhem. And then the next day, Cooney, playing first base, drove in the winning run in the fourteenth inning, as Wertz and Larry Benton shaded Sherdel and Alexander, 5 to 4. That left the Birds tied with the Reds for first place with a .577 percentage; St. Louis was idle on the fourteenth, but Cincinnati defeated Brooklyn and took the lead for the last time.

Hornsby next moved his club to Baker Bowl, the former lair of the old tailend Phillies, for a six-game series, and while the flag was not clinched in Philadelphia, that series really was the pay-off. Before losing the sixth game, the Cardinals really swung their maces, winning by scores of 9 to 2, 23 to 3, 10 to 2, 10 to 1 and 7 to 3. By winning the 10 to 1 decision on the 17th, as Frankie Frisch—who a year later was to become a distinguished Redbird—bowled over the Reds with a tenth inning homer on the Polo Grounds in New York, St. Louis took undisputed possession of first place, and from there on never was headed.

It was during this Philadelphia series that Hornsby pulled one of his smartest bits of baseball psychology. Several of his players began riding the Phillies, and belittled them on their feeble showing. "Don't do that," warned Rog. "Don't do anything to get them sore at us. Get one of these tailenders riled, and they play their heads off against you. Let 'em alone, and they stay dead."

It was during this same series that Catcher Jimmy Wilson, later a Cardinal great, and his Philadelphia manager, Art Fletcher, a chap from Collinsville, Illinois, across the river from St. Louis, were bounced by Umpire Bill Klem from the first game of a double-header, and the famous "Catfish" sign appeared from a clubhouse window. Bill is allergic to anything that even remotely resembles a catfish. Fletcher was suspended by President Heydler for the remainder of the season, and during the suspension Art was fired by Baker, the Philadelphia owner. Fletcher really took the rap for Jimmy, the real culprit, who hung out the sign before the manager even reached the clubhouse. However, it was a good break for Fletcher, who caught on with the Yankees, where he has shared in ten rich World's Series.

From Philadelphia, the Redbird trail led to Brooklyn, where they were stopped for a day by Jesse Petty, the Dodger lefthander, winning a close 4 to 3 decision from Sherdel and Alexander, September 21. The Redbirds came back with a vengeance next day, clouting Jesse Barnes, the former Giant star, for 15 hits as they won, 15 to 7. Lester Bell, the third baseman, had a field day with three triples and a double, while Bottomley and little Thevenow hit homers.

The last nail was hammered into the pennant pole on the Polo Grounds, Manhattan, September 24, as the Cardinals, with Rhem and Sherdel pitching, defeated the Giants, 6 to 4, in the championship-clinching game. Southworth's late inning homer was the winning punch. The happy Redbirds raced into their clubhouse under the New York stands, singing, cheering, delirious with joy. They gathered around Hornsby and yelled: "You told us in Texas in the spring, Rog; you told us, Rog!"

"Yes, but we've got another job ahead: that other New York club —the Yankees," he said. "But we can take them, too."

To the press Rogers gave out a statement in which every word breathed the spirit of Hornsby: "We felt confident from the beginning. It was confidence that won for us; that's half of any battle. The boys got nervous at times, but what cost us most in games lost was the inexperience of some of our players. I had just one policy all year, and that was to try our best for each game which was played. I gave our pitchers all the chance in the world for each game. We refused to get excited, and I guess that's how we won."

116

The Cardinals eventually beat out Cincinnati by two games. St. Louis won 89 games and lost 65 for a percentage of .578, the lowest to win a pennant in the 68-year career of the National League. Cincinnati finished second with 87 victories and 67 defeats for a percentage of .565. St. Louis' first pennant victory was helped by the virtual collapse of the Reds on the home stretch, the Cincinnati club winning only two of its last nine games. Carl Mays, a 19 game winner, became ill, and the Red pitching staff cracked up. In desperation, Hendricks overworked his star, Pete Donohue; he pitched Pete in all three games of his final series in New York, while the Cards were having their soft touch in Philadelphia. Donohue started that series with a shutout, relieved in the second game, and was knocked out when he started the third.

5

St. Louis went into a frenzy when the news came over the wires and radio that the Cardinals were National League Champions on the afternoon of September 24. It was a long, long trail, starting just exactly fifty years before. It also was St. Louis' first baseball championship of any kind since Von Der Ahe's Browns had won their last American Association pennant in 1888. No wonder the town went completely berserk, got pie-eyed and had a terrible hangover the next morning. Parades in the downtown streets lasted long after Sallee's old milkmen buddies delivered their morning milk. Only St. Louis' celebration which marked the Armistice of November 11, 1918 was comparable to it.

But, it had been tough going all the way! Hornsby did not have a good season—at least, not up to former Hornsby batting standards. His average dropped from .403 to .317, and after leading the league for six straight years, he surrendered the National batting crown to Bubbles Hargrave, the Cincinnati catcher. Val Picinich, the other Red catcher, slid forcibly into Rog at second base, knocked several vertebrae out of place in his spine, and Hornsby couldn't get the old power behind his swing.

Bottomley also fell off sharply in his hitting in the close race, dropping to .298. The booed Bell of the spring was the club's batting leader with .325, followed by Southworth's .320. Douthit hit .307 in his first season as a regular and Blades, .305. This runnin'est kid finally crashed into the right field wall at Sportsmans Park in pursuit of a line drive, badly cracking a kneecap. He was out for the season and would have been out permanently but for the skill of Dr. Hyland, the club physician, who performed one of his ablest feats of baseball surgery on the maimed knee.

Bob O'Farrell, the catcher obtained from the Cubs in 1925, had a truly magnificent year, catching 146 games, and hitting .293. He was Hornsby's successor as the National League's most valuable player. Little Thevenow also had a remarkable season at shortstop; Tommy did not miss one of his team's 156 games, and handled 1,013 chances, 105 more than the next shortstop. But he trailed the Cardinal regulars at bat with .255.

The South Carolinian, Flint Rhem, easily topped the pitchers; he was credited with 20 victories against only seven setbacks. It was the Carolina boy's big year. Including seven spring games with the Cubs, Aleck's record was 15 wins and seven reverses. Sherdel chalked up 16 victories against a dozen defeats, and Art Reinhart had a Woolworth record—five defeats and ten victories. Jesse Haines had a 13-4 showing, and Herman Bell, used largely as a relief man, broke even in 12 decisions. Sothoron won three and lost three, but one of his scant winning crop was that important and vital job against the Pirates, August 31. At the foot of the class was Willie Hallahan, later one of the club's superdupers, with one win and four defeats.

XVI ✇ THE FIRST BLUE RIBBON

I

THE CARDINALS FINISHED the league season in New York. Between the clinching date and the opening of the World's Series at Yankee Stadium on a Saturday, October 2, Rogers Hornsby received bad news from Texas, the kind of news that bowls over the average man. His mother died in the Lone Star State. Hornsby announced he would not attend his mother's funeral, but would remain with his ball club. Some thought it was heartless, lacking in the finer sentiments. But it was just like Rogers Hornsby. He was all baseball, and baseball was to him just like a war. He felt the same grief over losing his mother as does any man in a similar situation, but he was preparing to lead his Cardinals into World's Series battle. He could no more have left his players than a commander about to lead his troops on a beach attack could walk out on his command after getting bad news from the home front.

By an odd shuffle of the baseball cards, Miller Huggins, manager of the Cardinals from 1913 to 1917, now was leading Ruppert's crack Yankee team against his old St. Louis club, directed by his greatest find and erstwhile pupil, Rogers Hornsby. The 1926 Yankees were not as highly regarded as World's Series opponents as some of their famous successors. Little Hug's World's Series record in New York had been only fair. He lost his 1921 and 1922 series to the Giants, failing to win a game in the latter year, and in 1923, his Yanks defeated McGraw's clan, four games to two. Miller's entry was the club which had made the sensational leap from seventh place in 1925 to Pennantland in 1926.

"They've got a good ball club; that guy, Ruth, is always tough, but he isn't going to get many good balls to hit," Hornsby told his players before the series. "The only pitchers they have who will bother us are Pennock and Hoyt. But, we can take them—just as we took the best in the National League. And no matter what the score is, we're going to keep fighting and hustling."

The first game turned out to be a left-handed pitching duel between stout-hearted Sherdel and the graceful Yankee southpaw star, Herb Pennock. It was to be the start of Willie's World's Series bad luck, as he dropped the decision to the Squire of Kennett Square by the narrow margin of 2 to 1. Neither of these mauling crews showed their vaunted punch, as the Cardinals made only three hits, and the Yankees twice that many. Two of the Redbird hits came in the first inning; Taylor Douthit opened on Pennock with a double to right and raced home on Bottomley's pop fly single over Joe Dugan's head. The only other St. Louis hit was Bottomley's second single in the ninth inning.

Sherdel started off with a flurry of wildness, the American League champions scoring a hitless run in the first, immediately getting back the Douthit run. Willie walked Combs, Ruth and Meusel, filling the bases, and Earle, the fleet-footed lead-off man, scored when Gehrig forced Meusel at second. Lou also singled home the winning Yank tally in the sixth after Ruth opened the inning with a single and Meusel shoved him to second with a sacrifice bunt.

Some of the Cardinals were sympathetic with Sherdel on his "hard luck." Hornsby overheard it. "The hell with yapping about hard luck," he snapped. "That one's gone; we'll even it up tomorrow."

His pitcher for the second game, played on Sunday before a then record crowd of 63,600 fans, was Grover Cleveland Alexander, making his first World's Series appearance since he pitched for the Phillies against the Red Sox in 1915. Aleck's opponent at the start was old "Red Neck"—Urban Shocker, the former Brown star. Before the game was over Huggins called in Bob Shawkey and Sam Jones, as old Pete tied up the series by bringing home a 6 to 2 victory.

New York was the first to score, getting two runs off Aleck in the second inning on singles by Meusel, Lazzeri and Dugan and Alexander's wild throw as he tried to break up an attempted double steal. However, after Combs opened New York's third inning with a single, Grover gave a masterful exhibition. Not another Yankee reached base. Twenty-one of Huggins' men walked to the plate and as many paraded back to the bench again.

The Redbirds, in the meantime, had tied the score on Shocker in the third inning on Douthit's safe bunt, Southworth's single, Hornsby's sacrifice, and Bottomley's two-run single. The game remained tied until the seventh when Southworth shot a homer into the right field bleachers with O'Farrell and Thevenow on base. Billy and Tommy were heroes with Aleck; each came out of the game with a homer and two singles.

Thevenow's home run was one of the most amusing of World's Series history. There used to be a groove at Yankee Stadium between the right field boxes and the old wooden bleachers (now torn down); New York sports writers termed it "bloody angle." Tommy lined a ball into bloody angle for what should have been an everyday two-base hit. While nearly two-thirds of the fans could see the ball from the stands, Ruth—playing right field, couldn't find it and groped all around "the angle" for the ball while Tommy ran joyfully around the bases. Returning to the Yankee bench, the big Bambino blustered: "I kept yelling out there: Where is that stupid ball? Where is that stupid ball? And not a son of a sea cook out there would tell me."

THE TEAM THAT STIRRED ST. LOUIS TO FRENZY IN 1926

SUNNY JIM BOTTOMLEY

being presented with $1,000 bag of gold by former president John Heydler for being voted the National League's most valuable player in 1928.

With each team in possession of one victory, the Cardinals moved on to St. Louis to make their first appearance at Sportsmans Park since Art Reinhart won the sixth game of that vital Pittsburgh series, September 1. Before they opened the Sportsmans Park end of the series, the Redbirds got a reception back to St. Louis which might have knocked a less stable outfit off its red-draped pins. The entire front page of the *St. Louis Globe-Democrat* was given to the homecoming under such streaming banner lines as: "Tumultuous Thousands Welcome Cardinals." "Greatest Demonstration in City's Baseball History Staged as Frenzied Multitudes Lionize Baseball Heroes Amid Bedlam of Noise and Joyous Enthusiasm."

The *Globe-Democrat* baseball writer, Martin J. Haley, himself a veteran of World War I, wrote: "The reception was even more impressively enthusiatic than that accorded the noble sons of the Mound City on their victorious return from the World War seven and a half years ago."

The Cardinals were to prove next day that the reception hadn't turned their heads. They still had their feet firmly on the ground, October 5, when Jesse Haines hurled a 4 to 0 shutout against Dutch Ruether, Bob Shawkey and Myles Thomas in the first World's Series game played in St. Louis since 1888. To make Pop Haines' triumph additionally sweet for the 37,708 fans, who came from all over the Middle and South West, the popular pitcher wrecked Ruether himself, hitting a fourth inning home run into the right field pavilion with Thevenow on base and two out.

Huggins' New Yorkers came back with a vengeance in the fourth game, when St. Louis was treated to a one-man hitting display such as seldom has been seen in the history of American baseball. Ruth broke out like a pent-up bull on a rampage. Though Rhem had a 20-6 record for the championship season, Hornsby had a dread the Yankees might blast his fast ball, especially the two dangerous left-handed hitters, Ruth and Gehrig. Rog's fears were not unfounded. Rhem, opposing Waite Hoyt, fogged through his fast one and fanned Combs and Koenig in the first inning. But Ruth was hot this day from the very outset, and sent the first pitch high over the right field pavilion some 15 feet in from the foul line. When Babe came up again in the third inning, Flint tried a slow ball and

Ruth crashed this one over the roof in right center for his second homer.

In the sixth inning, with big Herman Bell on the mound, and Combs on base, Ruth smashed a three and two pitch for the longest home run ever seen in St. Louis and No. 3 for the day. It struck far up in the bleachers in direct center field. The ball had traveled well over 500 feet when it struck the bleacher and still had plenty of carry behind it. By the end of that day, Ruth had established eight new World's Series records. Inspired by that tremendous one-man show, the Yankees tied up the series by winning the game, 10 to 5, though the Cardinals matched the 14 Yankee hits off Rhem, Reinhart, Bell, Hallahan and Keen with the same number off Hoyt. To make it an even worse day for the Cardinals, Taylor Douthit, the brilliant center fielder, crashed with Hafey in going after a line drive, and while the California collegian gamely played out the game, his shoulder was so badly tied up that he missed the remainder of the series. Waddie Holm, the young catcher-outfielder, replaced him.

"It was just another ball game; forget it," said the Rajah, after it was over, "but that big guy doesn't get any more good balls to hit."

St. Louis fans filed sadly out of the park when the fifth game was over. After trailing one game to two, the Yankees took the important three to two edge and were going home to wind up the Series in their own park. Sherdel and Pennock put on a St. Louis return engagement of their first game tussle at Yankee Stadium, and the outcome was the same—only this time Herb had to go ten innings before he won, 3 to 2.

The hitting was brisker than when these clever southpaws met in the first game, each team getting nine hits. It was nip and tuck and see-saw all the way. St. Louis twice was in the lead. Bottomley drew first blood, scoring in the fourth on his double and Bell's single. The Yanks had luck in tying it up in the seventh. Pennock got a double when Hafey fell in going after his fly ball. Later O'Farrell had Herbie picked off second base, but Thevenow spilled the throw. Combs walked and Koenig came through with the single which drove in Pennock.

The Redbirds were gleeful when they regained the lead in the seventh on Bell's two-bagger and O'Farrell's single, but luck again was with the American Leaguers when they tied the score in the ninth. Thevenow backed into left for Gehrig's short fly. The sun blinded Tommy and a stiff wind blew the ball away for a double. Lou reached third on Lazzeri's safe bunt, and scored when Paschal, batting for Dugan, lined a single to center.

The disappointing end for St. Louis fans came in the tenth when Hornsby tried to match wits with Huggins, and the old master won. Koenig singled and reached second on a wild pitch. Rog ordered Sherdel to walk Babe Ruth. Meusel advanced the pair with a sacrifice, and then Hornsby instructed Sherdel to hand out a second intentional pass, this one to Gehrig, filling the bases. However, Lazzeri brought in what proved to be New York's winning run with a long fly to Hafey.

3

The Cardinals were a pretty sober bunch of players as the Series returned to New York. The Yankees were tough on their own ground; they had two chances to win; one more defeat would eliminate the Cardinals. But Hornsby would concede nothing. Before the sixth game, played at Yankee Stadium on a cold Saturday, October 9, the Rajah addressed his team in the clubhouse: "If we don't do it today, there ain't any more series. But, there is going to be more series. We've got to win today and we've got to win tomorrow. So, get out there, fight your heads off; knock the ball down the pitcher's throat, and don't concede a thing."

Knock the ball down the pitcher's throat; the Redbirds followed instructions to the letter. Huggins picked Shawkey, Shocker and Thomas, and the Cardinals got to the trio for 13 hits, which were all unlucky for the Yankees. Alexander, making his second start, breezed in by a score of 10 to 2, the Redbirds having two especially fat innings—the first, when they scored three runs, and the seventh, when they tallied five. Lester Bell was the big gun, with a homer, two singles and four runs batted in.

The seventh game, one of the historic contests of baseball, was played on a wet, raw Sunday, October 10. It rained almost up to game time; a morning report in New York said the game had been postponed and the crowd was only 38,093. It was a titanic struggle, won by the Cardinals, 3 to 2, when they got a series of breaks to score their three runs off Waite Hoyt in the fourth inning. Jesse

Haines was Hornsby's slabster, and Ruth had given the Yanks a 1 to 0 lead with a towering home-run blast into the right field bleachers in the third inning.

Hornsby was the first out in St. Louis' big fourth, grounding to the infield. Bottomley singled to left, and Bell was safe on Shortstop Koenig's fumble. Hafey raised a fly to short left; Koenig and Meusel couldn't decide who should take the ball and it dropped safe for a single, filling the bases. O'Farrell followed with a line drive to left center; both Meusel and Combs went after it; they almost collided and when Earle stepped away at the last moment, Lanky Bob muffed the ball. It enabled Bottomley to score the tying run, and left the bases still jammed with eager Cardinals. Little Tommy Thevenow—a Yankee thorn throughout—then came through with the most telling blow of the series, a single over second, which scored Bell and Hafey.

That was the extent of St. Louis' run-getting as Hoyt held the Cards back in the fifth and sixth, and after Waite yielded to a pinch-hitter, Pennock pitched shutout ball in the last three innings.

The big problem was whether the Yankees could get those two big runs back. They scored one off Haines in the sixth on Dugan's single and Severeid's long double and it looked as though the seventh would be their inning. Combs led off with a single, and was put in position to score the tying run on Koenig's sacrifice. Hornsby again refused to give Ruth anything to hit and ordered Jesse to walk the Babe. Meusel forced Ruth at second, Combs advancing to third. Haines couldn't get them over for Gehrig, and the pass to Lou filled the bases.

Hornsby walked in to the pitcher's box, and asked: "Can you make it, Jesse?"

Jesse showed him his fingers. He had been bearing down so hard pitching his knuckler that he had rubbed the skin off one finger. Blood was dripping from it.

The preceding inning, Alexander had picked up his glove and walked out to the bull pen. Reinhart and Rhem also were warming up, but when Hornsby beckoned to the bull pen, the man who answered the call was the forty-year-old Alexander, who had pitched nine innings the preceding day. And feeling his work for the series over, Aleck had had his usual Saturday night celebration.

Hornsby walked out to short left field to meet him; he looked in the veteran's eyes, saw they were clear, slapped Alexander on the back, and said: "You can do it, Pete."

What happened is recorded for posterity on the Alexander plaque at baseball's Hall of Fame at Cooperstown, N. Y. Though Lazzeri hit only .275 in 1926, his freshman year, he was murder in the pinches, ranking second only to Ruth in runs batted in, with 114. Tony took the first strike; he connected sharply with the next pitch and drove a vicious foul down the left field line; it was less than a foot in foul territory as it sped past third base. "A foot made the difference between being a hero and a bum," Alexander said later. Grover didn't "fool around" with the California Italian. He sent another strike over the outside corner: Tony swung furiously for the third out. Even the partisan New York crowd sent up a cheer for this exhibition of courage and skill which reverberated all through the Bronx.

Alexander set down the Yankees in order in the eighth, and he got Combs and Koenig in the ninth. Then Ruth walked after a two and three pitch. Aleck walked to the plate and asked Hildebrand, the American League umpire: "What was wrong with it?" "It was just that far outside," said Hildebrand, almost touching his fingers. "If it was that close, I'd think you'd have given an old geezer like me the break," said Grover.

While Alexander was pitching to Meusel, Ruth, on his own, made a break for second base on an attempted steal, but O'Farrell's stout peg to Hornsby shot him down and the great series was over. Hornsby's Cardinals not only were National League pennant winners, but World's Champions. Judge Landis, also league President Heydler, Sam Breadon, Rickey and other National Leaguers tumbled over each other to reach the Redbird clubhouse and congratulate the happy victors. As for St. Louis, even though it was a Sunday night, the city on the Mississippi went on another wild orgy. It was unfortunate that after waiting so long to win a National League flag and a World's Championship, both the clinching of the pennant and the Series should have taken place in New York.

Despite the comparatively poor crowd which saw the last dramatic game at Yankee Stadium, the attendance record for that series, 328,-051, still holds today, and the receipts, $1,207,864, stood up for ten years as the record and have been exceeded only twice. Proving that the last shall be first, Tommy Thevenow, weakest hitting regular on the two clubs, led both teams at bat with a fancy average of .417. Hornsby hit .250 against Ruth's .300, but to show how well Hornsby kept his pitchers from feeding Babe good balls, the crack Yankee slugger walked 12 times in the seven games.

4

The winning of the 1926 World's Series by the Cardinals in October had a wild and tumultuous sequel two months later, when to the amazement—and consternation—of St. Louis and the entire baseball world, Sam Breadon traded the playing manager of his new World's Champions, Rogers Hornsby, to the New York Giants for McGraw's able second baseman, Frankie Frisch, and Pitcher Jimmy Ring. It was one of those things which simply was unbelievable. St. Louisans wondered whether their eyes were deceiving them, or were those glaring headlines in the newspapers some crazy prank?

But, it was the truth—the full truth. The trouble between Breadon and Hornsby went back to early September, when the Cardinals went east for their pennant-winning trip. Early in the season, Breadon had booked a September Sunday exhibition game in New Haven, where the club was then owned by George Weiss, now head of the New York Yankee farm system.

Breadon wrote to Weiss, asking him to cancel the agreement to play the game. Weiss declined, saying he had put out $500 to advertise the contest. Sam said he gladly would reimburse Weiss for the advertising, but George again said: "No." He wired back: "If you were down, you would expect us to keep our end of it. Now, you are up and the attraction, and you will have to keep your end."

By a strange coincidence, it was in Pittsburgh, where Hornsby was promoted to the management shortly before Decoration Day, 1925, that the storm broke on Labor Day, 1926, which was to bring an end to Rogers' meteoric career as manager of the Redbirds.

Breadon told Hornsby in Pittsburgh of his correspondence with Weiss, that he was unable to break the agreement, and that the exhibition game must be played.

Hornsby was furious; he was a fellow who always was outspoken and never held back his punches. "You're more anxious for a few exhibition dollars than to win the championship," Rog yelled. "You want to fritter away the pennant."

"I want to win the pennant twice as badly as you do, but an agreement is an agreement," shot back Sam.

There were more hot words, and before it was over Breadon made a mental note that, win or lose, Hornsby was through as his manager. Speaking of it years later, he said: "I came to the decision that if I was president, my chief must work with me. If he didn't, either he or I must get out, and I wasn't ready to leave the club."

There also had been some friction over Rickey. The 1923 feud never had completely healed; Hornsby didn't want to work with Branch. Breadon terminated one of these arguments with the flat declaration: "You manage your end—the ball club. I'll take care of the other end."

Winning the last game of the 1926 World's Series was the big thrill of Breadon's baseball experience, yet before him arose the vision of the storm which would follow Hornsby's removal as manager.

Perhaps the final blow-up might still have been averted if it hadn't been for a salary squabble which followed. In 1926, Hornsby served the last year of a three-year contract calling for $30,000 a season. In half-hearted negotiations after the World's Series, Breadon offered Rogers a one-year contract for $50,000, which Hornsby refused, demanding a long-term contract.

At the December, 1926 meeting in New York, Breadon and Rickey talked to Stoneham and McGraw of the Giants on a possible Hornsby deal in the event Breadon wished to dispose of him. Sam said he didn't want money, but New York's crack second baseman, Frank Frisch. So, a Hornsby-Frisch-Ring deal tentatively was set up.

Breadon and Hornsby held their last meeting in the Cardinal offices, December 21; the air was as frigid inside as outside, and Rogers left in a huff. Breadon immediately called up Stoneham, but the Giant president couldn't be located until 6 o'clock, St. Louis time. When Breadon got the connection, he said: "Well, you've wanted Hornsby for a long time. You can have him now for Frisch and Ring."

St. Louis wasn't only stunned; it was wild with rage and indignation. Breadon's name was anathema in the Mound City. Boiling him in oil would have been light punishment. Fan groups and clubs held indignation meetings and threatened to boycott the club; bitter fans hung crepe on the doors of his private residence and his automobile business. He had to disconnect his telephone to protect his ears from vitriolic abuse. Newspapers printed denunciatory editorials, and the club's loyal of loyal baseball writers, Jim Gould, then of the *Star*, vowed he never would see another Cardinal game so long as Breadon was head of the club. He stuck to his vow for years. Of all the writers, Sid Keener, sports editor of the *Times*, was the only one who had a half-friendly word for Sam. He realized there must have been real provocation to have given Breadon, a smart baseball man, the courage to arouse all of these roaring lions.

The troubles of Breadon and Stoneham weren't over with the trading of Rogers to New York. There still was the vexing problem of Hornsby's Cardinal stock, and under baseball law a man can't own stock in one club and play with another. And Rogers knew the winning of the World's Championship had greatly enhanced the value of his holdings. It took a special meeting of the National League and the personal intervention of league President Heydler to iron out the matter shortly before the start of the 1927 season. Heydler and Hornsby met in Pittsburgh, a neutral spot, and Rogers, a shrewd bargainer, held out until he was paid $116,000. Of this amount, Breadon put up $80,000, and the National League and the Giants, $18,000 each. The stock then was placed in the St. Louis club's treasury; it never has been brought out since. Rogers' two-year profit was $66,000. It was the half interest in Fuzzy's Anderson's original holding, which went to Rogers in a double play, Fuzzy, to Rickey, to Hornsby.

XVII ⊛ IRISH BOB AND DEACON BILL

I

FOLLOWING THE TRADING of Hornsby to New York, Breadon offered the managerial job to Bill Killefer, Hornsby's first lieutenant on the 1926 team, who had five years of managerial experience behind him in Chicago. But Bill turned it down, saying: "Rogers is too good a friend of mine for me to be taking his job." Killefer then signed with the Browns as coach, eventually succeeding Dan Howley to the management of that club.

Breadon next offered the post to Bob O'Farrell, the team's great catcher and the league's most valuable player. That took some of the curse off Sam, as Bob had become very popular through his great work the year before. The collapse of the Pirates late in the 1926 season cost Bill McKechnie his job in Pittsburgh; he was succeeded by Donie Bush, the former great Detroit shortstop, and Deacon Bill caught on in St. Louis as Irish Bob's coach and first assistant. Announcement also was made that Frankie Frisch would be team captain in the new set-up. The town still was cool, and indifferent toward Frisch; Frankie was a good player, yes, but he couldn't tie the laces of Hornsby's cleated shoes.

Yet, Breadon had great confidence in his 1927 team, and felt surer of the pennant that spring than any which followed until 1943. Maybe the New Yorker in him enabled him to appreciate Frisch, the Bronx boy, better than did most of the other native-born Missourians at that time. The truth is that but for two mishaps, the 1927 Cardinals would have won by a dozen games. Despite the fact that Tommy Thevenow broke a leg after playing only 53 games, and O'Farrell, the 148 game catcher of 1926, suffered from a sore arm all season, taking part in only 59 games, the club carried the race until the last Saturday of the season, and eventually was beaten by only a game and a half—a mere nine points, in a great three-cornered race with the Pirates and the Giants. The final standing showed the three leaders bunched as follows: Pittsburgh, .610; St. Louis, .601; New York, .597.

The tough break for the St. Louis club came on June 21, when the day's news on the surface was good: "With Haines winning a tough 6 to 5 decision from Chicago, and Flint Rhem breezing home by a score of 12 to 3, the Cardinals advanced to within two and a half games of first place. Unfortunately for the victors, the club's able shortstop, Thevenow, fractured his ankle in the fourth inning of the second game, and was replaced by Toporcer."

The ankle was more than fractured; it was a bad break, which healed slowly and poorly. Tommy never was the same player after the accident. He played no more ball that year, and when he tried to come back later, the old snap in his play was gone.

O'Farrell's big problem after June was the hole at shortstop. The 1927 record of National League shortstops showed that Thevenow played in 59 games at the position, Jake Flowers in 65, Heinie Schuble in 65, Specs Toporcer in 27, and Rabbit Maranville in 12. Of course, in many games O'Farrell used two or three of them. During the most crucial part of the race, Schuble, a nineteen-year-old boy, tried to fill the gap; he was a product of the club's farm in Danville in the Three-I League. Heinie covered a lot of ground, had a strong arm, which still was untamed, and hit .257.

Near the close of the season Rickey brought in Maranville, one of the game's most colorful characters, from Rochester, after the close of the International League season. The Rabbit had been one of baseball's great shortstops, also one of the game's top playboys. The year in the minors helped bring about his reformation. He played brilliant ball for the Cards in the last fortnight of the season, and St. Louis critics say if he had been brought in a month earlier, St. Louis would have won the championship.

Irish Bob's catching problem was almost as acute as his gap at shortstop. As in the season before, O'Farrell expected to do most of his catching, yet the throw which stopped Ruth's steal for the last play of the 1926 World's Series was Bob's last great peg in a long time. Early in the season, Rickey regained Frank Snyder from the Giants, but Pancho was well past his prime and hit only .257. A local boy, Johnny Schulte, also was engaged for service behind the bat and hit rather sharply—.288 in 64 games; Johnny now is Joe McCarthy's battery coach on the Yankees.

However, Frisch had a truly phenomenal year and carried the team. "In all the years I have had the Cardinals, no player ever played such ball for me as did Frank Frisch in 1927," said Sam Breadon.

A brilliant athlete at Fordham, Frisch always had great competitive spirit. He hates to lose, and even today cries more over a defeat than any other manager in baseball. He was put on the spot when he came to St. Louis. He was taking the place of the town's baseball idol, the man who led his league's batting parade in six of the previous seven games. Frisch's determination was not only to fill the second base hole in the Cardinal infield, but to make the town forget Hornsby. And wonder of wonders, he succeeded.

After Frankie had burned up the Polo Grounds with his scintillating fielding and lashed out hits to all fields in a 1927 Giant-Cardinal series, McGraw, the manager who brought him out and played him on four championship clubs, remarked rather ruefully: "I guess that Breadon isn't so dumb."

Frisch was the son of a German-born linen importer, a prominent and dignified member of New York's Linen Exchange. After one of Frankie's greatest World's Series with the Giants, some of the other linen men congratulated him on his famous son. "Yes, you send your boys to college, and they play feet ball and baseball," was the elder Frisch's none-too-enthusiastic observation. Frankie has a brother who tried to follow in his athletic footsteps.

Frisch hit .337 that season, scored 112 runs, hit 31 doubles, 11 triples and ten home runs, and stole 48 bases. Hornsby hit .361 in his one year in New York, and in a deal which still is somewhat of a mystery was traded to Boston. Yet the figures do not tell half the story of the ball the Fordham Flash flashed in St. Louis that season. The town not only warmed up to the New York boy, it sizzled and before long Frisch was as big a favorite as Hornsby ever was.

It might even be said that Frisch made possible Breadon's continuation in baseball. Had Frank flopped, the resentment against Sam would have become more bitter as the team flopped with him. But where the club drew 681,575 at home in 1926, its first championship year, the attendance jumped to 763,615 in 1927, the second best in the history of the club.

"After the season of 1927, I never again was afraid to dispose of a player, regardless of his ability or popularity," remarked Breadon. "I knew after that year that what the fans want is a winner, and that a popular player is quickly forgotten by one who is equally popular."

Pretty good testimony that it was Frisch and the pitchers who held up the 1927 club and kept it in the race right to the wire is the fact that the former slugging Cardinals dropped to sixth in club batting. Hafey began to climb as a hitter, banging away at .330; Blades, with his leg again patched up by Dr. Hyland, hit .316, but was in only 61 games, and Bottomley hit .303. However, Douthit dropped to .262 and Lester Bell slumped to .259, the third baseman playing in only 115 games. Hornsby seemingly had Lester hopped up for his one great season, 1926, as Bell never was the same ball player after that year.

The pitching held up brilliantly all season. Alexander, in his first full season as a Redbird, won 21 games and lost ten; Haines enjoyed his best year, 24 victories and ten defeats, and faithful Sherdel checked in with 17 wins against 12 defeats. Rhem, who frequently wandered off the reservation, fell off sharply, from 20 victories in 1926 to 10 winning efforts and 12 defeats.

Rhem presented an alibi that season for reporting three sheets to the wind which still is a baseball classic. The Cardinals were quartered in Boston that year at the old Elks Club, which had just been converted into a hotel, and now is the Bradford. Prohibition was in full swing, but there was a sort of night club on the third floor. Without consulting O'Farrell, a new hotel manager threw a party at "the club" for some of the fun-loving Redbirds. When it was over, Rhem, in the language of his native Southland, was "beautifully lickered up." Called on the carpet next day, Flint didn't deny it, but pleaded: "They were passing drinks to Aleck so fast, I had to drink 'em up. I wanted to keep him sober; he's more important to the club than I am."

Hard-hearted Sam Breadon refused to accept this estimable bit of self-sacrifice. There was a good conduct clause in Flint's contract, whereby he was to get one sum if he remained on "the straight and narrow," a lesser sum if he strayed off the reservation. There had been some lesser breaches which the club had winked at. This time Flint was fined and advised that he had sacrificed the higher salary by violating the good conduct clause. The Carolinian left the team in a huff, but soon returned, the "sacrifice hit" costing him approximately $1,500.

The night after Jakie May, the former chubby little Redbird left-hander, knocked the Cardinals out of the pennant with a 3 to 2 victory in Cincinnati, a tornado almost blew down the Cardinal ball park. It ripped diagonally through the town, did damage in the millions, raised the roofs of near-by houses and blew the debris into the ball-yard and blew the roof of the pavilion into Grand Avenue. Had the Cardinals won the pennant, Breadon and Rickey would have had a job to get their park in shape for a World's Series.

Sam Breadon, who changes managers as another man changes his ties, had his third manager in three seasons as the Cardinals started another pennant hunt in 1928. Despite the fact that O'Farrell had lost the 1927 flag by only one and a half games, Sam felt Bob did not possess real managerial qualifications. Maybe he was right as O'Farrell had only one other managerial opportunity in the majors, with the Reds in 1934—and then he was released in midseason. Breadon also thought the worries of managing the club had taken something out of Bob's catching and was responsible, in some de-degree, for his mediocre play of 1927. However, he gave Bob a $5,000 raise as a player to show appreciation of his general work of 1927.

The new manager was Deacon Bill McKechnie, who had won a National League pennant and World's Series with Pittsburgh in 1925, and was O'Farrell's first adviser in 1927. Though he had a long career as a player, Bill was a full-time regular in only three seasons in the majors. Mac always was light with the stick. In most of his career, he was in the National League, but he was with the Yankees for half of the 1913 season, when he had an especially horrible time at bat, hitting only .134 in 44 games. Yet Frank Chance, the manager, picked Wilkinsburg Bill as his particular companion on the team.

Asked why he selected such a pygmy hitter as his crony, Husk barked: "Because he's the only man on the club with whom I can talk baseball. He has brains and knows what it is all about."

McKechnie always had a wise head on his shoulders, and was particularly smart with pitchers. The millionaire oil man, Harry Sinclair, first recognized that the Deacon had managerial talents; he put him in charge of his Newark Federal League team in 1915. At the end of the Federal League war, McGraw bought McKechnie for the Giants, but later traded him to the Reds. Off and on, Bill played for Pittsburgh, his home town team, usually as a utility infielder. He was a Deacon and choir singer in the church back in Wilkinsburg, a Pittsburgh suburb, which helped him with Rickey.

Several changes were made on the 1928 Cardinal club. Lester Bell, after slipping so badly in 1927, was traded to Boston for Andy High, a former St. Louis sand-lotter—a mite, who at times played a lot of good ball for the Redbirds. O'Farrell again failed to regain his 1926 form, and on May 10 he was traded to the Giants for Outfielder George Harper. And on the following day Rickey closed the deal which practically assured the club the 1928 pennant; he landed Catcher Jimmy Wilson, then one of the game's best, from the Phillies for Virgil Davis, a husky young catcher, and Outfielder Homer Peel. Breadon also salted the deal with some of the money he made in 1927. Davis was a husky Alabaman, and a robust hitter. Ed Barrow and Miller Huggins of the Yankees thought they had him tucked away in the minors in 1926, when wily Rickey caught Davis in the draft.

In June, the Cardinals also purchased Clarence Mitchell, baseball's only lefthanded spitballer, from the Phillies. Mitchell is the chap who hit into five putouts in two times at bat for Brooklyn in the 1920 Dodger-Cleveland World's Series, one of them Billy Wambsganss's unassisted triple play. From the Cardinal farms, Rickey also brought in Pitchers Tony Kaufmann, Sylvester Johnson and Carlisle Littlejohn. Fred Frankhouse and Harold Haid, up before, were given more work this year.

Outfield acquisitions were Wally Roettger, another St. Louis kid, now baseball coach at the University of Illinois, and two later prominent Gas House Gangsters, Ernie Orsatti, and one John Leonard Martin, of Temple, Okla., better known as Pepper, who was to write a few chapters of Cardinal history himself. But, perhaps the most vital change was the installation of the picturesque veteran, Rabbit Maranville, as the regular shortstop.

The 1928 race was another beauty, one of those real National League humdingers. The Cardinals were in it from the first ball pitched by Jesse Haines against Pittsburgh on April 11, when the Birds won, 11 to 7, until they clinched their second flag, September 29, a day before the final gong. At the finish, their winning margin was exactly the same as in 1926—two games ahead of the second place club, this time the Giants. The final standing showed the three top clubs lined up: St. Louis, .617; New York, .604; Chicago, .591.

McKechnie's club led most of the way, but it was hand-to-hand fighting from day to day. The Cardinal lead never was more than a few games at any stage of the race. The Redbirds were tied with the Giants, April 15, and then McGraw's band held on to the first rung until April 26. Robbie's Dodgers poked their noses in front for a few days, to be dislodged by the Reds. Cincinnati and the

FRANK FRISCH
Boss of the Gas House Gang.

PEPPER MARTIN

© Acme

GROVER CLEVELAND ALEXANDER

Cubs were tied May 15 and 16, McCarthy's Chicago club led from May 17 to 22, and Jack Hendricks' Reds led the pack from May 23 to June 14.

On June 15, the Cardinals pushed out in front, and from there on, they held the lead to the finish, with the exception of four days in the late summer, August 19 to 22, when the Giants occupied first place.

George Harper, the outfielder McGraw traded for O'Farrell in the spring, just about saved the pennant for St. Louis in a big three-game late September series at the Polo Grounds. The Cards went into Gotham two games to the good, and met McGraw's gang in a double-header, September 20, before a packed house. Harper practically won the first game single-handed, as he birched three home runs into the right field stands, and St. Louis won 8-5, Sherdel outlasting Larry Benton, Jack Scott and Dutch Henry. It was to be a series of home-run clouting as Hafey also banged one for the Birds and Shanty Hogan reached the stands for New York.

It looked as though Alexander would give McKechnie a double win in a battle with Carl Hubbell in the second game; Aleck went into the eighth inning leading by a score of 4 to 2. But the Giants pulled it out with a vicious rally, scoring five runs in the eighth. After one run trickled in on an error by Maranville, Shanty Hogan hit a grand slam homer, one with a Giant on every sack. McGraw had procured Hogan, big 250-pound catcher, from Boston for St. Louis' old favorite, Hornsby. Hafey again homered for the Cards.

New York also won the third and deciding game, September 22, by a score of 8 to 5, home runs by Reese and Cohan being the decisive factors as Fitzsimmons, relieved by Hubbel in the closing innings, vanquished the Cardinal lefthanders, Mitchell and Sherdel. It cut St. Louis' lead to one game, but try as they might, the Giants could whittle it down no further. The end came in Boston, September 29, when Sherdel, assisted by Rhem, defeated the Braves by a 3-1 score. On the same day, the Giants—hanging on to the bitter end—defeated the Cubs. The Cardinals and Giants wound up the season with a single game in New York, September 30, and it is just as well for McKechnie's crew the race didn't hinge on that contest. With Hubbell opposing young Frankhouse, the New Yorkers were victorious, 4 to 3.

Where Frisch was the great spark on the gallant second place club of 1927, the driving force of this new Cardinal champion was Jim Bottomley. While his batting average was no higher than .325, he was a dynamo, scored 123 runs and drove in 136. Sunny Jim was elected the league's most valuable player, giving the Cardinals three winners in a space of four years. Hafey led the club's regulars with .336, while Frisch hit an even .300.

Haines had another great pitching season, winning 20 games and losing eight. Alexander won 16 and lost nine; Sherdel had that Woolworth record, ten and five; Rhem won 11 and lost eight, and Mitchell, including his early Philly games, won eight and lost nine.

And the Cardinal turnstiles played music that season as never before—and as never since. It was the year before the Wall Street crash; people still had plenty of money; St. Louis fans were happy with another pennant winner, and two years after the trading of Hornsby the club enjoyed its all-time home attendance high of 778,147, not including the World's Series.

There was nothing to mar Sam Breadon's happiness until the second Cardinal-Yankee World's Series, and then Sam wasn't happy at all.

3

The 1928 World's Series still is one of St. Louis' touchy baseball subjects. The 1928 Yankees, pretty much the same club that lost to the Cardinals two years before, were not regarded as supermen on the eve of the series. The Yankees almost blew a 13-game July lead in their own league, just barely limping in ahead of a fast-coming Athletic team. And the New York club was riddled with injuries. Herb Pennock, the pitcher, who had won two of the three New York victories in 1926, was out of the series with a lame arm. Earle Combs, crack center fielder and lead-off man, who had hit .357 in the 1926 event, was out with a broken finger. Huggins was planning to start Lazzeri, but Tony's arm was so dead he could scarcely get the ball to first base. And even Ruth supposedly was hobbling on one ankle. St. Louis licked its chops in happy anticipation; this was going to be good!

With Babe Ruth and Lou Gehrig putting on the greatest two-man show of all World's Series play, it proved a lark for the rampaging New Yorkers. They won four straight games, repeating the dose they handed Pittsburgh the year before. But, it was how the Cardinals lost which hurt Breadon and the St. Louis fans; the Birds were blown out of their roost by scores of 4 to 1, 9 to 3, 7 to 3 and 7 to 3. Ruth rose to his World's Series heights, and hit .625, getting three home runs, scoring nine runs and driving in four. Unlike Hornsby, whose pitchers walked Babe 12 times in 1926, McKechnie let his pitchers pitch to Ruth, and he walked only once. It was good sportsmanship, but it was fatal. Young Gehrig was almost as tough as the "Big Guy," hitting .545, his six hits including four homers and a double. The young first baseman walked four times, scored five runs and drove in nine. There was no doubt that the Yankees earned their marbles; they outhit the Cards, .308 to .207.

Sherdel, who lost a three-hitter to Pennock to start the 1926 Series, again ran into a three-hit game, this time pitched by Hoyt in the first game in New York, October 4. The Yankees won handily, Bottomley's homer accounting for the lone Redbird run. Bob Meusel homered for Huggins.

Alexander, now forty-one years old, tried to repeat his second game victory of 1926, but Gehrig promptly showed old Grover that this was another year, when he lashed the veteran for a four-bagger in the first inning with Durst and Ruth on base. The Cardinals gave the National League fans something to crow about in the second inning, when they tied the score with three runs on young Pipgras. George walked Harper as a starter, and Wilson's double, Maranville's single and Lazzeri's wild throw on Aleck brought in the runs. Unfortunately, it was to be the last time Cardinal rooters had a real chance to shout in the series. Pipgras settled after that, allowing no further scoring; the Yankees regained the lead with a run in their half of the second, and then knocked Grover out with four runs in the fourth.

When the series shifted to St. Louis, October 7 and 9, it was more of the same, the Cardinals twice going under by the same lop-sided score. Jesse Haines, the 1926 whitewasher, tried to stop New York's thunderers in the third game, but was also clubbed out, Gehrig hitting a pair of round-trippers. Huggins got away with this one with old Tom Zachary, a Washington southpaw discard, in the box.

In desperation, McKechnie benched Center Fielder Douthit, who had made only one hit, in the fourth game, putting in the rookie Ernie Orsatti, while Earl Smith, the former Giant, went behind the plate in place of Wilson. Those moves worked well, as Ernie hit a double and single and Earl three singles, but it couldn't change the verdict. Hoyt again vanquished the unlucky Sherdel, as Willie went down to four defeats in two series.

This was the game of the famous quick pitch, which nettled the Cards and finally sent the deck crashing all over the field. St. Louis stayed in this game longer than in the others, leading 2 to 1, as the Yanks came up in the seventh. Sherdel had two strikes on Ruth, and then shot a "quick return" right over the heart of the plate. The Cardinals and the crowd thought it was a strike-out, but Pfirman refused to allow it. In his instructions to the umpires, Judge Landis had ruled against this quick pitch. Ruth, amused at the annoyance of Sherdel, McKechnie and Frisch, knocked the next pitch into the stands for his second homer of the day, and Gehrig followed with an even longer one. For good measure Babe hit his third four-bagger off Alexander in the eighth, matching his great three-homer performance at the same park two years before.

With Lazzeri suffering from his lame arm, Huggins relieved him in each of the four games with a pesky flea of a rookie infielder, who rode the Cardinals unmercifully. He was later to become a great shortstop on the Redbirds in another World's Series—Leo Durocher, the famous Lip, now manager of the Brooklyn Dodgers.

The most disappointed man in all St. Louis was Sam Breadon. He couldn't understand it; he admitted the Yankees were good, but not that good. He could take defeat, but four straight shellackings left an ugly taste in his mouth. All during the series he felt his club lacked inspiration.

So, he demoted his manager, Bill McKechnie, to the class AA farm in Rochester, and brought Billy Southworth, playing manager of the Rochester Red Wings in 1928, to St. Louis for Billy the Kid's first fling at the Cardinal managerial job.

4

Billy Southworth had been one of the boys when he was with the Cardinals, sang with them, occasionally knocked off a prohibition-forbidden highball. In short, he had been a good guy. But, in a varied major league career, he had been under some tough managers, Joe Birmingham in Cleveland, George Stallings in Boston, John Mc-

Graw in New York and Rogers Hornsby in St. Louis. A fellow with a naturally sweet disposition, he felt he had to emulate these men—to be tough with his former fellow players to command their respect. He since has admitted it was his big mistake in his first major league managerial venture.

The Cardinals trained in Avon Park, Florida, in 1929. Most of the players had been in two rich World's Series in 1926 and 1928; they were signed for good salaries—and were in the dough. A number not only had their wives at the camp but their cars. The Birds had an exhibition game scheduled in Miami, and Billy heard some of his players were contemplating driving there.

He held a meeting in his clubhouse and said: "We go to Miami tomorrow, and we go by train. There won't be any riding in automobiles to Miami with your family and friends. I hope everybody gets that."

Hafey and Bottomley, two jovial roommates, snickered. Jimmy Wilson, the catcher, spoke up: "Billy, Mrs. Wilson is down here, and she has been looking forward to that Miami trip ever since we landed in Florida. I, for one, am driving to Miami."

"Oh, is that so," said Southworth. "Well, so long as you've gone on record, I'll go on record, too. You can drive to Miami, but if you do, it will cost you $500."

As the meeting broke up some one said "Heel" under his breath, but loud enough for all to hear. Later Southworth, believing that two players were having a party in their room, entered the chamber, only to find both men in bed. It didn't make him any more popular with the squad.

Despite this training-camp discord, Billy's 1929 edition got off to a good start. Through May and June, they fought the Pirates, the 1927 champions, tooth and nail, and on June 4, the Redbirds still were first. A week later, June 11, the Pirates were leading by two points, .622 to .620, and seven days later, the Redbirds had a two point edge. By June 15, the Cards had fallen back to third, Chicago having nudged into second, and after the Fourth of July games, the Redbirds were fourth with .545. After that St. Louis never threatened again as the Cubs went on to win an easy pennant victory, Joe McCarthy's first major league flag. St. Louis eventually finished a mediocre fourth, with 78 victories, 74 defeats and a percentage of .513.

By July, Breadon decided he had made a mistake after all, and had brought Billy the Kid back to St. Louis as manager without sufficient minor league experience. He switched the two Bills again, returning Southworth to Rochester, and putting McKechnie back in the driver's seat on the Cards.

During the latter part of the season, McKechnie did considerable experimenting with young pitchers. Frankhouse did well, winning seven and losing only two, while Bill Hallahan, back from additional courses at Houston, broke even in eight games. Sylvester Johnson was the biggest winner during the Southworth-McKechnie season, with 13 victories and seven defeats.

And poor Aleck, the 1926 hero, was sent back from the club's last eastern trip in August for being constantly out of condition. Sam Breadon talked to him like a Dutch uncle, paid him off in full and sent him back to his home in Nebraska. "So long as Alexander was on the Cardinals, we never took a penny from him in fines," said Breadon. "We knew his weakness, as he knew it. Once he told me: 'I know I've let you and the club down. But it has been a weakness in our family, and I guess it's just too much for me.' "

The unfortunate part of Alexander's last lapse is that he closed his career with 373 victories, tied with Christy Mathewson for most victories in the National League. He needed only one more victory for a new record. He lost six valuable weeks late in the 1929 season, and, traded back to the Phillies the following winter, he never won another game.

On the constructive side of the 1929 picture was the farm system coming up with another great young shortstop, Charley Gelbert, a Lebanon Valley collegian, who joined the Cardinals after only a season and a half of minor league ball with Topeka and Rochester. Though tucked away in a small Pennsylvania college, he attracted sufficient attention as a backfield star for the late Walter Camp to place him on one of his last All-America elevens. His father, Charles Saladin Gelbert, of Penn, was Camp's All-America right end in 1893-4-5, his associate end being the great Hinkey of Yale. Frisch took an immediate fancy to young Gelbert, taught him the finesse of big league play, and they immediately became a superb second base combination.

In his first year as a regular, Orsatti blew up his batting average to .337. He was a Hollywood doubles and stunt man during the off-season, and now is an actor's agent. Ernie's pal, Johnny Martin was sent back to Rochester for more experience, much to Pepper's disgust.

XVIII ☻ THE OLD SARGE WINS
A PAIR

I

GABBY STREET, Walter Johnson's old battery mate in Washington, had been engaged as a pitching coach in the 1929 season at the recommendation of Blake Harper, the colorful concessions chief.

"Gabby has knocked around baseball a long time, and I think he can do us a lot of good, especially with the young pitchers Mr. Rickey is bringing up," suggested Blake.

Charley Street, a fellow Southerner from Huntsville, Alabama, was an old friend of Harper's. In addition to catching for Washington, Street had been with the Cincinnati Reds and the Yankees. He took Johnson's fastest ball, once caught a ball dropped from the top of the Washington Monument, had a good arm, but never threw much of a scare into a pitcher at the plate. He was a salty likable character, who enlisted in the Regular Army in the first World War, saw a lot of action in the Argonne, and came out a top sergeant. From then on baseball knew him affectionately as the Old Sarge.

Gabby started the 1929 season in St. Louis as second coach, but Greasy Neale, the first coach, was let out in midseason (they say he talked too much football), and Gabby moved up a notch. McKechnie was running for town assessor in Wilkinsburg, and knocked off the last few days of the season to do some campaigning. Street took over the Cardinal reins in those few games.

According to Breadon, McKechnie could have stayed on in St. Louis in 1930, but Judge Emil Fuchs, the then president of the Braves, offered Bill a five year contract to build up his Boston club, and Singing Sam gave the Deacon permission to accept it. Breadon liked what he had seen of Street's work in 1929, and put the Old Sarge in charge of his aggregation. For the fifth successive year, the St. Louis club started out with a new manager.

Few thought of the Cardinals as a pennant contender in Avon Park in the spring of 1930. The general impression was that the championship club of 1926 and 1928 was breaking up, especially in pitching, and that a lot of rebuilding needed to be done. But a happy series of events completely changed the picture. After knocking around the Cardinal farms for years, coming up every so often for a brief fling under Sam Breadon's main tent, Wild Bill Hallahan, the Binghamton boy, suddenly tamed his wild shoots and became one of baseball's greatest left-handers. He won 15 and lost nine that year.

In June, Breadon and Rickey pulled another master stroke, obtaining Burleigh Grimes, Old Stubblebeard, from the Braves for Willie Sherdel and the promising kid, Frankhouse. St. Louis was sorry to see little Willie go, but Grimes paid rich dividends. Burleigh had a salary dispute with Dreyfuss of the Pirates the previous winter, and Barney—in a huff—traded him to the Braves. But the hefty spitballer was unhappy in his second division surroundings; he welcomed a chance to get back with a club which was going places. Rhem was back after having been sent to Minneapolis and Houston to mend his ways.

George Watkins, an outfielder with a home-run bat, joined the Birds after taking Rickey courses in applied baseball in Marshall, Tex., Houston and Rochester. Little Sparky Adams was purchased from the Pirates to play third base, and Gelbert improved daily at shortstop. Judge Landis also did the club a real good turn when he nixed a deal whereby Rickey tried to send Gus Mancuso, the Texas Italian catcher, to Rochester. The Judge ruled Branch had sent Gus out once too often, and would either have to keep him or turn him loose. It proved a lucky ruling, as Mancuso hit .366 in 76 games, and when Jimmy Wilson was injured in the grueling pennant fighting late in the season, Gus jumped in and did a noble job.

Even so, for a good part of the season, the 1930 Cardinals were just a good first division team, running fourth as Brooklyn led most of the way. The main Dodger opposition came from Chicago and New York.

When the Giants came to St. Louis for an August series, Sam Breadon threw a party at his suburban farm for the New York writers. It was the picnic at which Sam sang his theme song about night ball: "It makes every day a Sunday." One of the features was a ball game between the New York and St. Louis writers. Martin "Mike" Haley hit a ball down the left field foul line, which Gabby Street, umpiring the game, ruled a fair ball, and Marty got a triple. He scored on Roy Stockton's single. "The next time we play here, we'll bring our own umpire," beefed Buck O'Neill, then of the *New York Journal*.

The party picked up enthusiasm as it went along. "It's too bad our club didn't start a little earlier; I would have all you guys back here for a World's Series," said Breadon. "We're playing the best ball in the league right now, but we're too far behind to make up the ground we lost earlier in the season."

But Sam didn't know how good and determined that club really was. It was August 17, and the Redbirds were 10 games behind the then leading Cubs. The Redbird uprising, which was to thrill the nation, had started just a week before. Brooklyn came west for its last western trip, riding proudly in the van of the procession. The Daffiness Boys easily knocked off the Redbirds in the first tilt of a five-game series, 11 to 5. The victory gave Brooklyn 66 wins against 41 defeats for a percentage of .617. The Cardinals had just one more victory than defeats, 53 to 52 reverses. Street's club trailed the leaders by 12 games, with the Cubs and Giants in between. Who then would have given a nickel for the Redbirds' chances?

Perhaps that 11 to 5 shellacking was just what the Cardinals needed to arouse them. They turned sharply on Brooklyn, August 9, and knocked the Dodgers off the top perch by scoring four successive victories, St. Louis pulling out the last one, 7 to 6, with three runs off Thurston and Phelps in the ninth inning. The Cardinals then won three out of five from the Braves, and split a big-scoring Sunday double-header with the Giants. With Mitchell, a St. Louis cast-off, pitching for McGraw, the Giants won the first game, 12 to 4, but Burleigh Grimes came back to win an even split for St. Louis, 13 to 4. Breadon's picnic, at which he regretted there wasn't sufficient time to catch the leaders, came the following Monday—an open date.

The Cards kept on coming. They divided the next two games with New York, George "Showboat" Fisher, a Giant cast-off, beating

McGraw in the second game with a pinch home run. Then the Phillies came to town, and the Redbirds really feasted. It was like that fat fall series of 1926 all over again, as the Cardinals won five in a row by 16-6, 10-8, 9-6, 9-4 and 6-4. Against the East, the Gabby Streeters won 14 and lost five. Maybe, there still was time after all!

The race daily grew more hectic. From the time the Cardinals knocked Brooklyn off the top perch in mid-August, McCarthy's Cubs led until early September. Then Brooklyn regained the lead, with the Redbirds coming faster and faster. For the third time in five years, if they wanted the pennant they had to win it on their last eastern trip.

2

Eventually Street took his club into Brooklyn, for a big three-game series, September 16, 17 and 18. To make it even more dramatic, the other two contenders, the Cubs and Giants, were battling at the Polo Grounds at the same time. When the series started, the Dodgers were one game ahead, with the first three teams lining up: Brooklyn, .583; St. Louis, .577; Chicago, .573.

On the eve of the Cardinal-Brooklyn series came the most bizarre of all the Flint Rhem incidents. Flint was going strongly at the time; he was effective against the Dodgers and Gabby planned to pitch him early in the series. But the colorful South Carolinian disappeared.

He showed up the morning of the first game, bleary-eyed and disheveled—with one of baseball's weirdest tales. He was standing in front of the Cardinal hostelry in New York, when two men called him over to a taxicab. Naïvely, he walked over to see what they wanted. Before Flint knew what was up, he was pushed into the cab, and covered with a gun. The men drove him under the Hudson tube to a house on the New Jersey side. There, one gunman pressed a revolver against his ribs, while accomplices compelled Flint to guzzle cups of raw whisky.

Rhem still sticks to his story. The Cardinal management half believed it; they had the police investigate, but Rhem never could find the place in New Jersey where he said he was taken. It made banner heads in all the New York newspapers—a gamblers' plot to beat the Redbirds and give Brooklyn a break in the big series.

However, the St. Louis newspapermen with the Cardinals were skeptical. Roy Stockton, able writer of the *Post-Dispatch*, still has a twinkle in his eyes when he discusses it. "Flint said he was kidnaped; who am I to spoil his good story?" asks Roy.

To complicate matters for Gabby Street, the day before the first game, Bill Hallahan caught a finger of his left hand in a taxicab door, raising a big blister on a pitching finger. Rhem would have opened the series had he been fit to pitch.

Every game in Brooklyn was a sellout, and Dodger fans still get a sinking feeling when they think of what happened. The Cardinals took the series three straight, and the Daffiness Boys never stopped reeling until they wound up in fourth place. Wild Bill Hallahan, blistered finger and all, beat Dazzy Vance in the opener in a sensational ten-inning duel, 1 to 0. Andy High, hot all during the streak, doubled in the tenth and scored on Douthit's single. Brooklyn filled the bases on Wild Bill in its half with one out, but Catcher Lopez ended the game by hitting into a double play. It was on a ball to Adams in deep short. "It took Al exactly fifteen minutes to get down to first base," moaned Uncle Robbie when it was over.

The second game was another humdinger, with Syl Johnson, Grabrowski and Lindsey wearing down the Cuban, Luque, 5 to 3. St. Louis tied in the eighth, and won with two runs in the ninth. That put the Redbirds in the lead by the width of a thread, but they clinched their hold when Grimes won over Babe Phelps and Thurston, 4 to 3, the next day.

From then on, every one knew it would be St. Louis. A week later, September 26, the Cardinals clinched the flag at Sportsmans Park with a 10 to 5 victory over Pittsburgh, and curiously enough at the finish they had their customary two-game margin over the second place club. It was 92 and 62 for the Cards and 90 and 64 for the Cubs, with the former Redbird chief, Hornsby, replacing McCarthy as Chicago manager in the last week of the season. From the time the Redbirds aroused themselves against Brooklyn, August 9, they won 39 games out of 49 for a percentage of .796.

"You're the new miracle man of baseball, Gabby," congratulated the St. Louis captain, Frankie Frisch.

"Forget that miracle man stuff, Frank," said Street.

"Forget it nothing," shot back the Flash. "How can you? You'll go down in baseball history as one of the miracle men of the game. Your name always will be linked with that of George Stallings of the 1914 Braves."

"You're damned right, Frank," chimed in Sunny Jim Bottomley.

With the pennant safely tucked away, on the last day of the season, Sunday, September 28, Gabby Street let the St. Louis fans see a young twenty-year-old Redbird pitching farmhand, who had acquired quite a strikeout reputation in St. Joe and Houston. He held the Pirates to three hits, defeated Larry French, 3 to 1, and catching the Pittsburgh infield out of position, bunted a ball into left field. His name was Dizzy Dean.

3

St. Louis was pretty well steamed up over the World's Series with Connie Mack's later-day Athletic champions, the team built around the two great pitchers, Lefty Bob Grove and George Earnshaw; Left Fielder and batting champion Al Simmons; the aggressive catcher, Mickey Cochrane; clubbing broad-shouldered First Baseman Jimmy Foxx and the loquacious third sacker, Jimmy Dykes. They had taken McCarthy's Cubs, four games to one, in the Series of 1929. But, Cardinal fans were asking, would that parallel with the 1914 Braves continue to hold? Stalling's team knocked off what many considered an even greater Athletic team four straight sixteen years before.

For the third time the Cardinals had to start the World's Series in the American League park. It was Burleigh Grimes against Lefty Grove in the opener at Shibe Park, Philadelphia, October 1; old Stubblebeard gave up only five hits, but what hits! All were for extra bases—homers by Simmons and Cochrane, triples by Foxx and Haas and a double by Dykes. Each was good for a run, and the Athletics won, 5 to 2.

With Earnshaw pitching a masterful game, the Philadelphians also bagged the second game, 6 to 1, Mack's Big Moose defeating Rhem, Lindsey and Syl Johnson. Cochrane hit another home run, while St. Louis' only run was a four-bagger by young Watkins.

"It's a breeze for the Athletics," said the critics, as the teams moved on to St. Louis. Bozeman Bulger, the popular New York baseball writer, was taken with an appendix attack on the World's

Series caravan. Dr. Hyland later snipped out his appendix in St. Louis. Boze's old pal of *New York Evening World* days, Irvin Cobb, wired: "Congratulations on being the first baseball writer ever to get a cut in a World's Series."

However, the Cardinals weren't in much mood for joking. "Forget those two defeats, and remember how we pulled out the pennant," said Gabby Street, and to the great joy of St. Louis, the Redbirds tied the series by winning the third and fourth games at Sportsmans Park.

Catcher Jim Wilson was out with an injury when the series started; young Gus Mancuso did a good fill-in job, but the pitchers worked better as the more experienced Wilson returned to work in the third game. Bill Hallahan, the boy who had been a long time coming, turned in a shutout job in this one, just as Jesse Haines had done in the first home game of the 1926 series. Bill won, 5 to 0, his lefthanded shoots handcuffing all but Bishop, the little "A" lead-off man, and the slugger, Simmons, the pair getting five of the seven Philadelphia hits. Lefthanded Rube Walberg, Bill Shores and old Jack Quinn pitched for Mack, and one of the ten St. Louis hits was a homer by Taylor Douthit.

Jesse Haines then came through when Grove tried to repeat for Mack and the series was All Stephen when Pop won a 3 to 1 verdict over tall Mose. It was a light-hitting affair, with the Athletics garnering only four hits and the Redbirds getting only one more. Young Charley Gelbert was the fly in Grove's ointment; he hit a triple and single, drew a walk, scored one run and drove in another. And Haines made his third inning single good for a run. The greatest St. Louis World's Series crowd, 39,946, shouted itself hoarse as Jesse tied it up.

Then came St. Louis' heart-breaker, a great pitching duel in which Earnshaw and Grove finally outlasted Grimes. But Burleigh was brilliant in defeat. For eight innings, neither team scored. Mack thought he saw a chance in the eighth, when Jimmy Moore batted for Earnshaw, but Stubblebeard walked the pinch-hitter, filling the bases, and then set down Boley and Haas, the top of the Athletic batting order. Earnshaw had given up only two hits in seven innings; Grove gave up one in the last two.

As for Grimes, he had yielded four hits up to the ninth. Then

147

he walked Cochrane, the first man up, and the crowd gave a sigh of relief when the dangerous Simmons popped out. And then, curtains! Brawny Jimmy Foxx swung those Maryland East Shore shoulders at the first pitch, and there never was a moment's doubt where the ball was going. It sailed far up into the left field bleachers for a homer. The park was so still one could hear the feet of Cochrane and Foxx as they pattered around the bases. The Birds couldn't come back in their half and the A's won, 2 to 0.

The clubs moved back to Philadelphia to wind up the series, and after Grimes's defeat, the sixth game proved an anticlimax. The Mackmen won easily, 7 to 1, behind another well-pitched game by Earnshaw, and again were World's Champions. Hallahan developed an early blister on a pitching finger and retired after two innings; Street sent in a pitching parade of Wild Bill, Johnson, Lindsey and Bell. The Athletics again made only seven hits, but as in the first game, they were loaded with dynamite. Again all were for extra bases. Simmons and Dykes hit homers; Miller hit a pair of doubles, and two-baggers flew from the flails of Dykes, Cochrane and Foxx.

The St. Louis heroes of the series were young Gelbert, who hit .316, Haines, Hallahan and Grimes, even though Burleigh lost two games. Frisch hit only .208, and Douthit and Bottomley fell down the hardest, even though Taylor hit one home run. His average was .083 and Sunny Jim's was scarcely visible to the naked eye—.045.

4

Most St. Louisans consider Gabby Street's 1931 club, which easily repeated for the National League championship, the best of the Mound City's pennant winners. The Old Sarge goes even further. "I've seen a lot of great ball clubs in my day, but for pitching, hitting, spirit and all-around balance, I would back my 1931 Cardinal team against any of them," he says proudly.

Unlike the St. Louis championship clubs of 1926, 1928 and 1930, who had to fight to the wire, the 1931 club had a pennant romp. It excelled from the start, and never was seriously threatened. From April on, there wasn't a week-end that the club wasn't in first place. It won 101 games, the first National League club in eighteen years to get in the century win class. The club eventually finished 13½ games ahead of the second place New Yorks, but the general feeling was that if it really had been pressed, it could have gone up to 110 victories.

Despite the one-sided race, the season of 1931 produced the greatest crowd in St. Louis' baseball history for a Sunday double-header with the Cubs, July 12. The crowd, which fought its way into Sportsmans Park that day, was given officially as 45,715, about 13,000 in excess of the park's seating capacity. Bill DeWitt, then the club's treasurer, called it 7,419 better than the best previous attendance for a St. Louis league game. And above the din of that crowd could be heard the raucous exhorting voice of Mary Ott, the Cardinals' No. 1 feminine fan and a St. Louis institution. The crowd swarmed all over the field, massed along the foul lines, and stood so thickly in the outfield that the outfielders played on the heels of the infielders. The games proved farces, with any kind of a pop fly falling into the crowd for a ground rule double. The Cubs won the first game, 7 to 5, in a contest of nine doubles. But the real two-bagger harvest came in the second tilt, won by the Cardinals, 17 to 13. This one produced 33 hits, of which 23 were doubles, a major league record for one game. Jim Collins and Gus Mancuso of the Cards and Gabby Hartnett and Woody English of the Cubs each blew themselves to three of the plentiful two-base crops.

On top of the strong pitching of 1930, the club's farm system turned up with its annual jewel, this time a strong husky right-hander from Kentucky, Paul Derringer. He had been in the farm chain four years, two at Danville and two at Rochester, and in 1930 won 23 games for the Red Wings. He was six feet, four inches tall, gustful, and from the start quite a personality. Oom Paul fetched in 18 victories, of the 200 he had at the end of the 1943 season, with the Cardinals in his freshman year.

Chick Hafey, the left fielder, won the batting championship that year with .3489 in the closest batting race in major league history. A washcloth could have covered the three leaders. Bill Terry of the Giants was second with .3486, and Hafey's pal, Sunny Jim Bottomley, followed with .3482. Despite Bottomley's strong going, the club brought up another first baseman, Jim "Rip" Collins, of Altoona, Pa., who had slugged his way up from the farm club in Rochester. Bottomley frequently was injured, and "the Ripper" clouted .301 in 89 games. Mike Gonzales was regained for the third time from Minneapolis and helped Wilson and Mancuso as third string catcher.

And the club finally had to give regular work to Pepper Martin—on his own insistence. He had been shunted back and forth to the minors, and early in 1931, he still was doing utility and pinch-hitting chores. He burst into Rickey's office one spring day, insisting: "I'm tired riding that bench; I want to get into the game or I want you to trade me to some club that will play me." Rickey cleared the way for Pepper to play center field, June 15, by trading Douthit to the Reds for Wally Roettger.

For years thereafter, Martin was the club's most colorful figure outside of the pitching department. He was a bundle of energy, couldn't sit still for a moment, and was unpredictable. His major league debut in 1928 was typical of Pepper. Bought originally by Rickey for $500 from the class D Greenville, Texas club, Martin hitchhiked his way from Oklahoma to the Cardinal training camp at Avon Park, Fla. Riding the rods, he was picked up in Thomasville, Ga. and spent a night in the clink. When he reported at the Florida resort in khaki trousers and hunting jacket, he had a week's growth of beard, and his face was smeared with dirt and oil.

Later, after he became a star on the Redbirds, he often reported for work looking much the same. He took up midget auto-racing, and spent the early morning tinkering with his car. He would just have time to reach the park for batting practice, his face, hair and hands still covered with grease. When the club forbade him to race at night, Martin employed a night driver, but he still continued to give his midget its morning workouts.

He was superstitious and always looking for hairpins. They supposedly brought him luck. In a later pennant campaign, wishing to bring Pepper luck, also to have a little fun, Roy Stockton and Ray Gillespie, St. Louis baseball writers, scattered a packet of hairpins around the lobby of the Cincinnati hotel where the team was housed. Joe Medwick came along and started picking up the pins. "Hey, those are for Pepper Martin," exclaimed Roy. "Let Pepper find his own hairpins," replied the unsentimental Ducky.

The Athletics of 1931 won 107 games, the highest victory total of their career; Al Simmons won another batting championship with a .390 average; and Lefty Grove had his greatest year, 31 victories against only four defeats, and one winning streak of 16 straight. Yet, this year the Redbirds wore them down, and won back baseball's proudest emblem in a scintillating seven-game World's Series.

It was the series in which Pepper Martin, the Wild Horse of the Osage, ran amuck. His name became a household word in the nation as he hit .500, his 12 blows including four doubles and a homer. And he virtually stole the shin guards from Mickey Cochrane, valiant Athletic catcher, getting away with five stolen bases. He bagged all of his hits in the first five games, and as the teams were being whisked back to St. Louis, fans gathered at all stations where the Cardinal Special paused, to get a look at the rollicking Wild Horse. He accosted Street, and asked: "Say, Gabby, ain't I the same guy I always was?"

This time Bill Hallahan wove his lefthanded magic so well over the Athletic bats that they got to him for only one run in 18 1/3 innings, while Burleigh Grimes's spitball was equally tough for the Mackmen.

Street gave them his fast ball freshman, Paul Derringer, in the first game, Oom Paul going in against Lefty Grove at Sportsmans Park, October 1. For the first time in four Series, the Cardinal fans were seeing the first two games. Paul didn't go so well, the Athletics ganging up on him for four runs in the third, and two more in the seventh when Simmons followed a Cochrane single with a home run blast into the left field bleachers. The Redbirds lost, 6 to 2, but they took comfort from the fact that they belted Grove, the American League ace of aces, for 12 hits, Martin starting on him with a double and two singles.

Hallahan evened it up for St. Louis next day, by hurling a 2 to 0 three-hit shutout against Earnshaw. The Athletics' Big Moose gave up only six hits himself, two of them to Martin, who stole second each time and converted the hits into the two St. Louis runs.

Before the game was safely deposited in the Cardinals' bat bag, Catcher Jimmy Wilson gave the St. Louis fans an awful scare with one of the World's Series' worst boners. With Foxx and Dykes on base and two out in the ninth inning, Hallahan struck out Jim Moore, the Athletic pinch-hitter, who took a swipe at a low strike. Wilson picked the ball out of the dirt, and to the consternation of the crowd hurled it down to Jake Flowers, standing some distance from third base. Jimmy thought the game was over. Moore stood at the plate for a few moments, but the wide-awake Athletic coach, the veteran Eddie Collins, going through gyrations like a wild Comanche, motioned Moore to run to first. He did, without a play being made on him. Hafey, Gelbert and other Cardinals, believing the game was over, had started to run off the field. If Flowers hadn't been on the alert, and caught the unexpected throw, all the runners on the bases could have scored.

There was wild excitement and a lot of bickering and jawing with the umpires. But Nallin, the man behind the plate, called Moore safe on first, and ordered the game resumed with a Mackman on every sack. Fortunately, Hallahan's sang-froid was not ruffled; he was equal to the occasion and snuffed out Max Bishop on a pop foul to Bottomley.

There was a three-day lull before the series was resumed in Philadelphia, October 5, and Grove again was ready to shoot over his fire-ball. Grimes was Street's pitcher. It was a pleasant day on the Redbird bench; the Cards again massaged Mose's southpaw wares freely, reaching him for 11 hits in eight innings, and won by a score of 5 to 2. Grimes hurled a two-hitter and had a shutout until two were out in the ninth, when Cochrane walked and big Simmons poled a homer over the right field fence. This time Pepper had two hits in four attempts.

Earnshaw, a really great World's Series pitcher, tied it up for Mack by hurling a two-hit shutout (both hits went to Pepper) and winning, 3 to 0, from Syl Johnson, Lindsey and Derringer. But before the clubs left Philadelphia, Hallahan had given Street the three to two edge by winning, 5 to 1, from Waite Hoyt, the old Yankee star, Walberg and Rommel. Martin again turned this game inside out with a homer and two singles; the Oklahoman batted in four of the five St. Louis runs.

The clubs returned to St. Louis to wind it up, and Mack had his two stars, Grove and Earnshaw, primed to give him his third straight world's title. And, it looked pretty good for him when Grove got away with the sixth game, an easy Philadelphia victory, by a score of 8 to 1. Young Derringer failed again; the Athletics had the knack of getting to him for blocks of four runs, and Paul went out after a four-run blast in the fifth, while Jim Lindsey was shot up for four more in the seventh.

With Mack having Earnshaw, deadly effective against the Birds for two years, ready for the seventh game, the betting odds favored Philadelphia in the final. But they didn't reckon with a stout-hearted Grimes, pitching the game of his career. Burleigh again had the Athletics shut out with three hits until two were out in the ninth, when his famous arm weakened and Bill Hallahan had the distinction of extinguishing the last Athletic rally as the Cardinals won, 4 to 2.

Earnshaw went down pitching a great game and all the breaks went against him. Both High and Watkins reached base in the first inning on pop flys, which somehow dropped safely for singles between Simmons and Mack's novice shortstop, Dib Williams. Frisch advanced the pair on a sacrifice, and High scored on a wild pitch, Watkins advancing to third. Earnshaw walked the dangerous Martin, who promptly stole second. George then fanned Orsatti, but Cochrane dropped the third strike, and had to throw out Ernie at first. When Foxx made a poor return throw to the plate, Watkins scored.

In the second inning, High reached base on another Texas Leaguer behind the infield, and Watkins lined a home run to the roof of the right field pavilion, the only solid hit off Earnshaw. After that, big George was invincible, retiring the next 15 batsmen before he moved out for a pinch-hitter.

The fans saw spirited action in the ninth, and the A's had the tying runs on base when, quite appropriately, Martin, the Series hero, snagged a fly ball for the last out. Working doggedly and determinedly, gallant Grimes held the fort until two were retired. He walked Simmons, but Foxx popped out and Miller forced Simmons. Only one putout needed for a three-hit shutout victory, and the precious World's Championship! Then Dykes walked and young Williams arched a single over High's head, filling the bases.

Roger Cramer, then a rookie outfielder, batted for Walberg, who had succeeded Earnshaw, and whistled a single to left center, bringing in Miller and Dykes. Street walked slowly out to the box, talked for a few moments to Grimes, and then beckoned to the bullpen and summoned Hallahan. As an early fall dusk was engulfing the ball park, little Bishop hit a Hallahan pitch solidly, but Martin came in fast and speared the ball in left center.

And St. Louis was ready for another World's Championship celebration! Maybe, it wasn't as spontaneous as 1926, but it was quite a spree, lasting far into the night.

After the big series, Pepper Martin was a national hero, and was engaged for an extensive vaudeville tour at $1,500 a week. After four weeks, Pepper suddenly called it off in his Louisville dressing room, tossing away $7,500 for five additional weeks, with the remark: "I ain't an actor; I'm a ballplayer. I'm cheating the public and the guy who's paying me the $1,500. Besides, the hunting season's on in Oklahoma, and that's more important business."

Martin had one more honor as the year came to an end. He was voted the "Athlete of the Year" in the Associated Press's annual sports poll.

The National League's most valuable player prize, however, went to Frankie Frisch, the Cardinal's dashing captain. He was the fourth Cardinal to win it in seven years. The National League abandoned its $1,000 bag of gold for the winner after Hornsby won it for the second time in 1929, but the Baseball Writers' Association continued the practice, later in conjunction with *The Sporting News*.

XIX ⊖ THE GREAT DIZZY DEAN

I

IF THE CARDINALS' 1930 pennant victory came as something of a surprise, the reaction which followed the sensational blue-ribbon victory of 1931 was even more unexpected; it was the most disappointing year under Breadon's ownership. Almost without exception the nation's sports writers handed Singing Sam the 1932 pennnant before a ball was pitched. Sam believed them; so did Rickey and Street. Instead, the Cardinals finished in a tie with the Giants for sixth place. The 1932 edition of the Redbirds, which ate up one of Breadon's highest pay rolls, lost ten more games than they won; their record was 72 victories against 82 defeats for a percentage of .468.

The club started like a champion; it set the pace for a few weeks in middle May and was back in first place again as late as the first week in July. But, from then on, the Birds started flying in reverse, the retreat eventually turning into a debacle as the St. Louis team skidded deeper and deeper into the lower recesses of the second division.

There were some accusations that the owners sacrificed a contender to greed and avarice, inasmuch as Grimes, the club's ace righthander of the two previous pennant-winning years, and Hafey, the new batting champion, were disposed of during the off-season. Yet, for years that was the fixed policy of the club, to sell or trade high-salaried aging stars when they still had considerable value, to make room for younger stars coming up from the farms.

Grimes, always a difficult man to sign, and in constant salary wrangles with such former club owners as Charley Ebbets and Barney Dreyfuss, had advanced his pay dirt to $20,000 for 1931. Old Stubblebeard and Frisch—also getting $20,000—were the highest salaried players on the team. Burleigh now was thirty-eight; young pitchers from Houston and Rochester were demanding their chance, so at the December, 1931 National League meeting in New York, Breadon sold Grimes to the Cubs for a handsome price. The front office also ran into salary differences with Hafey, and just before the new season started Chick was traded to the Reds for Outfielder Harvey Hendrick, a former New York Yankee, Pitcher Benny Frey, and a sizable check. A month later, Frey was sold back to the Reds.

One might almost suspect that Breadon and Rickey had consulted a soothsayer before making these deals. That near-shutout, in which Grimes had pitched his heart out to give the Redbirds the right to fly the World's Championship "blanket" from their center field flagpole in 1932, was just about Old Stubblebeard's last great game. Though Lord Burleigh pitched for another championship club, Charley Grimm's 1932 Cubs, he won only six games while losing 11. Hafey was ill during a good part of the 1932 season, and participated in only 83 Cincinnati games. It wasn't the loss of these two outstanding 1931 stars which sent the Cardinals reeling into sixth place.

The biggest single factor in the collapse of the 1931 World's Champions was the flop of their great hero of the series, Pepper Martin. If Pepper hadn't remained "the same guy" after his big World's Series, the 1931 "Athlete of the Year" would have been badly deflated in 1932. It was one of the few times in Pepper's career that he was lost for words, and his dauber was pretty low. He hit only .235 in 85 games; again had to ride the bench a good part of the season, and he stole only nine bases—four more than in the Series of 1931.

The Oklahoman had a contagious personality; when he was good, he could carry an entire team with his enthusiasm, but when Pepper was low, the whole ball club suffered with him.

Showboat Orsatti, the stunts man, was the only Cardinal who hit consistently throughout the season, and finished with .336. The league's most valuable player of 1931 also had a mediocre year— that is, for a Frank Frisch. Injuries limited the Fordhamite's play to only 115 games, and he hit .292. Catcher Jimmy Wilson also was off in his work, with Mancuso taking over in 103 games and hitting .284.

2

Though the Cardinals were low in the standing, the 1932 season had its redeeming features—Dizzy Dean and Ducky Medwick. In his first complete season in the league, the great Dizzy pitched the most innings, 286, led in strike-outs with 191, and won 18 games while losing 15. Brought up in the fall from Houston, Medwick showed he was a natural righthanded slugger and potentially great out-fielder; the then twenty-year-old Jersey boy hit .349 in 36 games. The pair were destined to star on the defense and offense for another great Cardinal team which already was in the making.

A Dizzy Dean comes to a club only once in its lifetime. The Athletics could have only one Rube Waddell; the Yankees only one Babe Ruth; and the Cardinals only one Dizzy Dean. Of all the rich colorful characters in the Cardinal Cavalcade—Von Der Ahe, McGraw, Donlin, Bresnahan, Hornsby, Frisch, Martin, Dizzy easily went to the head of the class. For what sports writers term color— and ability to make the newspaper headlines in activities other than baseball, Dizzy was topped only by Ruth.

Dean was a smart, shrewd operator, fully aware that he was a great pitcher. He had the knack of saying and doing things that were entirely unexpected—a born showman. He was quick on the trigger —never at a loss for a comeback. Even Ring Lardner, that genius of the press box, whose "You know me Al" baseball stories once delighted the nation, could not have thought up Dizzy Dean.

When he first came up with the Cardinals, he gave three different reporters as many birthplaces in as many states—Oklahoma, Texas and Arkansas. To one he gave his name as Jay Hanna Dean; to another he was Jerome Herman Dean. In the *Sporting News Register* of today, he is Jay Hanna Dean, born in Lucas, Ark., January 16, 1911, and in *Baseball Magazine's* Who's Who, he is Jerome Herman Dean, born on the same date in Holdenville, Okla. He said his mother liked Jay because that was Jay Gould's name. An older brother died, so the family gave him the name of the deceased as well as his own. But he prefers Dizzy, and never did a player have a more appropriate nickname.

Later he remarked, "One of those Oklahoma sandstorms was blowing when I was born," which may help explain the gusto of this fascinating diamond personality and how all state lines were obliterated at his birth. His father, Albert Monroe Dean, was a semi-pro player, and a cotton-raising share-cropper when he wasn't pitching or playing third base.

Once Dean said: "If I had finished the second grade in school, I would have went a year longer than my old man." But, on another occasion, he told how when he was twelve, he and his brother Paul, then ten, playing for the Spaulding, Okla. High School, helped defeat Oklahoma State Teachers' College. Dizz pitched and Paul knocked in the winning run.

· He had an uncle, who was an itinerant country preacher—the Rev. Bland R. Dean, who had an early influence on his famous nephew. "I think I once took up the collection for him after a sermon in a tent," said Dizzy. "Well, anyway, it was either me or Paul. I was always solemn like after listenin' to him. He could make things sound awful real."

Pitching a game after hearing the Rev. Bland preach, Dizzy was so impressed that he remarked: "The Lord he had his arms around me all the time; yes he did. Like to have choked me, he held me so tight. Whenever I was gonna go wild, He just patted me on the head and the next guy popped up."

He enlisted in the Regular Army in his teens, and pitched for the Twelfth Field Artillery team at Fort Sam Houston, San Antonio. The San Antonio Public Service Corporation said they would pay him $30 a week to pitch for their club if he could get out of the Army. He told his dad about it, and Pop Dean prematurely sold his cotton crop to raise $100 to get Jay Jerome out of service. Dizz fogged in his fast one with such speed that he won 16 straight games, when a Cardinal scout, Don Curtis, caught up with him. Don signed him for the Redbirds' Houston club, then managed by Frank Snyder, the former Cardinal catcher.

At the start, they called him "Foggy" because he used to talk of fogging in his fast one. But soon it became Dizzy. He didn't stay in Houston, but was sent to the Cardinal farm club in St. Joe, where he left a wake of strike-outs. Prior to his season in St. Joseph, he spent the winter in Charleston, Mo., with Oliver French, business manager of the St. Joe club, his semi-official guardian. Dizzy rarely took a drink; he wasn't a bad kid, just a harum-scarum youngster, with no sense of the value of money. He would give I.O.U.s all around town and trust a good Providence and the Cardinal organization to redeem them.

From the start he was a strange combination of temperament and genius. He had the modesty of Lardner's fictional character, Jack Keefe. Dizzy not only told you he was good, but he was good. Following a great season with St. Joe and Houston in 1930, and his three-hit game against the Pirates late in the season, he never would have been sent to the minors again but for his pranks at Street's 1931 training camp at Brandenton, Florida. Street ordered a morning practice, but Dizzy just went on and slept. Reprimanded, he said: "Let some of the other clucks work out for the staff; nobody can beat me." And he believed it.

At the same camp, Dean was much annoyed when he became the original "Dollar a Day" man. Dizz again had signed chits on bits of paper all over town—even on the backs of cigar coupons. He signed them at the haberdasher, the druggist, the town's café—not only for himself, but for any pals who happened to be along. So, Clarence Lloyd, the Cardinal secretary, sent word to the Brandenton merchants that Dean's I.O.U.s no longer were to be accepted. Each morning Clarence gave him a dollar bill, and Dizz had to sign a memorandum: "Received today, $1.00. Dizzy Dean." Naturally that was humiliating to the great one, and he resented it.

He was heartbroken when Rickey sent him back to Houston. He couldn't believe it—why, he could fog that ball through faster than any of the guys in that so-called "big league." However, he didn't let his peeve interfere with his work; he had another great Texas League year, winning 26 games and losing only ten.

And he married Miss Patricia Nash, a hosiery saleswoman, that season. It was to have been a wedding at the home plate at Houston, and was so publicized all over the country, though Dizz says today the actual ceremony didn't take place at the plate. However, his marriage was one of the best things that happened to him. Pat didn't cramp his style, but furnished the balance wheel for the family. She became his financial adviser.

Promoted to the Cardinals in 1932, Dean became an immediate National League sensation. The Redbirds were down, but they were a draw whenever Dizz was scheduled to pitch. Dean also was in big demand on the barnstorming circuit, but he never cared much for exhibition pitching when he was worked so frequently in league games. The Cardinals had an off day in going from New York to Pittsburgh. Rickey filled it in with an exhibition game in a Pennsylvania town. Street listed the players who were to play, made up partly of regulars and substitutes. Dizzy was one of the pitchers. The club left New York in three Pullmans; one was switched off at Harrisburg for the exhibition town, and the other two remained on the regular train for Pittsburgh.

When the train reached Pittsburgh the next morning, Dizzy and his wife, Patricia, were in the Pittsburgh car. Dizz looked out of the window, and inquired: "What town is this?" When told it was Pittsburgh, he said: "That can't be right; I ought to be in ———."

Gabby Street wasn't impressed with Dean's story that he awoke in the wrong car, and fined him $100. Again Dizz resented it, and said he wouldn't stand for the fine.

The Cardinals returned to St. Louis shortly afterwards, and were scheduled to open with Brooklyn. "If I go in and shut out Brooklyn for you, will you call off the fine?" Dean asked Street.

"I don't know; I'll see," said Gabby.

He pitched Dean in the first game, and sure enough Dizzy hurled a shutout. Street sent word up to the press stand: "That fine on Dean for missing the exhibition game is off."

In a *Liberty Magazine* article, "I Was No Pop-Off," appearing under Dizzy's signature, he claims that Branch Rickey and Sam Breadon, especially the former, inspired his conduct, to make people curious about him, and therefore, make him a greater attraction. But Dizzy needed no such inspiration; popping off was as natural for him as peep-peeping for a sparrow, crowing for a rooster and roaring for a lion.

Joe Medwick wasn't as colorful a figure as Dean, but he was no shrinking violet, had a temper as hot as Hungarian goulash, and had plenty to say when things didn't suit him. Strong as a bull calf, he was a born athlete, and could have gone high in college football if he hadn't become interested in professional baseball. Product of Magyar stock, he was an All-New Jersey scholastic half back, playing for Carteret High, and had numerous offers of college athletic scholarships, when he signed in the Cardinal organization and played his first season under the name of King, with Scottsdale in the middle Atlantic League, where the eighteen-year-old hit .419.

Medwick went from there to Houston and a .354 average with the Buffs in 1932 sent him to the Cardinals before the season was over. He went so well in Houston that a girl fan, enraptured by his play, fastened his nickname on him when she remarked: "Isn't he the ducky wucky?"

Like Hornsby, Joe was more or less of a lone wolf on a ball club. He played hard; he played to win, but never forgot Joe Medwick. He later formed an intimacy with Leo Durocher, a friendship which was stretched rather thin when Leo became manager of the Dodgers and Joe served under him as a high-salaried private. As Medwick's skill sent him into the ranks of the top-flight stars, he proved a good business man, and each spring gave Sam Breadon many anxious moments before Ducky signed on the dotted line.

3

Following their poor 1932 season, the Cardinals received another severe jolt. On November 16, Charley Gelbert, the club's great young shortstop, went rabbit hunting near McConnellsburg, Pa. His foot caught in a vine; the player half-stumbled and his gun hit a rocky mountain side. There was an explosion and the full charge entered Gelbert's legs four inches above the left ankle. The calf was badly riddled with No. 6 shot, several nerves were shattered and the left instep blown away. Gangrene set in, and for some time it was feared an amputation would be necessary. Charley fought against it with all his mental strength, and at Hahnemann Hospital, Philadelphia, the leg was saved by Dr. A. B. Webster.

It was two years before Gelbert again could play ball, and though his pluck and determination later enabled him to resume a baseball career, he never was the star he had been before the accident. Clubs picked him up when they needed an emergency infielder, but the foot eventually healed so well that he was commissioned a Lieutenant in the Navy.

However, the injury left the St. Louis club without a shortstop when the 1933 season opened. With Gelbert only twenty-six at the time of his injury, the Cardinals had no suitable replacement in their farm system for the Lebanon Valley collegian. Rickey hastily acquired Gordon Slade, a Salt Lake City youth, from Brooklyn. Never much of a hitter, Gordon was especially inept at bat for the Cardinals, hitting only .113 in 39 games.

After a few spring games, Slade proved he couldn't handle the assignment and on May 7, the Redbirds swung a deal with the Reds whereby they acquired Lippy Leo Durocher to fill the shortstop gap. Rickey gave up plenty to get The Lip; Pitchers Paul Derringer and Allyn Stout and Infielder Sparky Adams went to Cincinnati in exchange for Durocher and Pitchers Frank "Dutch" Henry and Johnny Ogden. The release of Derringer, later one of the great National League pitchers, has been criticized as one of Rickey's biggest mistakes, but Branch needed an experienced shortstop badly, and Leo filled the bill in fine style for the next five years.

After two seasons with the Yankees as utility infielder and later part-time regular, Durocher, a stormy petrel, had been waived out of the American League after Miller Huggins' death in 1929. Leo was Miller's "boy" on the Yankees; others didn't think so highly of the flamboyant, talkative rookie. In Cincinnati, Lippy Leo became the foremost defensive shortstop of his league, but he couldn't lose the sobriquet the New York writers had fastened on him: "the All-America Out."

The Cardinals also put Rogers Hornsby back on the pay roll. The fiery Texan had been let out as playing manager of the Cubs in August, 1932, and the Chicago club went on to win the National League pennant under Charley Grimm, the former St. Louis score-card boy. The Chicago players even refused to vote their deposed manager a share of their World's Series money. Despite his big salaries and his $66,000 profit in his Cardinal stock transaction, the great infielder and former batting champion was broke. One game Rog never could win was with the bookies.

Breadon and Rickey showed a nice touch of sentiment in letting bygones be bygones, and remembering Hornsby's great deeds for the Cardinals. The old master got into 46 games at second base and as pinch-hitter and showed he still had the old batting touch by hitting .325. Breadon gave him his release in July, so he could take over the management of the Browns, where oddly enough, he succeeded Bill Kellefer, who had been his coach on the Cardinal World's Champions of 1926.

During the previous winter, Rickey also put over a big deal with the Giants whereby the Cardinals gave up the promising young catcher, Gus Mancuso, and Pitcher Ray Starr for the return of Bob O'Farrell, also a pair of lefthanded pitchers, Bill Walker and Jim Mooney, and Outfielder Ethan Allen, now of the National League's promotion department. The deal apparently worked much better for New York than for St. Louis, for whereas the two clubs were tied for sixth in 1932, the Giants were World's Champions in 1933 and the Cardinals had to be content with a fifth place finish.

In another winter deal, the veteran first baseman, Jim Bottomley, was sent to Cincinnati for Outfielder Estel Crabtree and Pitcher Owen Carroll, a college wonder-hurler at Holy Cross, who never came up to expectations. Sunny Jim was sent on his way to clear the first base job for Jim Collins. Brooklyn's old fireballer, Dazzy Vance—by this time fairly well washed up—came to the Redbirds with Slade in a deal for Jake Flowers and Carroll, the pitcher procured from the Reds. It gave the Cards a Dizzy and a Dazzy, while Burleigh Grimes was regained from the Cubs in an August waiver transaction.

Dizzy Dean, again working like a truck horse, won 20 games and lost 18 in his second season in the league and struck out 17 Cubs

PAUL DEAN, JAMES HARRY "DIZZY" DEAN, FORMER OGLE-
THORPE COLLEGE NO-HIT STAR, AND JEROME "DIZZY" DEAN

JOSEPH M. (DUCKY) MEDWICK

on July 30, 1933, for a modern National League record. Tex Carleton, a newcomer from Houston, who had a continual feud with Dizz, won 17 games, while losing 11. Despite this fine pitching by Dizzy and Tex, healthy averages well over .300 for Medwick, Frisch and Jim Collins, and Pepper Martin's 78-point batting jump as the club's new third baseman, the 1933 Cardinals again were a disappointment. The Birds won ten more games than in 1932, but Bill McKechnie's Braves, usually habitual second division dwellers, nosed out the Cardinals for fourth place, .539 to .536, on the last day of the season.

Sam Breadon, who changed managers after the club won pennants, couldn't sit idly by while his Redbirds finished in the second division two years in succession. Gabby Street, the miracle man of 1930, was paid in full on July 24, and his managerial job was turned over to Frankie Frisch, the hustling aggressive captain and second baseman of the club. The Cards had gotten off to a poor start, winning only six games out of 15 in April, and then, shortly after Durocher braced the infield, it looked as though the Redbirds really had snapped into it. They tore through May, winning 19 games and losing seven, and held first place in early June. Then another big recession set in, and Gabby went out with it.

"Street was a far better manager before he won his World's Series in 1931 then he was thereafter," said Breadon. "Somehow, he figured his World's Champions could do no wrong, and thereby lost control of his team. The players got out of hand, and a change had to be made. Gabby did a good job, but his turn had come."

Frisch, the new manager, has been termed New Rochelle's Town Crier. If his club is on a winning streak, and wins 17 games in 20, he will moan more over the three losing efforts than rejoice over the 17 games that are won. But Frisch was—and still is—a smart, positive manager, a distinct personality, and a character who contributed much to colorful Cardinal baseball. He was what baseball men term "a natural" for managerial promotion. Before retiring from the active management of the Giants in 1932, John McGraw, Frisch's old New York boss, tried to get Frankie back from St. Louis with the idea of installing the Fordham boy as his successor. Breadon wasn't interested; he had his own ideas for Frankie's future, and the Giant job went to Bill Terry.

163

XX ⊜ THE GAS HOUSE GANG

WITH DUE RESPECT to the powerful Yankees of the Babe Ruth era, the most colorful, picturesque club of modern baseball was the Cardinal World's Champion outfit of 1934, the famous Gas House Gang of St. Louis. In the sense that the Gas House Gang was a bunch of rowdies, who played dirty, "anything-goes" baseball after the fashion of the old Baltimore Orioles and St. Louis' transplanted Cleveland Spiders, the name was a misnomer. Frisch always played hard-driving, heads-up baseball, but his tactics are clean.

The main cogs on the Gas House Gang were frolicsome, exuberant spirits, with boundless energy—Pepper Martin, Dizzy Dean, Rip Collins, Lippy Durocher, Ernie "Showboat" Orsatti, Joe "Muscles" Medwick, Bill "Kayo" DeLancey, etc. And they had the perfect manager for that kind of a team in Frisch. They got right down into the dirt, and played hard—winning ball. Pepper always perspired freely, especially on a hot St. Louis afternoon, and a nicely laundered uniform looked as out of place on him as a Lord Fauntleroy suit on a freckled Irish kid from St. Louis' old Kerry Patch.

"Now listen, you guys. We aren't gonna let anybody in this league run over us," Frisch addressed his players before that season started. "Do you fellows get that? You've got to win those ball games, especially the close ones. I'm not going to be a detective and watch over you at night. Your nights are your own, but your days belong to me. Now, if you'd rather go back to the mines and dig for coal or ride around the country in Pullmans and live in the best hotels at the expense of the club, speak right up. We haven't any room for softies, and no holds are barred. That's the way we're going to play ball."

"You said more'n a mouthful, Frank," approved Dizzy Dean.

Oddly enough, the term "Gas House Gang" did not originate in St. Louis, but first was used by Frank Graham in the *New York Sun.* And Frankie attributes it to Leo Durocher. Graham was visiting the Cardinal bench while the team was in New York, and Dizzy Dean remarked that the Cardinals could take up the lowly Brown percentage and still win the pennant in the American League.

"They wouldn't let us play in that league," snapped Durocher, the former Yankee. "They'd say we were a lot of gas house ball players."

Bill Corum, a Missouri boy with a soft spot in his heart for the Cardinals since he was in rompers, took up the term in his widely-read column in the New York *Journal-American* and it quickly spread over the country.

There never was another major league race exactly like the National League Marathon of 1934, and it will be years before baseball sees anything just like it. While the Cardinals held on tenaciously, until they got into the World's Series, no team ever blew a pennant as badly as did the Giants of that year. The New York club was considered "in" to such a degree that a national magazine, in its issue coming out after the World's Series, had the Giants battling the Detroit Tigers in the Series, with full-page illustrations of the New York players. It took brilliant pitching by the Dean boys, especially in the last fortnight of the race, for the Cardinals to win their fifth championship, but they needed collaboration on the part of the Giants, who lost six of their last seven games to the fourth place Braves, seventh place Phillies and sixth place Dodgers.

Even after blowing a seemingly fool-proof early September lead, the Giants still could have won the pennant by winning their two closing games from Brooklyn. It was the year Bill Terry, the New York manager, made his famous facetious wisecrack: "Oh, Brooklyn, are they still in the league?" a remark which was to plague him for years. Brooklyn upset the Giants in their last two games, while the Cards were downing the Reds, and at the finish the new St. Louis Champions had their proverbial lead of two games. With the exception of a few days in the spring, the Cardinals never were first until the day before the close of the season. The final standing showed St. Louis with 95 victories and 58 defeats for a percentage of .621, and New York with 93 wins and 60 setbacks for .608. The Chicago Cubs, a contender most of the way and the league leader in April and May, fell back at the finish, winding up third with 86 victories, 65 defeats and a .570 percentage.

2

Frisch's club didn't start out like a prospective pennant winner, and lost seven of its first 11 games. On the eleventh day of the season, the Redbirds were tied with the Phillies for last place. Then they followed the pattern of the 1933 club and experienced a remarkable May, winning 21 games and losing six. That reserve of victories later served in good stead as the club played mediocre ball through June and a good part of July. For weeks the Giants rode well out in front; Terry was getting great pitching from Hubbell, Schumacher, Fitzsimmons and Parmelee, and it looked as though New York, the 1933 World's Champion, would repeat in a breeze. Chicago was the club which was chasing Terry's lads, with the Cardinals running third.

There came a substantial St. Louis upsurge in August; Frisch was exhorting the team, driving, scolding, moaning, praising his players, in turn, and the Gang began dreaming of the pennant. The dreams faded pretty dim on Labor Day, September 3, when the Cards blew a double header to Pittsburgh. Paul Dean was knocked out of the opener, as Larry French won easily, 12 to 2, and Hoyt and Meine wore down Walker, Dizzy Dean and Hallahan in the second game, 6 to 5. After the Labor Day games, the Giants led St. Louis and Chicago, tied for second place, by exactly six games. With the advantage of playing most of their September games on their friendly Polo Grounds, the pennant really looked to be all wrapped up in Bill Terry's bat bag.

As one St. Louis reporter put it: "The Cardinals kept hustling and fighting to beat out Chicago for second place, and before they knew it, their hustle and the Giant flop put them in the World's Series."

3

Frisch made only a few changes from the club which finished fifth in 1933, but those changes were important, noteworthy and made the subsequent successful September campaign possible. Dizzy Dean's younger brother, Paul, a year and a half Dizz's junior, was advanced to the Cardinals after getting his minor league education in Houston, Springfield, Mo. and Columbus. His Columbus battery mate, Catcher Bill DeLancey, came up with him. Until his health broke down two years later, requiring him to go to Arizona, Bill looked like a catcher who might rank with Bresnahan, Kling and Dickey. Jack Rothrock, who had been shifted around from the infield to the outfield for the American League's tailend Red Sox, was acquired and became the regular Cardinal right fielder.

The preceding winter, Jimmy Wilson, who always seemed to be shuttling back and forth between Philadelphia and St. Louis, was released to the Phillies so that he could take up the managerial reins of that club. Some thought Jimmy would get the St. Louis job when Street was released. Wilson was traded for Catcher Virgil Spud Davis, the erstwhile Redbird, and Infielder Eddie Delker. Two guys named George exchanged uniforms; George Watkins was traded to New York for George "Kiddo" Davis, a former New York University star, while Chick Fullis, another outfielder, also was picked up from the Giants.

However, the great move was the graduation of Paul Dean to the Cardinals' main show. Almost from his first connection with the Redbirds, Dizzy Dean had insisted: "I got a brother that's pitching and he's faster'n me." And it was on Dizzy's recommendation that the St. Louis club first signed Paul. In the World's Series of that year, after Schoolboy Lynwood Rowe had pitched a particularly meritorious game against the Cardinals, Dizzy remarked: "With the wind behind him, Rowe was almost as fast as Paul"—no mean compliment. For the next few years, "Me and Paul" became the two great pitching names of baseball. Unlike the loquacious Dizzy, Paul seldom spoke. Some sports writers tried to fasten the nickname, "Daffy" on Paul, but it fitted him as well as if they had tried to call the elder Dean, "Clarence." Paul had a tremendous admiration for his older brother, and Dizz never ceased being his idol and hero. Paul's curve was only a "wrinkle" in baseball parlance, not nearly as sharp as Jay-Jerome's fast-breaking curve, but he had a blinding fast ball, and for two years he was quite a pitcher. Like Dizzy, he could fog 'em through, and make batters look silly.

Between them, "Me and Paul" turned in 49 winning games that season, the elder Dean winning 30 games and losing seven, while Paul notched 19 victories against 11 defeats. Dizz is the only National League pitcher to win 30 games in a season since Grover Alexander turned the trick for the Phillies in 1915, 1916, and 1917.

In the final pennant spurt, the pair were magnificent. When the Cardinals made their last sensational drive through the east, which carried them within striking distance of the Giants, it was Pop Albert Monroe's two sturdy lads who carried the ball for Frisch.

167

There was that memorable double-header in Brooklyn, September 21. After Dizzy won the opener, 13 to 0, Paul came through with a no-hit game in the second tussle, winning, 3 to 0.

"I wish that kid had told me he was going to pitch a no-hitter," said Dizz. "I wouldn't have given 'em none either." Dizzy gave up three.

Then, in that final glorious week at home, when every game—every play, meant so much, the Deans pitched in five of the six games. On September 25, Dizzy defeated Larry French, Pirate southpaw, 3 to 2. The next day, Waite Hoyt, the former Yank, now pitching for Pittsburgh, won a 3 to 0 shutout from Paul. That left the Cardinals with only four more games with the Reds. There was only one Deanless game, Walker, Vance and Carleton staggering in to an 8 to 5 win over Derringer on September 27. On September 28, Dizzy pitched a 4 to 0 whitewashing against Frey and Stout; that put the Cards in a tie with the Giants.

Paul won the next day, the 29th, by 6 to 1, giving the Redbirds the lead by a game, and before a crowd of 37,402, on Sunday, September 30—the last day of the season—Dizzy came back to put the final crusher on the Reds, 9 to 0, as Collins and DeLancey helped with homers. Before the game was over, the scoreboard showed Brooklyn had defeated the Giants, assuring the Cardinals of the pennant, but Dizz never eased up and pitched his seventh shutout of the year.

Despite their great pitching, the Dean boys staged a mid-season two-man strike. It was over that old St. Louis vexation—an exhibition game. As the club returned from its first eastern trip, Breadon scheduled an exhibition in Detroit. The Deans were advertised to pitch. Instead, they took a train back to St. Louis. Both players were fined and suspended.

Dizzy appealed to Judge Landis, and this time the Mountain came to Mahomet. Instead of holding court in his Chicago office, the Judge went to St. Louis to hold his hearing. There the elder Dean, the Oklahoma farm boy, tried to match wits with two lawyers, Landis and Branch Rickey, the shrewd Breadon, and the college-educated Frisch. The pitching pair eventually was reinstated with a reprimand, and Dizzy celebrated his return to good standing the next day with a sensational 1-0 victory over New York.

Dizzy did all the talking for the Dean side at the hearing, and Frisch, as manager of the club, had to argue the St. Louis club's case against Jay-Jerome and Paul, their insubordination, the breach of discipline, and added a few words on the problem of managing the difficult Deans.

Paul didn't say a word during the entire controversy; he sat in a chair staring out of the window. However, when it was all over, he made his only comment. "Dizz," he said to his brother, "why didn't you pop that Dutchman (Frisch) right on the nose?"

4

Perhaps nothing shows better the spirit of the Gas House Gang than the marriage of Leo Durocher, the club's aggressive shortstop, in the last week of that hectic season. Leo was very much in love with Grace Dozier, a fashionable and prosperous St. Louis dress designer. The Lip always had a keen eye for good looks and good clothes, and Miss Dozier was quite an eyeful. No other player but Durocher would have selected such a week to press his suit, and no other club but the Gas House Gang of that period would have encouraged a marriage under such conditions. Fifteen out of sixteen club owners probably would have said: "Can you imagine a guy thinking of love and marriage, when his every thought—awake and asleep—should be on the daily ball games, and winning the pennant?"

But maybe that's where Rickey showed himself to be more of a psychologist. Miss Dozier wasn't entirely unreceptive to Leo's campaign, but she was a red-hot Cardinal fan, and wasn't sure whether she should marry the Redbirds' crack shortstop at such an important stage in the club's fight for the pennant.

Durocher appealed to Branch, as the Rickeys were old friends of Miss Dozier. Leo had it bad; it was one of those cases where he just "couldn't live without her." It preyed on his mind, when he should have been concentrating on the baseball situation at hand. So Branch telephoned Grace and suggested that if she had any serious intentions with Leo, she had better marry him then and there, and free the young New Englander's mind for baseball.

With the matter presented in that light by Cupid Rickey, what was a lady, a good Cardinal fan, to do? She gave in, and Grace and Leo were married on the morning of September 26, the day Durocher's old Yankee teammate, Waite Hoyt, gave the Cardinal pennant chances a stiff jolt by shutting out St. Louis. Grace cried over the defeat; so did Frankie Frisch. "Can you imagine picking a time like this for a wedding?" he moaned. But, after his marriage The Lip's mind was cleared for baseball; he was a veritable ball of fire on the Cardinals' infield, as the St. Louis club swept their last four-game series with the Reds. It is regrettable that a romance which had such a dramatic beginning should have ended in the divorce courts nine years later.

5

In bringing in the 1934 pennant, the Deans had most pitching help from Tex Carleton, and the former Giant southpaw, Bill Walker. Tex won 16 games and lost 11, and Bill won 12, while losing four. Hallahan had lost a lot of his stuff; even with a champion Wild Bill could fetch in only eight winning efforts against 12 defeats. Old Pop Haines still was around, breaking even in eight decisions.

Rip Collins, the new first sacker, was fourth in National League batting with .333 and second in runs batted in with 128. Ducky Medwick was getting better and better, hitting .319, with a robust collection of 40 doubles, 18 triples and 18 homers. DeLancey, the new catcher, hit .316; Manager Frisch was listed at .305; and Pepper Martin, again playing third base, got a lot of power out of a .288 average. The farm system came up with a most promising infielder, a collegian who looked as though he might develop into another Frisch—Burgess "Whitey" Whitehead, a Phi Beta Kappa man from the University of North Carolina.

One name, which didn't get into Cardinal box-scores, but who had a prominent place in the victory was the Redbird trainer, "Doc" Harrison J. Weaver. Ever since he first joined the St. Louis outfit in 1927, "Doc" Weaver, known as "Bucko" in his college football days, has been one of the most colorful of the Cardinals. He, too, was a natural on the Gas House Gang. A chiropractor, he is a graduate of Rickey's old college, Ohio Wesleyan. The Ohio Wesleyan song is the winning chant of the Redbirds; "Doc" plays it on his clubhouse phonograph after every victory. He made one trip with the

Birds in 1927—to help out Rickey in a pinch, and Bucko hasn't missed one since.

Weaver knows more hexes, jinxes and whammies than a Haitian voodoo doctor. He had to work double in 1934, to put one hex on the teams opposing the Cardinals, and a long distance whammy on the Giants. How well he succeeded, Bill Terry and his 1934 New York crew remember only too well.

XXI ⊗ FRESH WORLD'S SERIES LAURELS

I

THE OPPONENTS of the Redbirds in the 1934 World's Series were the Detroit Tigers, who won their first American League championship in twenty-five years under the leadership of the dynamic catcher, Mickey Cochrane, who had been behind the bat for Mack in the Series with Street's Cardinals of 1930 and 1931. In one of the greatest series on record, the Redbirds won their third blue ribbon, defeating Cochrane's team in a stubbornly contested seven-game series. In a way, it was 1926 repeating itself. The Redbirds were trailing, three games to two, when they were obliged to invade the lair of their enemy to finish the series—and pulled it out by winning the sixth and seventh games.

St. Louis' heroes again were the two Deans, each of whom won two games, along with the same players who wrought most havoc with their war clubs during the season. Martin wasn't quite the standout that he was in the 1931 victory, but he hit .355, stole the Cards' only two bases, and as the St. Louis lead-off man scored eight runs, more than any other player on either side. He rapped out 11 hits in the seven games, as did Medwick and Rip Collins. The new bridegroom, Durocher, fielded a phenomenal game at shortstop, accepting 30 chances without a slip. After living up to his title of the "All-America Out" for three games, Leo's hitting in the sixth game was the deciding factor in the St. Louis victory and made a seventh game possible.

The series started in Detroit, October 3, before a 42,505 crowd, and Dizzy won in a romp, 8 to 3, from Alvin Crowder, Fred Marberry and Chief Hogsett. The Birds lashed the Tiger trio for 13 hits, and there wasn't an unlucky bingle among them; Ducky Medwick blew himself to four, including a homer, and even Dizzy's bat spouted forth a two-bagger.

Detroit tied it up next day, as Lynwood Rowe, the big schoolboy from Eldorado, Ark., pitched one of the Series classics in bringing home the victory for Cochrane, 3 to 2, in 12 innings. Despite Hallahan's mediocre showing during the season, Frisch pitched the old Cardinal World's Series ace, and Bill fought off the tall schoolboy until the Tigers tied the score at 2-2 in the ninth. Bill Walker, another lefthander, relieved him, and lost the game in the twelfth on his lack of control, when the Detroit G-men finally got him. With one out, he walked Gehringer and Greenberg, and Goose Goslin singled home Detroit's great second baseman. From the third inning, when St. Louis scored its second run, no Cardinal reached base until Martin doubled in the eleventh inning, Rowe retiring 22 successive Redbird batsmen.

The series shifted to St. Louis for the third game, October 5, and Paul Dean put the Cardinals back in the lead, winning a well-pitched effort from the capable Tommy Bridges by a score of 4 to 1. The Cardinals collected only one more bingle than the Tigers —nine hits to eight, but Pepper Martin was the usual one-man blitz against the American Leaguers, hitting a triple and a double, with Rothrock, the Red Sox discard, driving him home each time.

2

Cochrane's crowd had its field day in the fourth game, jumping on five St. Louis pitchers, Carleton, Vance, Walker, Haines and Mooney, to win as they pleased, 10 to 4. This time it was Detroit, who hammered out 13 hits, and Hank Greenberg, the tall Bronxonian, who belted four hits, two doubles and a pair of singles. The Cardinals really left an odor of stale fish in this one, piling up five errors, three by Martin at third base. Eldon Auker, of the submarine delivery, scored an easy victory for Cochrane.

What for a time threatened to be even more costly for St. Louis than the loss of the game was Dizzy Dean being knocked cold in the fourth inning. Working on the idea that his Dizziness had an inspirational effect on the Cardinals, Frisch used him as a pinch-runner for Virgil Davis, the slow-moving catcher. As Billy Rogell, Detroit shortstop, tried for a double play, his peg collided with Dizzy's dome. Jay-Jerome went out like a light, had to be carried to the clubhouse, where he inquired: "Where am I at?" but fortunately was not seriously injured.

In fact Dizzy was ready to return to the wars the very next day, when he hurled against Tommy Bridges, the game little curve ball man from Tennessee, and this time Dizz was thrown for a 3 to 1 setback. Each club cracked out only seven hits, but one of the Tiger blows was a homer by the mechanical man, Charley Gehringer. St. Louis' lone run resulted from DeLancey's seventh inning home run with none on, coming when Detroit led, 3-0.

Leading three games to two, as they returned home, Cochrane and his Tigers felt pretty cocky. The best crowd of the series, 44,551, was out at Navin Field, Detroit, October 8, to see Schoolboy Rowe, the sensational second game winner, wind it up. But Redbird teams never have gone down easily!

"The hell with that Rowe; we're the better ball club; we pulled out the pennant, and we can pull this out," Frisch had said on the way to Detroit, giving his Redbirds an old Fordham pep talk. "It's just like it was when we played the Yankees in 1926, and you know what we did to them," volunteered Pop Haines. "Paul'll take 'em in the next one, and I'll set 'em back on their cans in the seventh game," said Dizzy. "That's talking, Dizz," from Pepper Martin, "why, it's in the bag."

It had to be Paul Dean against Rowe, and fortunately for Paul, this was the game in which the "All-America-Out" broke out. After going hitless in the first three games and getting only two hits in 18 times at bat in the first five, Bridegroom Durocher became a hitting fool for a day. Paul's 4 to 3 decision over Rowe was achieved largely on Leo's three hits; he scored two of the St. Louis runs and put another in scoring position. With the score tied, 3 to 3, and one out in the seventh, The Lip lashed out a steaming double and Paul won his own game when he drove in the chattering shortstop with a long single.

The seventh game was one of those never-to-be-forgotten games of baseball, though Judge Landis doesn't like a recollection of it, and it still leaves a nasty taste in the mouths of Detroit fans. When Paul Dean won from Rowe, all the pitching advantage went to Frisch. He had Dizzy, the year's leading boxman, to shoot against Auker, Cochrane's fourth game winner.

Auker fought off Dean for two innings, but the Redbirds dropped depth charges on Eldon's submarine ball in the third, piled up seven runs, and from there on, it was a hilarious joy ride for the merry Cardinals. Eventually, they won, 11 to 0, as the desperate Cochrane vainly followed Auker with Rowe, Hogsett, Bridges, Marberry and Crowder. The Redbirds closed the series with a 17-hit barrage, Rip Collins getting four, Dean two; Durocher following his sixth game attack with a triple and single. Dizzy pitched a six-hit shutout.

During St. Louis' seven run assault in the third inning, Joe Medwick hit a triple, and as he slid into third base, he had an altercation with Marvin Owen, the Tiger third baseman. Marvin didn't like the way Joe came into the bag, and Ducky thought Owen put the ball on him with unnecessary roughness. There were hot words, a few wild swings, but Bill Klem, the third base umpire, prevented any real fisticuffs.

As Detroit's cause became darker and darker, the Tiger fans, especially those in the left field bleachers, worked themselves into an ugly mood. Most of their resentment was directed against Medwick. They bombarded him with vegetables, fruit, rolled-up newspapers and score-cards—even a few pop bottles. Several times, attendants cleared the field, only to have a fresh volley burst from the stands.

Umpires and players pleaded with the crowd to cease throwing edibles, but their pleas fell on deaf ears. It got so bad in the seventh inning that Ducky couldn't take his regular position. Judge Landis then summoned Medwick, Owen and the umpires and held court in his box. The Commissioner requested Medwick to leave the game and Frisch assigned Chick Fullis to left field. Landis said he took this action "to protect the player from injury and permit the game to proceed." However, many at the game felt this was not one of the Commissioner's best decisions.

The entire series drew 281,510 persons, with a gate of $1,031,341; Sam Breadon's cut of it was $143,811. Despite the great finish by the Cardinals, Singing Sam needed his World's Series cut to show a profit on the season. After the Cardinals' spring flurry, few St. Louisans figured the club had a chance until late September. The club drew only 327,000 for its 77 National League games at home, one-fourth of it in the last week of the season. That was 451,000 less than the St. Louis National League Champions of 1928 drew to Sportsmans Park.

Of course, Dizzy Dean couldn't miss joining the host of Cardinals who have been selected for the National League's most valuable player award. He also was voted the Player of the Year by the New York Chapter, Baseball Writers' Association of America, and dolled himself up in his first Tuxedo to go to New York to bring back his plaque to Patricia.

At the end of the season, with his Cardinals again perched at the top of the baseball heap, Sam Breadon, the lad from New York's lower West Side, came close to selling his Redbirds to Lewis Haines Wentz, a Ponca City, Oklahoma oil millionaire, with Pittsburgh connections. Branch Rickey had been acquainted with Lew Wentz for some time. Negotiations reached a point where a price was agreed upon for the St. Louis franchise, but broke down over Breadon's high valuation of the Cardinal farm properties. Had Wentz been successful in buying the club, he would have brought Fred Clarke, the old Pirate manager, into the Redbird picture.

XXII ⊜ FRISCH'S FROLICSOME FOLLIES

I

IF THE CARDINALS of 1934 thought they blew the pennant on Labor Day, the Redbirds of '35 thought they had assured themselves of another shot at World's Series glory on labor's early September play-day. As in the preceding season, Terry's New Yorkers ran first for the greater part of the distance. For a spell here and there, Charley Grimm's Cubs shoved their stubby snouts in front, but to all the Cards—from Frisch down to the bat-boy—the Giants were the club to beat.

The Cardinals led New York by a full game, with Chicago trailing the Giants by a half game, when the St. Louis club opposed the Pirates at Sportsmans Park before a shouting enthusiastic crowd of 30,849. Reversing the order of Labor Day, 1934, the Birds scored a double knockout. With Paul Dean finishing the first game for young Heusser and Hallahan, Frisch's team wore down the perennial schoolboy, Waite Hoyt, in 16 innings to win, 4 to 3. Dizzy Dean then took care of the nightcap, 4 to 1.

The Cardinals were tired but happy boys when they rushed into their clubhouse and scrambled for the showers. The scoreboard showed the Giants had been rained out in New York, and that the Cincinnati Reds had held Chicago to an even break. The Cards were two full games in front of New York, and two and a half ahead of the Cubs.

"That was it, gang," said Frisch, happily. "From here on, we go places."

"You said it, boss," echoed Pepper Martin. "We won't let up on 'em."

But the club which wouldn't let up was Grimm's grim Cubs, who soon went on one of the most amazing winning streaks in baseball history. The Cardinals could have beaten an ordinary club; they soon outdistanced the Giants—who broke again in September; but the Gas House Gang was stymied by a club which just refused to lose. The Cubs went on a 21-game winning streak which carried almost to the final game of the season. In the third week of September, banjo-playing Charley's inspired players shot by the Redbirds.

"They can't keep that up; they're not that good. We just got to keep hustling and fighting, and catch them at the finish," the Flash encouraged his gang, as day after day the scoreboard boy posted additional Chicago victories.

The Cub winning streak had reached 19 straight when they met the Cardinals in St. Louis on Friday, the 27th, two days before the close of the season. The Birds still had a chance, especially if they won the double-header scheduled for that day. They even got Dizzy Dean two runs off Bill Lee in the first inning of the first game, but it wasn't enough. The Cubs were a pennant-crazed club, and defeated the great Dizz, 6 to 2. Bill Jurges, the Cub shortstop, was all over the place and accepted 13 chances. It was the Cubs' pennant-clinching game and their twentieth in a row. Just to make the pennant pole even more secure, they bagged the second game, 5 to 3, for No. 21, the second longest winning streak in the 68-year-old history of the National League.

When the final returns were in two days later on Sunday, September 29, the three leaders ranked: Chicago, 100 won, 54 lost, percentage .649; St. Louis, 96 and 58, per. .623; New York, 91 and 62, per. 595.

Even though the two Deans again enjoyed a great season, Frisch didn't have enough pitching strength behind his Oklahoma aces. "Me and Paul" were his only pitchers to appear in as many as ten complete games. Dizzy fell two behind his imposing 1934 total, winning 28 games and losing 12. Paul hit his 1934 victory total, 19, right on the nose, and lost 12. Bill Hallahan made something of a comeback with a 15-8 record, while the other lefthanded Bill—Walker—was right behind him with 13 and eight. Ed Heusser and Roy Harrell, a pair of kids, and the veteran Haines helped out. As the season advanced Rickey tried to bolster the staff by obtaining Phil Collins, a fair right-hander, from the Phillies. The previous winter, Rickey also had traded Pitcher Tex Carleton to the Cubs for Pitchers Bud Tinning and Dick Ward and cash, with emphasis on the greenbacks.

Medwick showed even greater improvement than in 1934, hitting .353; Muscles was third in league batting, and fired an extra-base shower which included 46 doubles, 13 triples and 23 homers. He hammered home 126 Cardinal runs. Terry Moore, perhaps St. Louis' greatest homegrown player, and the Tris Speaker of modern center fielders, made his bow with the club; on September 5, while the Cardinals feasted on the Braves, 15 to 3, the kid outfielder collected six hits in as many times at bat. The game but unlucky Charley Gelbert came back to play 60 games at third base, while Frisch started to break in young Whitehead as his successor.

2

The 1936 Cardinals had an odd record. They took the year's series from every club in the league with the exception of the lowly sixth place Bostons, then termed the Bees. Frisch's hustlers defeated the champion Giants, 12 games to ten; they took Chicago, tied with St. Louis for second place, 13 games to nine, but could win only nine from Boston, while the second division Bees stung them 13 times. Despite unforeseen happenings, the Cardinals could have won if they had enjoyed greater success against these pestiferous Bees, still managed by Bill McKechnie.

The race again was between the same clubs which provided the fireworks in 1934 and 1935, New York, St. Louis and Chicago. As the clubs dashed past the half mile post, the contest seemingly was between the Cards and Cubs. In early summer, the Giants dropped as far as ten games behind. Then, from July 27 to August 28, the New Yorkers really stepped on it, winning 26 games out of 28, and Carl Hubbell, a 26-game winner, closed the season with 16 straight victories. The Giants, reversing the order of the two previous seasons, finished in high, and came in five games ahead of St. Louis and Chicago. The Cubs tied the Gas House Gang for the runner-up spot on the last day of the season, Sunday, September 27, when the Bruins, with Warneke opposing Dizzy Dean, won by a score of 6 to 3.

There was considerable bickering between Dizz and "the Dutchman," Dean's term for his manager, during the season. Dizzy claimed "the Dutchman" had been picking on him, and hinted that some of Frisch's strategy was not exactly master minding.

"Imagine that guy popping off," said Frankie. "I put it up to him to win second place for us, and he couldn't even do that."

If Frisch could blame the loss of the 1935 flag on the Cubs' 21-game September winning streak, he could excuse his failure to win in '36 on brother Paul's lame wing. After two 19-victory seasons, the younger Dean suffered with a lame arm all season, and closed with a record of five victories and as many defeats. Paul never did regain stardom. Dizzy had to carry the staff, winning 24 games and losing 13. The winter before, Rickey tried to strengthen the Cardinal staff by trading Burgess Whitehead, the promising second-string second baseman, to New York for Pitcher Roy Parmelee and Phil Weintraub, a cumbersome fielder who carried dynamite in his bat. Roy failed to come up to expectations, breaking even in 22 games, while he pitched only nine complete contests. A young fellow, Jim Winford, helped, though his record was only 11 wins against ten

178

defeats. Even George Earnshaw, Mack's former World's Series ace, was picked up from Brooklyn in July in an effort to brace the staff.

In addition to Paul Dean's disability, Frisch received another crushing blow when he lost Catcher Bill DeLancey. Bill contracted a lung disorder, which made it advisable for the brilliant young catcher to seek Arizona's crisp dry climate. "You can't lose a catcher like that, and not have it hit your entire ball club," said Frisch. "It was as though Joe McCarthy had lost Bill Dickey in his prime." Virgil Davis took over the first line catching duties; Spud hit a powerful .317 but was slow as Stepin Fetchit, while Bruce Ogrodowski, a San Francisco Pole, was advanced from Columbus to help the stricken catching department.

Ducky Medwick set a new National League doubles record that season which still stands—64 two-baggers. Jersey Joe again was red hot; he lashed out 223 hits, scored 115 runs, and drove in 138, tops for the league. The slugging first baseman from Georgia, Johnny Mize, couldn't be kept in the minors any longer, and Rickey brought him up. By cleverly shifting Mize and Rip Collins between first base and the outfield, Frisch managed to get Johnny in 126 games and the Ripper in 103. Mize broke in with a .329 average, 30 doubles and 19 homers.

Old Pop Time—and a spike wound in Frisch's foot which went back to his Giant days, finally brought down the Fordham Flash. His activity was confined to 93 games, only 60 at second base. With Whitehead traded to New York, it left quite a gap at the midway. Stu Martin, a Guilford, N. C. collegian, and a young Italian, Art Garibaldi, did their best to fill it. Don Gutteridge, the present St. Louis Brown second sacker, came up in the fall and was a ball of fire in 23 games at third base, hitting .319 and running bases in the most approved fashion of the Gas House Gang.

The Gang still was functioning, and pulled one of its greatest pranks that season. It happened at the Bellevue-Stratford, swank Philadelphia hostelry, where Sam Breadon puts up his Redbirds. A large and dignified banquet was in progress, when pandemonium suddenly broke loose in the banquet hall. Three men, wearing overalls and box-shaped carpenters' caps, entered the room, carrying ladders, hammers and other accessories. One climbed up the ladder and began hammering loudly on the ceiling. The other two scraped and tossed chairs across the room. The toastmaster, the men at the head table, and the other diners were in a high dudgeon of indignation.

"What is the meaning of this outrageous interruption?" demanded the toastmaster from the leader of the gang. You guessed it; the boss was Pepper Martin, and his assistants were Dizzy Dean and Rip Collins.

"Why, I have instructions from the manager to make a thorough clean-up job," said Pepper, continuing his hammering.

Some one ran down to the hotel manager, started to give him a good dressing down, when the manager, smelling a Gas House Gangster, made post-haste for the banquet hall. He came in, just as the workmen were leaving. He exploded all over the place, but the best part of it was that when the banqueters learned the identity of the culprits, they treated it as a huge joke and invited Pepper, Dizzy and the Ripper to occupy seats at the head table. However, the trio received letters from Sam Breadon and league president Frick not to give a repeat performance.

3

The 1937 season was a great one for Joe Medwick, also for Johnny Mize, the new first baseman, but not so good for the Cardinals. They won five of their first six games, ran first in April, second in May and a part of June, and then fell back and wound up a mediocre fourth with a percentage of .526, only six points ahead of the fifth place Braves. The Giants won again, with the Cubs and Pirates also topping the Cards in the standing.

However, Ducky had one of those seasons a ball player dreams about; he just about turned the National League inside out. He led it in practically everything. He was the batting champion with an average of .374, and the league's most valuable player. He led in runs scored, 111; hits, 237; total bases, 407; doubles, 56; runs batted in, 154 (39 ahead of the second man); and tied Mel Ott of the Giants in homers with 31. While the National League lost the annual All-Star game in Washington, 8 to 3, Medwick crashed four hits for the losers. Mize followed Medwick in the National League batting averages with .364 and hit 25 home runs.

After the 1936 season, Trader Horn Rickey swapped Rip Collins and Parmelee, the pitcher procured from the Giants for Whitehead, to the Cubs for Lon Warneke, Chicago's pitching ace. It looked like a good deal for both clubs, and St. Louis fans believed it would bring them the pennant. Lon, known as the Arkansas humming bird, did his bit, winning 18 games while losing 11. Spud Davis, the heavy-hoofed catcher, was sold to the Reds, and to help fill De-Lancey's place on the catching corps, Mickey Owen was pulled in from Columbus after only two seasons in the minors. The kid probably was advanced a year too soon, and suffered from too much of a build-up.

Dizz was in constant hot water that year. During the training season, he got into an argument with big round Jack Miley, then sports columnist of the New York *Daily News*, in the lobby of the Tampa Terrace Hotel at Tampa. It since has been called the Battle of Tampa Bay. They began exchanging round-house swings. Irving Kupcinet, of the *Chicago Daily News* and a former North Dakota football star, tried to take a hand, when Mike Ryba backed him away, and Joe Medwick's fist came out from nowhere and clipped Kupcinet.

In a game with the Giants in St. Louis, May 19, Dean and Jim Ripple, then a New York outfielder, had a collision at first base, which resulted in a free-for-all between both clubs. Dizzy was hit from behind, but got up swinging. Don Gutteridge, trying to act as peacemaker, came out with two shiners. Giant Catcher Gus Mancuso was looking on from the side-lines, admiring a good fight, when young Mickey Owen plunked him on the chin. "Why did you pick on Gus?" some one asked after it was over. "Why, I thought every one was supposed to take out his man," replied Owen.

Then, in the sixth inning, Umpire George Barr called a balk on Dizzy. Ford Frick had put in a new rule interpretation that season, that a pitcher must come to a full stop after his wind-up stretch, when a runner was on base, before letting go his pitch. Barr said Dizzy didn't do it. Dizz argued five minutes that he did.

In his next game, May 23, against the Phillies, Dizzy announced he would follow instructions literally, if it took him three hours to pitch the game. After three long delays in the second inning, Beans Reardon called another balk on Dean for stalling.

Shortly afterwards Dizzy attended a father and son dinner at Belleville, Ill., and the following day, in the *Belleville Daily Advocate*, Dean was quoted as saying that Frick and Barr were "a pair of crooks." He spoke disparagingly of Frick, terming him "our great little president—but a pain in the neck to me."

Frick suspended Dean, and summoned him to New York. Dean denied he had made such remarks, but the young reporter from the *Advocate* said he had quoted Dean correctly. Frick wanted Dizz to sign a retraction, but Jay-Jerome left the meeting with his famous ultimatum: "I ain't signin' nuthin'." Nor did he, and after three days in the league doghouse, he was let out. The incident won Dean a lot of new friends in St. Louis, and Breadon announced Dean's "I ain't signin' nuthin'" vacation would cost him nuthin'. No salary deduction was made for the time he lost during the suspension.

Dean still was the best pitcher in the National League, and at the annual All-Star game in Washington, he opened against the American League stars, made up largely of Yankees. Dean held his own for two innings with McCarthy's Lefty Gomez. Dizzy had two out in the third inning, when Lou Gehrig toted his bat to the plate with Joe DiMaggio on base. The count on Lou worked down to three balls and two strikes, when Gabby Hartnett, the National League catcher, signaled for a curve. Dizzy shook him off, and tried to fog it past Larrupin' Lou. Gehrig swung and the ball sailed over Griffith's right field wall for a two-run homer. The next batter, Earl Averill, shot the ball back at Dizzy's right foot like a machine gun bullet. Dizz scrambled painfully after the ball, got his man and then limped to the bench.

An X-ray showed a broken toe. Dizzy next claimed that Frisch and the Cardinal management ordered him to pitch too soon after his injury. He said that in favoring the broken toe, he put an unnatural strain on his arm, and it became very sore. He really never was the same pitcher after that All-Star game, and closed the season with only 13 victories and ten defeats.

Paul Dean was another source of worriment for Frisch. Paul's arm still was sore and failed to respond to treatment, and the Cardinals sent him to Dallas in the Texas League in the hope that the hot Texas sun might boil out the trouble.

Among the new players brought in that season were big Bob Weiland, a left-hander who had pitched in the American League with Chicago, Cleveland and Boston; Pitcher Bill McGee, a right-hander, up from the Columbus farm; and Stanley "Frenchy" Bordagaray, an outfielder-third baseman, formerly with the White Sox and Brooklyn.

Along with Madcap Martin, the leader, and Warneke, these new-comers set the Gas House Gang to music, and formed the famous Mudcat Band.

Pepper was master of ceremonies and played a harmonica and guitar; Warneke played a guitar and sang; Fiddler Bill McGee naturally fiddled; Weiland blew into a jug; and Frenchy Bordaga-ray played a contraption which included a washboard, whistle, auto horn and electric light. The light went on when Director Pepper played. Max Lanier, with a good singing voice, was a later acquisition. The Mudcat Band rigged themselves out in cowboy attire, sombreros and dress boots. Frenchy even grew a thick mustache.

The band specialized on hillbilly and cowboy tunes, and made Bob Ripley's Believe It or Not radio show in New York. "Believe it or not," said "Rip" that night, "Fiddler Bill McGee has just pitched a one-hit game in Brooklyn, but he had to make two hits himself to win." The Fiddler had held the Dodgers to one blow, a bingle by Goody Rosen, but it scored a run. To offset that run, Bill had to drive in one run with a hit, and score another after hitting safely again.

One Cardinal who hadn't much taste for mountain music and hill-billy tunes was the slugger from Jersey—Joe Medwick. "What the hell are we any way; a ball club or a minstrel show?" groused Ducky. Maybe he preferred Hungarian rhapsodies.

4

Prior to the 1938 season, Branch Rickey pulled the banner trans-action of his career, the sale of Dizzy Dean to the Cubs for $200,000, and two capable pitchers, Curt Davis and Clyde Shoun, a left-hander. The Chicago club also tossed Outfielder Tuck Stainback, now with the Yankees, into the deal for $15,000, which reduced Phil Wrigley's check to Breadon to $185,000.

Dizzy didn't show anything on Frisch's 1938 training trip to St. Petersburg, Fla., the first spring the Birds worked out in Al Lang's "Temple of Sunshine." A winter's rest hadn't helped Dean's arm; it was sore as ever. and Dr. Hyland, the Cardinal's club physician, diagnosed it as bursitis.

However, Phil Wrigley, the chewing gum millionaire and Chicago club president, was hot to get Dean. Several of his lieutenants had sold him the idea that if he obtained one more winning pitcher the Cubs could win the pennant, and Clarence Rowland, the former Chicago scout, now president of the Pacific Coast League, was sent to get Dean at any cost. Dean was only 27; the Cubs felt his arm trouble was largely in his head, and that it could be remedied by Chicago specialists.

Rickey played the game strictly on the up and up, and hid nothing of Dean's condition from Rowland. In fact, as they completed negotiations in St. Louis three days before the start of the 1938 season, Branch had Rowland get Wrigley on the long distance telephone, and dictated an agreement that the deal was being made with both clubs knowing the physical condition of all players involved, and assuming all risks and hazards. Davis, one of the Cub pitchers involved, also had been a lame arm pitcher in 1937. Clarence signed the agreement for Wrigley and Dizz moved on to new territory.

Dizz's arm didn't improve in Chicago; it grew worse as time went on. He brought Wrigley only 16 victories in three seasons in Chicago, but in 1938, Dean was credited with seven victories against only one defeat. The Cubs nosed out Pittsburgh for the pennant in the last week of the season. Wrigley never complained, and still says the Dean purchase was money well spent. "The 1938 club won the pennant; we paid off the Dean purchase price that season, and still declared a dividend. What more could we ask?" said Phil.

Shortly before Dean left St. Louis for Chicago, Bill DeWitt, General Manager of the Browns, sued Dizzy for moneys due him on Dean's by-products in 1934, '35 and '36. DeWitt, former vice president of Cardinal chain clubs, had been business representative for the Dean boys, and got them $86,000 in those three years in side pick-ups, $70,000 of it going to Dizz. Dean took his first Cub check to DeWitt's office; they cashed it at a near-by bank; Dizz paid off his obligation, and Bill withdrew his suit.

During the 1937-'38 Winter League season, Rickey traded Leo Durocher, the acrobatic shortstop, to Brooklyn for Infielders Joe Stripp and Jim Butcher; Roy Henshaw, the pony southpaw; and the Fountain-of-Youth ball player, Johnny Cooney. A case of incompatibility had developed between Frisch and The Lip. The deflation of Durocher's batting average from .286 in 1936 to .203 in 1937 didn't help. Leo had access to the front office, and it came to a showdown— Frisch or Durocher. Leo went.

If the Cubs won the 1938 pennant with Dean, it was a dire season for the Deanless Cardinals. From fourth in 1937, the club continued the descent and slumped to sixth. When St. Louis clubs slip into the second division, Dr. Breadon has one remedy—a change in managers. Faithful, fretful, fuming Frisch was let out on September 10, ending 12 interesting and tempestuous years in St. Louis. The reason was partly financial. Despite the big check from Wrigley for Dean, the 1938 Cardinals lost money, and Frank still was working under that fat player-manager contract. Miguel Gonzales, the coach, serving his fourth engagement with the club, took over as acting manager for the balance of the season, the only Cuban ever to manage a major league club. After one season in Boston as a sportscaster, Frisch returned to the National League managerial ranks as skipper of the Pirates in 1940.

Medwick slumped considerably from his .374 of 1937, but his .322 was fourth in the league, and he still was good enough to score 100 runs and drive in 122. For the second year, Mize was runner-up to the batting champion with a .337 rating; the big boy led the league in triples with 16, and pounded out 27 home runs. The only other .300 hitter on the Cardinals was Jimmy Brown, the Carolina infielder, who was shifted all around the infield, and hit .301.

With Dean gone, there was no bull elephant for the pitching staff. Fiddler McGee was well up in earned runs, but could show only seven wins to 12 defeats. Curt Davis, the former Cub, won 12 games and lost six, while Shoun, the other pitcher in the Dean deal, broke even in 12 games. The records of Mudcats Weiland and Warneke were 16 and 11, and 13 and eight, respectively. Lanier, young left-hander from Denton, N. C., showed a lot of stuff and promise in the second half of the season.

XXIII ⊗ BLADES CUTS A FEW CAPERS

THE NEW CARDINAL manager in 1939 was Ray Blades, the little gamester, who was a member of Hornsby's first World's Championship team in 1926, and whose knee hinges were sewed back by the skill of the surgeon, Dr. Hyland. After his playing career, Blades did well in the Cardinal organization; he managed with success in Columbus—1933-4-5, and Rochester—1936-7-8.

Some said that Rickey's oratory sold Blades to Breadon. Sam says otherwise: "Rickey's first choice was Burt Shotton; I preferred Blades."

But throughout baseball, Blades was considered to be Branch's man, to a greater sense than any other Redbird manager. Rickey first saw the boy in 1913 when as manager of the Browns he umpired a game at Sportsmans Park for the city's grammar school championship and little Blades played for the Franz Siegel School. Ray first joined the Cards in 1922 under Rickey's management and the last two seasons he has been back with Branch as manager of clubs affiliated with the Brooklyn organization.

Blades played hard, and he would break a leg if breaking it meant winning a game. He had plenty to say as a player. And he had a fiery temper, somewhat tamed in later years. Once, when the Cardinals gave him word they were sending him to a farm club, he stormed into Rickey's office, kicked around the furniture and spared no language in telling Branch just what he thought of him and the organization. On another occasion, Blades ripped up his uniform. But Branch always had a forgiving nature; Blades stayed in the organization and prospered.

As usually happens when the Redbirds change managers, there was a sharp rise in the club's percentage and fortunes. From a sixth place finish in 1938, the club soared to a hot contender in 1939, and stayed in the race until three days before the end of the season. Blades had odd ways of running a ball club. No manager in major league baseball ever has made as many changes in his line-up as Ray did that season. It seemed to be a daily game how many players he could get into the box score. He thought nothing of employing four, five or six pitchers a game, and of his big staff only Curt Davis pitched in ten complete games. But, Ray was cutting capers—and going places; he was the managerial wonder of 1939.

After an uncertain April, the Cardinals landed second place in late May, held the runner-up spot through June, when they bogged a bit and after the Fourth of July games the club rested in fourth place with a .524 percentage. Then, the Birds started soaring again; they regained second place later in July and never let go. In a series in Cincinnati, August 19 and 20, they served notice on the first place Reds, led by their old Deacon, McKechnie, that they intended to make trouble. By holding Cincinnati to a 3-3 tie, and winning a double-header, 7-1 and 7-5, they cut the Red lead to three and a half games, and from then on were dogged pursuers.

They hacked off another game in September, reducing McKechnie's lead to two and a half games, but it was back to three and a half when the Redbirds went to Cincinnati for a four-game series in the last week of the season. The Birds needed to make it a clean sweep to take the lead; if they won three out of four, they still would be in the fight. The series opened with Gene Thompson winning for Cincinnati by a 3-1 score, which put McKechnie very much in the driver's seat, but the Cardinals came back gamely with the two pitching youngsters, Mort Cooper and Fiddler Bill McGee, hurling shutouts in the second and third games. In the fourth game, the Cards hit their 1930 star, Paul Derringer, with everything but the kitchen stove; they outhit the Reds, 14 to eight, but Oom Paul left 11 St. Louisans stranded on the bases and staggered through to the pennant-clinching victory by a score of 5 to 3. Blades threw in Bowman, Andrews, McGee and Shoun in a futile effort to stay in the race. Three days later the season ended with the Reds four and a half games to the good, with a record of 97-57 against St. Louis' 92-61.

The finish was a big feather in Blades' cap. The Cardinals again were hitting fools; their club batting average leaped 15 points, from .279 to .294, 16 points better than that of the champion Reds, second in that department. After running second for two seasons, burly Johnny Mize snatched the National League batting championship with an average of .349. Another hefty son of Dixie, Don Padgett, converted from an outfielder to a catcher at Rickey's suggestion, topped Mize by 50 points, hitting .399 in 92 games, but Don wasn't in sufficient times at bat to win the crown. Ducky Medwick was third among the regulars, and the second year outfielder, Enos "Country" Slaughter, fired away at .320.

With Medwick falling off 52 points in hitting from his 1937 high, Breadon clipped $2,000 off Joe's stipend when he sent out 1939 contracts. As a consequence Ducky was a holdout well into the training season, and disgruntled much of the year. The St. Louis fans got an idea he wanted to get away, possibly to follow his pal, Leo Durocher, to Brooklyn. Medwick had a midseason run-in with Blades, when Ray, with his penchant for putting names in the box-score, sent Lynn King, a rookie outfielder, faster than Muscles, to left field in the late innings of a close game to tighten the Cardinal defense. Medwick felt much aggrieved; he took it as a slight on his fielding and accused Blades of trying to show him up.

Curt Davis, the pitcher procured from the Cubs in the Dean deal, played the role of Dizzy on the pitching flock, and was the only St. Louis pitcher listed in the first group of National League hurlers. Worked like a Trojan, Curt won 22 games and lost 16. Shoun, the other Cub acquisition, did 53 relief jobs, setting a new National League record, which since has been surpassed by Ace Adams of the Giants, while big Mort Cooper, who had pitched a few games for Frisch in 1938, had a creditable record of 12 wins and six defeats.

2

Many picked the Cardinals to win in 1940 on the strength of their powerful 1939 batting and strong finish, but the Redbirds took one of those nose dives reminiscent of Huggins' up and down clubs. Blades had done well the year before by sticking half a dozen pitchers into a game, but in the spring of '40, the trick no longer worked. The system backfired, as the whole staff became disorganized and demoralized.

By the Decoration Day holiday, the club was riding seventh, with only the lowly Phillies beneath them, and there were rumors that Blades would be replaced. Branch Rickey gave out a statement that the little guy would be kept on the job and given a chance to work his way out of his difficulties. Maybe Sam Breadon didn't read it, for a few days later—June 7—without consulting Rickey, Sam fired Blades, brought on Billy Southworth from the Rochester club to take his place, and sent Estel Crabtree, the veteran outfielder, to Rochester as manager.

Just as the poor ticket sale for the post-Decoration Day Sunday in 1925 was a determining factor in Breadon relieving Rickey of the team management that year, so the Cardinals' first home night game, played June 4, 1940, was the back-breaking straw which finished Blades as manager. The game was well ballyhooed, and despite the Cards' seventh place position, it drew a 23,000 crowd. However, Brooklyn, led by Durocher, the former Cardinal shortstop, scored five runs in the first inning and went on to win easily, 10 to 1, as Blades trotted out Mort Cooper, Lanier, Shoun and Jack Russell.

The crowd booed, tossed bottles into the arena, held their fingers to their noses, and acted in general as though it considered Breadon's first night frolic an odoriferous party. Rickey pleaded for more time for Blades, but Sam made up his mind during the game—he would make another managerial change. Ray's successor was his fellow outfielder of the Cardinal World's Champions of 1926, Billy Southworth, who had had a varied career, in and out of the Redbird organization, since Breadon shunted him back to Rochester in 1929.

XXIV ⊝ BILLY THE KID RETURNS

I

I'VE LEARNED considerable since I was manager of the Cardinals in 1929; now I think I am ready to tackle this tough job," said Billy the Kid to Ray Gillespie, *St. Louis Times-Star* baseball writer, as he came to St. Louis for a chat with Breadon before taking over the club in early June, 1940.

In some respects Billy has been Breadon's most successful manager. From the time Southworth took command of the club, June 14, 1940, to the end of the 1944 season, his percentage has been higher than that of any Cardinal manager who preceded him. During that time the Redbirds were victorious 482 times while losing 242 games for a percentage of .666.

Good things come to Billy, but he is the kind of person who makes his own success. He learned much in managerial psychology in eleven years. Considerate, courteous and capable, he soon brought order out of the chaos of the early 1940 season, and despite the Cardinals' poor spring showing he brought home the club in third place. Southworth quickly captured the affections and respect of the entire club, and today the Cardinals give their manager a loyalty which is almost adoration. "He is the most considerate man I ever worked for," said one of his players.

He is the friend of every man on the team, and they know it. They come to him with personal problems, as well as those concerning baseball. Even if a man has made a stupid blunder, Billy doesn't bawl out the player until next day. Then both he and the athlete have had a night's sleep on it. He is a strict disciplinarian, but not in the sense that McGraw and George Stallings were clubhouse despots. The Cardinals just don't step out of the traces, because that wouldn't be playing fair with Billy. He is known as baseball's "little gentleman," but he can carry an iron fist in his velvet glove. No one puts anything over on him, and one of his first rules on the club was that no Cardinal should go to the front office except to get his pay check. That rule wasn't always in effect.

Before Billy took over his club in Boston, he was asked to attend a meeting at Sam Breadon's apartment. Branch Rickey and Larry MacPhail, Brooklyn's former fiery chief, also were there. "We've decided to trade Joe Medwick," Sam explained. "What do you think?"

It was putting the new manager on the spot, and naturally he had to be for it. "I hope we get something worth while," he observed.

Conversation went on well into the night, and the deal wasn't closed until Southworth was on his train for Boston. St. Louis included Pitcher Curt Davis in the deal and took largely cash in exchange—a neat sum of $125,000. MacPhail also tossed in a quartet of ball players—Pitchers Sam Nayhem and Carl Doyle, Outfielder Ernie Koy, and Third Baseman-Outfielder Bert Haas. Koy was Medwick's immediate successor in left field, but didn't last. Haas later turned into a pretty good ball player with the Cincinnati Reds.

The 1940 Cardinals had a .341 percentage when Billy the Kid took over. They finished with .549. In the 109 games under Southworth, the club played .633 ball, only a few points behind the pennant-winning pace of the champion Reds.

After Medwick left the club, Mize really got those broad Georgia shoulders behind his swing and his home run total zoomed to 43, 15 above his previous high. Johnny's big bat swept 137 Redbirds over the plate. Young Slaughter dropped 14 points to .306, but he did a lot of useful execution in the pinches. The graceful Terry Moore reached the .300 circle for the first time, hitting .304, while the inspiration of the old Gas House Gang, Pepper Martin, bowed out with an average of .316 for 86 games. Pepper left in the fall to take over the management of the Cardinal farm in Sacramento.

Redbirds who were to write new World's Series history later on joined the flock that season. The tall lanky Marty "Slats" Marion, called the Octopus by his mates, because his long arms reach in all directions, took over the shortstop job, while Johnny Hopp, of an athletic Nebraska family of the Five Hopps, played 80 games at first base and the outfield, and hit .270. Joe Orengo played second base most of the season, and in September Rickey brought up three brilliant kids, a Columbus battery of Ernie White and Walker Cooper, and Rochester's shortstop, Frank "Creepy" Crespi. White was a Carolina lefthander with plenty of moxie; Cooper, a young brother of Mort, the pitcher, and potentially a great catcher, and Crespi, a home-grown infielder, product of the St. Louis sand-lots. Lefty Max Lanier, who was with Frisch in 1938, also was yanked back from Columbus.

2

The 1941 season saw some of the worst series of breaks which ever befell a ball club and perplexed a manager. It was a difficult thing for Billy the Kid to keep smiling, but he did—and carried a strong Brooklyn team down to the wire. The race was not over until the last Saturday of the season, even though at times Billy almost had to play Coaches Mike Gonzales and Buzzy Wares and draft Catcher Rickey from the front office. How that 1941 St. Louis club held up in the face of its adversities still is one of the most brilliant chapters in all baseball history. Southworth's feat in finishing second—only two and a half games behind a Brooklyn club which won 100 games, was a greater managerial feat than winning the pennants in the two years which followed.

It was a two-team race between Brooklyn and St. Louis, with the remainder of the league always far behind. Both clubs started off strongly, with the Cardinals leading through the better part of May and June. At one stage both contenders had percentages above .700. Cardinal casualties knocked the club off the top perch, and after the Fourth of July contests, St. Louis trailed by three games. But, by July 24, the fighting Redbirds again were two games in front. Through most of August only a game separated the rivals, with the Dodgers holding the scant lead most of the time. Brooklyn started to push forward in September, and the race terminated September 25—three days before the end, when Whit Wyatt, caught by Mickey Owen, blanked the Braves, 6 to 0, while Max Butcher of the Pirates set back the Birds, 3 to 1.

Convinced that the club had the best young catcher in the country in Walker Cooper, Breadon and Rickey felt safe in listening to more of Siren Larry MacPhail's tempting conversation, and accepted $60,000, Pitcher John Pintar and the return of Catcher Gus Mancuso for Mickey Owen. Fiddler Bill McGee got off to a poor start in the spring, and on May 14, he was traded to the Giants for Pitchers Harry Gumbert and Paul Dean and cash. The New Yorkers had fished Paul out of the Texas League the year before in their draft net. It proved a good deal for St. Louis, as the Fiddler—who once had shown so much promise, won only two games that season and never regained his early form.

The nation's sports writers—everywhere but in Brooklyn, said it would have been the Cardinals—rather than the Dodgers, who would have met the Yanks in the 1941 World's Series if it hadn't been for Southworth's casualty list. Of the St. Louis regulars, only Shortstop Marty Marion, who played the full 155 games on the schedule, escaped.

Johnny Mize broke a finger and then hurt his shoulder; he couldn't get his old lift on the ball, and his home run production dropped from 43 to 16. Infielder Jimmy Brown broke a bone in his right hand, sliding into third base on a triple. Second Baseman Crespi was out for several weeks with a lesser hurt. The young catcher, Walker Cooper, broke his collar bone and a shoulder blade, and also was lost for valuable weeks. His pitching brother, Mort, was out of action from June 17 to August 3, and had to undergo a midseason operation as Dr. Hyland cut some growths out of the right elbow. It was a little miracle that Mort pitched any more that season.

However, the worst blow came in a Sunday double-header at

Sportsmans Park, August 10, when Enos Slaughter, the slugging right fielder, broke his collar bone after a collision with Terry Moore in front of the wall in right center. Both men went after a line drive; Terry caught it, but tumbled over Enos. Slaughter was as hot as a barn fire at the time, and was leading the club in home runs and runs batted in. The injury was even worse than was at first reported, and Slaughter was out for the season. Hopp, with a lacerated hand, had to fill in.

If that wasn't bad enough, the final straw came a fortnight later, when Art Johnson, a young Brave pitcher, exploded a fast ball against Terry Moore's skull, and put the agile St. Louisan into St. Elizabeth's Hospital, Boston. To make it hurt even more, Don Padgett, who was needed for substitute work at first base and the outfield, suffered a .152 point two-year batting drop from his .399 pace with Blades' 1939 Cardinal edition.

Billy Southworth, who was voted the Manager of the Year by *The Sporting News*, had his happy moments, especially with lefthanded members of his pitching staff. Ernie White, blond South Carolinian, won 17 games and lost seven. At one stage of the race, when the staff was badly battered, Ernie won three games from the Giants in successive days and was credited with four victories in five days. Rickey doesn't usually reach into a farm club during the playing season, but he plucked Howard Pollet, a New Orleans-born lefthander, from Houston, where he had a 20-3 record and the amazing earned run performance of 1.16. With the Cardinals, Howie won five games out of seven. A righthanded Howard—Howard Krist, also up from Houston, went through the season with ten victories and no defeats. Another of Dr. Hyland's famous operations had restored the use of Krist's pitching arm.

The veteran, Estel Crabtree, back from Rochester, did Herculean work, both as a pinch-hitter and extra outfielder, hitting .341 in 77 games. Hopp hit .303, and played well wherever Billy played him, while two great Polish kids, Stanley Frank Musial and George "Whitey" Kurowski, reported to Southworth in September. Both were moved up from Rochester. Musial, a late season replacement for the injured Slaughter, tore the league apart in the last fortnight of the race, hitting an amazing .426 in 12 games, getting 20 hits in 47 times at bat. And the Cardinals drew 646,000 fans at home, more than any season since the banner year of 1928!

The 1941 Cardinals also did their bit in making the nation vita-min-conscious. At the All-Star game played in St. Louis, July 9, 1940, Cliff Samuelson of General Mills, handed bottles of B-1 Vita-min tablets to Breadon and several of his cronies. Sam took them, found he had more pep and endurance, and his golf game showed a magic improvement. Breadon figured if B-complex could send his golf score down, it could send batting averages up. In the 1941 train-ing season at St. Petersburg, he sold his vitamin idea to Southworth, and Road Secretary Leo Ward left small flasks of bird seed in the form of thiamin pills in the Redbirds' rookeries. Leo continued to feed the Birds vitamin for the full season, and as the club rose above its difficulties, B-1 got much of the credit. Dr. Hyland kidded Singing Sam by calling him "Doctor" Breadon, but Sam knew what was good for him was good for his Redbirds. Sports writers took it up, sang the saga of the vitamin-pepped Cardinal cripples and gave the manufacturers thousands of dollars' worth of free advertising.

3

With injuries depriving the Cardinals of the 1941 pennant, they were top-heavy favorites for 1942. They rewarded their backers with victory, but not until the Redbirds had put on another of their hectic, packed-with-drama late season finishes. While the flag was not clinched until the very last day of the season, the Cardinals again practically won it with one of those rip-snorting drives through the East in September. Durocher drove his Dodgers to 104 victories in an effort to repeat, but the Redbirds soared to 106, the highest National League total in 39 years. Brooklyn was only the third major league club of this century to win 100 or more games and still lose a pennant. And, at the finish, the new Cardinal Champs were their usual two games ahead—as they were in 1926, '28, '30 and '34. The final standing showed St. Louis with 106 victories and 48 defeats for a percentage of .688. The Dodgers won 104 and lost 50 for .675.

However, for many weeks it didn't look like any World's Series for Sportsmans Park. The Dodgers got off to a running start, and blew up their lead as they went along. For four months, they looked unbeatable, and when Billy the Kid's team turned the tide and eventually won the race, it was 1930 all over again. When the Red-birds really started soaring, August 6, they were ten games behind, and all but the most optimistic St. Louisans long since had given up all hopes for the flag. But St. Louis won 43 of its last 52 games, a madcap pace of .813, which left Brooklyn's Daffiness Boys still daffier.

The winter before, Rickey made his last big St. Louis deal; he traded First Baseman Johnny Mize to the Giants for $50,000, Catcher Ken O'Dea, once a prominent Cardinal farm hand, Pitcher Bill Lohrman, and First Baseman Johnny McCarthy. Lohrman later was sold back to New York, and when Rickey assigned McCarthy to Columbus, Judge Landis queered the deal and recognized a prior claim by the Indianapolis club to the first baseman. There was more indignation and accusations that Singing Sam had sold his pennant chance for a mess of pottage. Breadon and Rickey felt safe in trading Mize, never a Chase in the field, as they had a great defensive first baseman in the organization, Ray Sanders, a former St. Louis softball player, who had knocked the wadding out of the ball in both of the Cardinals' Columbus farms—Georgia and Ohio.

Rickey and Sam also peddled Padgett to MacPhail, the Brooklyn impresario, for $20,000, but big Don joined the Navy instead of the Dodgers. Larry tried to get his check back, but this time Landis sided with the Cardinals. Early in the 1942 season, relief Pitcher Shoun was sold to the Reds, and in July, Warneke returned to the Cubs in a waiver transaction.

Southworth had some difficulty in arranging a satisfactory 1942 infield. He started out with Jimmy Brown on third base, Slats Marion at shortstop, Creepy Crespi at second and Sanders at first. Only Marion played that position in the subsequent World's Series, and Creepy and Sanders saw it from good seats on the bench. Billy hit his winning combination when he moved Brown to second, played the Pennsylvania Pole, Kurowski, at third, and Johnny Hopp at first.

According to Dr. Hyland, the Cardinal club physician, Kurowski is "one athlete in a million." He has shown X-ray pictures of Whitey's right arm to medical men from all over the world. To Hyland, it is a wonder Kurowski can throw at all—let alone possess one of the best infield whips in baseball. As an eight-year-old tot in Reading, Pa., Whitey fell off a fence among some broken glass and gashed his right arm. His father, a mill-hand with ten children, gave it only ordinary treatment. Two years later, the boy's arm became very sore—an acute case of osteomyelitis had set in. A good part of the ulna bone had rotted and the diseased part was cut away. As a result Kurowski has three inches of bone missing from his right arm, between the wrist and forearm, yet somehow nature grew such strong muscles there that they held the arm together. The carriage of the arm is affected, and the condition exempted Whitey from military service.

Another player who made Cardinal pennant history in 1942 was the freshman pitcher, Johnny Beazley, a cocky Tennesseean, now a Lieutenant in the Army Air Force. He came up from the Cardinals' former New Orleans affiliate and promptly won 21 games while losing only six. Mort Cooper, the big Missouri boy, had a magnificent year, 22 victories, ten of them shutouts, and only seven defeats. With an earned run record of 1.77, the best in the majors in years, Cooper won the league's most valuable player prize. Max Lanier, the singing southpaw, helped with 13 victories, and was especially good against Brooklyn.

Even the Cardinals recognized they had only an outside chance for the pennant when Brooklyn came to St. Louis for its last series, four games on August 24-25-26-27—two night games and two twilight contests. By diligent work, the Birds had shaved the ten-game lead of August 6 to seven and a half games. Lanier won the first one easily, 7 to 1, and the next night, before 33,527 fans, Mort Cooper struggled through 14 innings before being returned a 2 to 1 victor over Whit Wyatt, Larry French and young Les Webber. Beazley repeated by the same score over Max Macon, a former St. Louis rookie, the next day. In both of these tight games, the winning St. Louis runs came over when Dodger players, Riggs and Macon, fell to the grass trying to field infield pokes. Curt Davis, the former Cardinal, finally got away with the last game for Brooklyn by a 4-1 score. Despite their inspired play throughout the series—it drew 91,028 paid—the Cardinals still were five and a half games behind when Brooklyn left town.

However, that series was prime evidence that the Dodgers were not supermen, and the tumbles by Riggs and Macon convinced Southworth that Durocher's Dandies were tense, nervous and fretful of the Cardinal shadow looming larger and larger behind them. "We'll keep after them," said Billy, when the series was over, "and if we keep hustling on every play, we can pass them, and once we do, they'll never catch us."

The Dodger lead had been shaved down to two games when St. Louis called at Ebbets Field, September 11 and 12, for their last 1942 visit to Brooklyn. Before the mournful MacPhail clientele, all that remained of the once formidable ten-game Brooklyn lead was shot away as Cooper won a 3 to 0 shutout and Lanier followed with a 2-1 verdict over Macon and Davis, a homer by Kurowski being the decisive blow.

The two clubs were tied for first place as they took the field for Sunday double-headers, September 13. Bill McKechnie, the old Deacon of 1928 Cardinals, then did Southworth a good turn; his Cincinnati Reds bowled over Brooklyn twice, while the Cardinals broke even with the Phillies. It gave the Cardinals a one-game lead, and true to Southworth's prediction, the Birds never let go in the two strenuous weeks which followed. Larry MacPhail did send McKechnie a scorching telegram; he seemed to think the Deacon had primed his best pitchers for Brooklyn, and wasn't overly particular who pitched against St. Louis. McKechnie shot back a wire which even out-blistered MacPhail's effort. To their credit, the Dodgers hung on to the bitter end, and the race was undecided until the final day of the season, Sunday, September 27, when Ernie White, the plucky Cardinal southpaw, won the first game of a double-header from the Cubs, 9 to 2. Beazley followed by hanging up his twenty-first scalp.

"We won this one the hard way, and no one won it for us. We went out and won it ourselves," beamed the happy Southworth in the clubhouse between games. (His club had defeated the Dodgers in the year's series, 13 to nine, and in the crucial August and September hand-to-hand fighting had won five out of six from Brooklyn.) "And we'll go out and beat the Yankees the same way. One thing this young club isn't afraid of is reputations. All are great kids; they hustled and worked together, and it would be difficult—and unfair—to point to any one or two, saying they contributed most to victory."

The club, so different from Frisch's brash Gas House Gang, was the youngest ever to win a major league championship. Of the active players, Terry Moore was the oldest, and he was only 30 years old. The team was made up largely of Dixie boys, lads from Southern high schools and small colleges. Five to eight years before, they had been merely names in Rickey's card-index system, which long since had succeeded Branch's well-worn notebook. On the road, they were like a well-behaved team of Dixie collegians, playing under the supervision of a popular athletic-director coach. What a difference in a few years from Pepper Martin, Dizzy Dean, Rip Collins and that merry bunch of roisterers!

But they were similar in one respect. Like Frisch's Gas House Gangsters, they always were running. Unlike McGraw's 1911 Giants, who stole a pennant with 347 larcenies, Southworth's 1942 champions didn't go in much for stolen bases, but they ran on any pretext. It wasn't a "safety-first" ball club. No club ever took more reckless chances on the bases, and none had a higher percentage of successful risks.

4

The nation's sports writers, as well as the fans, knew the 1942 Cardinals were good—any major league club which wins 106 games is bound to command respect, but in the World's Series, they were meeting the mighty Yankees, and the Juggernaut of Yankee Stadium had become the most dreaded name in blue ribbon competition. Hadn't the famous Bronx Bombers swept eight World's Series since 1927, in which they won 32 games and lost only four? The Yankees had won 104 games in their own league, breezed to their pennant by 19 games, and rested for three weeks for the series. Who could stop them? Naturally, McCarthy's suave American League champs were made strong favorites.

But Southworth had said his team wasn't bothered about reputations. Many of these kids were too young to remember the earlier Ruth-Gehrig-Meusel Yankee teams. Billy remembered them; in fact, as right fielder for the 1926 Cardinals, he had helped give the Yankees their last World's Series pasting. "I'll say one thing," he said before the series. "They'll have to beat us out on the field, not in newspaper columns—and I don't think they will beat us on the field. When I played on the Cardinals in 1926, we weren't overawed, and Landis paid us the bigger checks."

The first game was played in Sportsmans Park, September 30, before a 34,385 crowd, and until the last half of the ninth inning it was a dreary spectacle for the Cardinal fans. Red Ruffing, the hefty Illinois righthander, going after his seventh World's Series scalp,

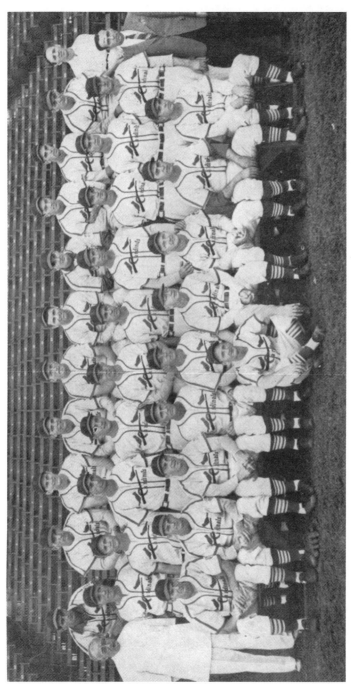

THE 1942 WORLD'S CHAMPIONS
They ran the Yankees into the ground.

© *Sporting News*

STAN MUSIAL

WALKER COOPER

© *Sporting News*

© *Acme*

MORT COOPER

was supreme for McCarthy's men; he didn't give up a hit until two were out in the eighth. The great Yankees were leading, 7 to 0; they knocked out Cooper in the eighth, and his successor, Max Lanier, had a flighty ninth when his two errors helped the Yankees to their last two runs.

Ruffing had two out with a man on first, when the fidgetty Redbirds suddenly sprang to life. Big Red needed only one putout for a two-hit shutout; he never got it, as a walk to Sanders, Marion's triple and singles by O'Dea and Brown sent him to the clubhouse thinking of the strange vagaries of baseball. McCarthy took no chances, and sent in Spud Chandler, his very best, to retire the side. Terry Moore and Slaughter cracked the Georgian for additional singles; four runs were in, and the bases were full, when Stan Musial —up for the second time in the inning, grounded to First Baseman Hassett for the last out.

Though defeated, that ninth inning rally—with two out, amounted to a moral victory for the Redbirds. They were anything but dispirited when they came out for the second game. Behind the plucky pitching of Johnny Beazley, they defeated the California giant, Ernie Bonham, 4 to 3. Southworth's boys showed their re-silient ability to bounce back in the eighth. With St. Louis leading, 3 to 0, in that inning, Keller dropped a three-run home-run bomb into the right field stands, tying the score. That didn't phase the Redbirds; they promptly regained the lead in their half, when Slaughter doubled, took an extra base on Rizzuto's muff of the throw-in, and raced home on Musial's single. A powerful bee-line throw by Enos Slaughter, from right field to third base, cut down Tuck Stainback in the ninth and spiked New York's last rally.

The scene shifted to Yankee Stadium, October 3, where, before a 69,123 crowd, the Cardinals took a two-to-one lead by winning a 2 to 0 shutout. Ernie White, the Carolina lefthander, won the decision in a tense duel with Spud Chandler; it was the first World's series whitewash job performed on the Yankees since Jesse Haines turned the trick in the third game of the 1926 Series. White had suffered from a lame arm much of the season, but he finished the season strong in August and September, and was in fine fettle. Ernie was helped by the brilliant support behind him, especially in the outfield. With Cullenbine on base in the sixth, Moore made an amazing sideways leaping catch of DiMaggio's low liner, snaring the ball almost at right angles to the course of its flight. Then, in the seventh inning, Musial backed to the left field boxes for Gordon's bid for a homer, and Slaughter made an even greater catch on the next batsman, Kingkong Keller, climbing up the right field screen to squeeze a liner which was ticketed for four bases.

Chandler suffered a tough defeat, as only four Cardinals reached base on him in his eight innings, and only one of the three St. Louis hits off his delivery was clean. The Yankees really talked themselves into this defeat. Spud walked Kurowski, first St. Louis hitter, in the third, and Marion apparently sent him to second on a sacrifice bunt, on which Slats was thrown out at first. However, McCarthy, Fletcher and Dickey argued so loud and convincingly that Slats' bunt was foul that George Barr, the umpire, requested Marion to bat over again. This time Marty tapped a fast ball for an infield single. So, instead of having a runner on second and one out, the Yanks now had Redbirds perched on first and second with none out. White's sacrifice bunt shoved Kurowski to third, and the Pole scored on Brown's infield out.

After Chandler retired for Pinch-hitter Ruffing, Marv Breuer, a Rollo, Missouri boy, proved a soft touch for the Cards in the ninth. He pitched to only three batters and gave up a run, two hits and a walk before McCarthy yanked him. Jim Turner came in with none out, and retired the side without any further St. Louis scoring.

The Cardinals followed up this victory with another emphatic success on Sunday, October 4, before a new record crowd of 69,902. This was a clouting carnival which the Cardinals won, 9 to 6. After New York tallied once in the first inning, the Redbirds gave Mort Cooper a seemingly safe lead when they scored six runs on young Hank Borowy and Atley Donald in the fourth inning. It was an inning in which the Redbirds really ran the bases, and McCarthy and the Yanks were dizzy watching the Cardinal Cavalcade roll by.

However, the Bronx Bombers had one big punch left. Mort Cooper, ineffective against the American League in both World's Series and All Star competition, went out in a five-run blast as New York tied the score in the sixth. Keller exploded his second three-run homer of the series. Again the Cardinals bounced back, as in the second game, and immediately regained the lead by scoring twice on Donald and Bonham in the seventh on a combination of hits and walks. Lanier, Billy's fourth pitcher of the game, held the Yanks safely in the last three innings, and was credited with the victory.

The amazing Redbirds made it four straight, by winning the fifth game, 4 to 2. This time young Beazley conquered the great Ruffing, who met only his second World's Series defeat in nine starts. The score was 2-2 in the ninth inning as an autumn mist settled over the Stadium playing field. Walker Cooper opened with a single and Hopp advanced him to second with a sacrifice bunt. Kurowski, the next hitter, had been lining dangerous fouls into the left field boxes all day, but McCarthy chose to let Ruffing pitch to him. The white-haired Pole with the crooked arm rifled a homer into these left field seats a few feet in from the foul line, and the Birds had a commanding two-run lead.

The Yanks had a chance to come back in their half, but fizzled out ignominiously. Gordon, who had a bad series, opened with a single—only his second hit of the five games, and Brown's fumble gave Dickey a life, putting two runners on base with none out. Just as Yankee fans began speculating on a game-tying rally, catcher Walker Cooper let go a lightning throw to Marion at second, and picked Gordon off the bag. The end then came quickly as Priddy popped out and Pinch-hitter Selkirk rolled to Brown, and for the fourth time in sixteen years St. Louis' colorful Redbirds roosted on top of the baseball heap.

Even with a bitter war raging on the Atlantic and Pacific, the nation was thrilled at this performance of Southworth's daredevil fast-running kids. They had run the great Yankees ragged, rolled them back four straight, and won as many games from the proud New Yorkers in four playing days as it had taken eight National League championship clubs to win in fifteen seasons between 1927 and 1941. It was a most popular victory, as the feeling of the country—especially in the great wide open spaces—was that the Yankees had held their lease on baseball's throne room entirely too long. And Billy Southworth, called a "heel" by one of his players in 1929, was at the top of the game, again named "The Manager of the Year," and more popular than ever—if that was possible—in the St. Louis clubhouse.

Doc Weaver, the Cardinal trainer, acquired fresh glory and distinction as a whammie man. The one time Ohio Wesleyan fullback gave the Yanks the double whammie in spades. He wiggled his thumbs and index fingers with such magic results that the Yankees were stymied in their tracks. So devastating was Weaver that McCarthy's first move after the series was to let out Doc Painter, his trainer of thirteen years; Painter just was unable to concoct any counter-voodoo. And during the series, Art Fletcher, the Yankee coach, had a game stopped long enough to have Butch Yatkeman, the Cardinals' veteran clubhouse man, tossed off the bench for practicing his own brand of whammy.

5

Less than a month after the end of the Series—October 29—Branch Rickey, the man whose name was in the seven hats in 1917, left the employ of the Cardinals, the club on which he had been such a factor, to accept the presidency of the Brooklyn Dodgers, succeeding Lieutenant Colonel Larry MacPhail, who had marched off to war. Rickey could have remained in St. Louis as executive vice president of his first love in major league baseball, the Browns, but the Brooklyn offer was one which Branch said "a man just couldn't turn down."

Breadon and Rickey had come to the parting of the ways a year and a half before. Ever since Breadon, the then young club owner, signed the manager with ideas to a five-year contract in the spirit of enthusiasm in January, 1923, Rickey had been re-signed for five-year periods. His stipend went up steadily, and he was cut in on a good share of the profits, and most Cardinal years, under Breadon and Branch, were profitable. His salary and percentage of the profits in 1941 was $88,000; in 1942 it was $65,000. Rickey, the farm boy and village schoolteacher, became an opulent man, with an estate in St. Louis County which was a show place.

Under the terms of the last contract, unless Rickey was notified by April 1, 1941, of its abrogation, December 31, 1942, the contract automatically would run another year. So in March, 1941, Sam advised Branch that it would not be renewed.

What brought about this severance after nearly a quarter of a century of close association? Among other things, Breadon saw the war coming, and felt the club couldn't carry Rickey's big salary in the difficult war years which were looming ahead. Others say Breadon decided Rickey's contract would not be renewed after Landis set free the multiple Cardinal farm hands in the famous

Cedar Rapids case, though Sam says he never reproached nor criticized his General Manager for getting out on this limb.

The truth is that while the two men were closely associated in business, there were many things on which they never saw eye to eye. Breadon recognized Rickey's talents and what he did for the Cardinals, but Sam isn't a man who can sit back and play second fiddle in his own organization. Too often the Rickey wits clashed with Breadon's business acumen. The time simply came when Sam and Branch no longer could live happily in the same ball park.

XXV ⊜ CARDINAL CAVALCADE ROLLS ON

1

THE WAR FLAMES LICKED deeper into the baseball structure after the 1942 World's Series. The Cardinals, made up largely of young fathers, had retained their manpower well up to that time, losing only rookies. But, in the winter of 1942-'43, the two crack outfielders, Captain Terry Moore and Enos Slaughter, the 20-game winner, Johnny Beazley, and Infielder Creepy Crespi entered the armed services. During the 1943 playing season, the Army also called up the new St. Louis Captain, Second Baseman Jimmy Brown, and Pitchers Howie Pollet and Murray Dickson. Pollet went out in a blaze of glory; he had pitched three successive shutouts and 28 consecutive scoreless innings when Uncle Sam beckoned.

Again the Cardinal farm organization proved adequate to take up this slack. Harry Walker, a brother of Brooklyn's Fred Dixie Walker, did a splendid fill-in job for Moore in center field, and Lou Klein, up from Columbus, played second base like a Frisch. Pitchers Harry Brecheen and George Munger also were advanced from Columbus, and after Pollet was drafted, the club came up with another prize left-hander from their Sacramento farm, Alpha Brazle, who won eight out of ten games in August and September. On June 1, Breadon made a deal with Bill Cox, the 1943 owner of the Phillies, whereby Sam gave Bill three outfielders—Coaker Triplett, Buster Adams and Dain Clay, for two—Danny Litwhiler and Earl Naylor. Musial was moved over to Slaughter's old beat in right; the newcomer Litwhiler installed in left, and Naylor sent to the farm in Rochester. Two veteran outfielders, Debs Garms and Frank Demaree, also were picked up as war replacements.

With these newcomers and what was left of the 1942 World's Champions, the Cardinals proceeded to spreadeagle the 1943 National League race. A curious jinx had followed National League World's Series winners since 1922. No National club to fly the world's baseball flag during that time had won its league pennant in the succeeding year. That included the Cardinal World's Champions of 1926, '31 and '34. But Southworth's club tore that superstition to shreds; it won by a margin of 18 games. The Redbirds clinched their flag on September 18, one of the earliest dates on record. They fell one short of their 106 victories of 1942, but 211 wins in two seasons was the greatest National League two-year total since Chance's Cubs won 223 games in 1906 and 1907.

The Brooklyns started as though they again intended to make a real race of it, and at one stage in June, the Dodgers got as much as three and a half games in front. By June 29, the Cards led by one game, .627 to .606, and after the games of the double holiday, July 4-5, the Birds had increased it to three games. The Dodgers then began slipping and shortly after trading Camilli to the Giants (Dolph never reported to New York), Durocher's clan went into a real nose dive, and fell out of the race with a ten-straight losing streak. After that it was only a question of how big St. Louis' lead would be at the finish; McKechnie's Reds moved into second place, but never were close enough to be a serious threat.

Major credit for the easy victory went to Stan Musial, the 23-year-old from Donora, Pa., who joined the club late in 1941. Stan is another proud product of the Cardinal system. A left-handed pitcher, he was plucked from a small city high school team at seventeen, and went through the Cardinal grades at Williamson, W. Va., Daytona Beach, Springfield, Mo., and Rochester. An injured shoulder, suffered in Florida, ended his pitching career and made him a full time outfielder. He shone in 1943 like a National League Ty Cobb, and had a season reminiscent of Ducky Medwick's big year of 1937. He topped Billy Herman, his nearest batting rival, by 27 points, as he led his league in hits, 220; total bases, 347; doubles, 48; and triples, 20, while he placed in run-scoring with 108. He was the tenth Cardinal batting champion since 1920, and as the new winner of the National League's most valuable player award, he followed that galaxy of Redbird stars—the great Hornsby, Bob O'Farrell, Jim Bottomley, Frankie Frisch, Dizzy Dean, Joe Medwick, and Mort Cooper.

Another brilliant worker was the big catcher, Walker Cooper, who was third in National League hitting with .319 and made the catching position on *The Sporting News'* annual All-Star team. Kurowski was an improved player at third; Marion fairly sizzled at shortstop, and Sanders, the softballer, started to prove his worth at first. On the offense and defense, the Redbirds were the class of the league; they easily led in club batting with .279, and their pitchers sparkled like jewels in a diadem. In the first group, pitchers in ten or more complete games, they had the three leaders, Pollet, Lanier and Mort Cooper, and in the secondary class, they placed the No. 1 and 2 men with Brazle and Brecheen. The three left-handers, Brazle, Pollet, and Lanier had the remarkable earned run averages of 1.53, 1.75 and 1.90, respectively.

2

Following their easy 1942 World's Series victory and their romp through the National League in 1943, the Cardinals hardly looked at another October joust with the Yankees with fear and trepidation. Some of the Birds arched their eyebrows and looked a little askance when the professional gentry again made the Yankees favorites to win the 1943 Series. Even many of the writers, including some of the reportorial lads from New York, asked: "How do they get that way? Are those professional betters getting fat in the head?" Certainly the vast majority of the nation's fandom again expected to see the Birds run the Yankees into submission.

McCarthy's team also had lost heavily to the armed forces since the 1942 Series—his star of stars, Joe DiMaggio, also Shortstop Phil Rizzuto, Pitcher Charley Ruffing, First Baseman Buddy Hassett, and Outfielder George Selkirk. Red Rolfe, the team's veteran third baseman, retired to take a coaching job at Yale, while Outfielder Roy Cullenbine and Catcher Buddy Rosar were traded to other clubs. Marse Joe's best pick-up was his new third baseman, Bill Johnson, later termed the rookie of 1943, while in the first half of the season Joe had experienced considerable success in converting a tall hefty pitcher, Johnny Lindell, into an outfielder. Pitcher Chandler, the Georgia Bulldog, enjoyed a phenomenal year.

Owing to war transportation restrictions, it was decided to have a "one trip" World's Series. As it was the American League's turn to open in their home city, it meant the first three games at Yankee Stadium; after that the series would end in St. Louis, regardless of its length. It was pointed out this might work to the disadvantage of the Cardinals, as the Yankees usually were toughest on their Bronx pastures. The Redbirds laughed it off. "We licked them three straight in their own park last year, and we can do it again," was their observation.

Despite the fact that the nation was nearly two years in the war, demand for World's Series ducats was unprecedented. The 1943 Series was short-waved to our armed forces on six continents and in the seven seas.

Southworth had a ticklish pitching proposition before the first game. Mort Cooper, his ace, again had been cuffed vigorously in the July All-Star game in Philadelphia; it marked the fourth straight time that the big Missouri boy had been shellacked by American Leaguers in important inter-league diamond warfare. But, in a nice gesture of loyalty, Billy announced to reporters in the Shibe Park clubhouse: "Don't think I've weakened on Mort. If I am lucky enough to get into the World's Series, he'll start for me."

However, so much was said and written about Billy and Mort being on the spot that Southworth opened the series with Max Lanier, who had been his most effective September pitcher, against McCarthy's No. 1 man, Chandler, at the Stadium, October 5. The Yankees won the game, 4 to 2. Lanier pitched well in spots, but his own muff at first base proved a damaging boot in the fourth frame, and two innings later he let fly a wild pitch, which enabled Crosetti to score from second and Johnson to race from first to a scoring position at third. The reason they made all this mileage is that Walker Cooper couldn't find the ball, but unlike Thevenow's homer in 1926, the ball didn't hide in Bloody Angle. It was only about fifteen feet in back of the plate.

In the early hours of October 6, the morning of the second game, the father of the Cooper brothers battery, Robert Cooper, a rural delivery mail carrier, died at his home in Independence, Missouri. A great fan and rooter and tutor for his boys, the elder Cooper had followed the radio controversy as to whether Mort should have pitched the first game and the criticism of Walker for not finding Lanier's wild pitch. Southworth promptly told the Coopers they could go home, but they elected to remain with the team, saying: "Dad would have wanted it that way."

With the nation applauding the plucky pair, the two Coopers went in as the St. Louis battery that afternoon, and Mort shook his American League jinx by tying up the series for the Redbirds, winning the second game, 4 to 3. Oddly enough, Bonham was the defeated Yankee hurler and he went down by the same score as when defeated by Beazley in the second 1942 game. The huge Californian had two rocky innings—the third and fourth, when the Redbirds showed their only real punch of the series. Marty Marion reached the left field stands with a homer in the third, and in the next frame Sanders's four-bagger into the right field bleachers was the big lick of a three-run St. Louis scoring drive.

Mort Cooper went into the ninth, leading 4 to 1, and just managed to survive a punishing Yankee finish. Bill Johnson hit a long double and ran home on Keller's 457-foot triple. The latter scored on an infield out, when Cooper clamped down on the rally.

The situation before the third game, played before a new record-breaking crowd of 69,990 at the Stadium, October 7, was exactly the same as when White faced Chandler in the same park in 1942 and Ernie sent the Birds to the fore with his 2-0 shutout. This time White was on the side lines with an ailing arm, and Billy the Kid gave the important pitching assignment to another left-hander, Alpha Brazle, the former Oklahoma cotton picker and sensational Sacramento mid-season pickup. McCarthy's pitcher was the former Fordham Ram, Borowy, who had taken the Sunday shellacking in 1942.

Brazle ran into the toughest luck of the series. The Cardinals gave him a two-run lead in the fourth, when after an intentional pass to Sanders, Litwhiler plunked Borowy for a single, driving in the Poles, Musial and Kurowski. Up to the eighth inning, tall redheaded Alpha had yielded only three hits, walked none, while the Yankee run in the sixth was tainted. Borowy scored on his double, a long fly and Kurowski's damaging fumble on Johnson came after two were out.

Lindell, the transplanted pitcher, opened New York's eighth with a single and took an extra base when Walker fumbled the ball.

Snuffy Stirnweiss, the former Mercury-footed North Carolina grid-iron end, batted for Borowy, and McCarthy ordered him to lay down a sacrifice bunt. Snuffy tapped it directly at Sanders, who steadied himself and pegged the ball across the infield to Kurowski for a play on Lindell at third. Beans Reardon waived Lindell out, but was compelled to reverse himself, when Whitey dropped the ball while putting it on the runner. However, Lindell, six feet, four inches of California brawn, hit Kurowski like a General Sherman tank rolling into a pill box. Both players were bruised and shaken up and there was some criticism of Lindell for the vigor of his slide. McCarthy snapped after the game: "It was no pink tea, and Lindell had the right of way."

As a result of the errors by Walker and Kurowski, the Yankees now had runners on third and first with none out. On Stainback's fly to Litwhiler, Lindell was held on third, but Stirnweiss moved up to second. Southworth then took a gamble, which later came in for a lot of chin music, from the grandstand and in press and radio. Billy ordered Brazle to walk Crosetti, veteran Yankee shortstop, only a fair hitter, but a pesky flea for the Redbirds all through the series. It brought up Bill Johnson, another "toughie" since the first game, with the bases full. Bill cleaned decks, lashing a triple through the alley between Litwhiler and Walker. Before the inning was over, Southworth rushed in Krist and Brecheen as the Yankees tallied five runs. When the dejected Brazle—his head hanging on his chest—walked off the field, the record Stadium crowd stood up to a man and gave Alpha a hand which reverberated throughout New York's Bronx.

Southworth wasn't sweet William in the clubhouse when it was over. He didn't cry about Lindell's slide, but he did point out to his players that the Yankees were pushing them around. In the first game there had been charges that Crosetti had given Lanier the hip which was responsible for Max spilling an important throw at first base.

"I'm tired of seeing you shoved around," said Billy. "We'll play that kind of ball from now on—if that's what they want."

There was an open date between the Brazle game and the fourth contest, played in St. Louis on a beautiful Sunday afternoon, October 11. Some of the faithful had stood in line twenty-four hours for the comparatively few unreserved seats. There was much talk that

St. Louis would see a new, aroused and inspired Cardinal team on their home grounds. Instead, the Redbirds were even more inept than they were in New York.

McCarthy took a daring gamble in the fourth game, pitching Marius Russo, his left-handed Long Island Italian. Marius had been plagued with a sore arm for two years, and his 1943 record with a championship club was most mediocre—five victories and ten defeats. However, Russo was at his best on this sunny Sunday, and won a close 2 to 1 decision from Max Lanier, who hurled another good game. The Yankee left-hander also hit two doubles and scored New York's winning run. Gordon's double and Dickey's single cooked up the first Yankee tally in the fourth. The Birds tied the score on two errors and Litwhiler's double in the seventh, only to have the Yanks regain the lead in the eighth on Russo's second two-bagger, a sacrifice and Crosetti's long fly.

The Cardinals weren't a pleasant bunch of well-bred Dixie college and high school boys when it was over, and Billy the Kid went completely out of character. "Ask your questions in a hurry, and get the hell out of here," he told the press gang who assembled around him for the clubhouse postmortem. And Walker Cooper, the Cardinals' third captain within a year, echoed Billy's sentiments.

Dick McCann, of the New York *Daily News,* was partly responsible for Billy's outburst, when he asked the Cardinal chieftain: "Have you looked at any left-handed pitching like that (the brand dished out by Russo) this year?" "Didn't you ever hear of such pitchers as Vander Meer of the Reds and Gerheauser of Philadelphia?" Billy fairly bellowed. "Besides, there are a few left-handers on this club who don't have to sit back for anybody." Being beaten by a five and ten left-hander was bad enough, but Dick's question was rubbing salt in the wounds. The situation wasn't helped the next day when the Cardinal clubhouse, which always had the welcome mat out for baseball writers, was closed to the press before the fifth game.

The Cardinal light went out in this fifth contest—another game which was painful for loyal St. Louisans to sit through. The Birds could hit Chandler, the 20-game winner, at any time except when hits meant runs. They got to the chunky Georgia boy for ten hits, but had no more runs at the finish than when they started. Mort Cooper tried valiantly to repeat his second game victory. He started out in a blaze of glory, striking out the first five men to face him, but his one lapse, in the sixth, was fatal. Keller slapped a slow-rolling single between Klein and Sanders, and Bill Dickey, New York's great catcher, met a Cooper fast ball cleanly and rocketed it to the roof of the right field pavilion for a two-run homer. It was the payoff blow, as the Yankees won, 2 to 0.

Trying to perk up his line-up for the last game, Southworth benched both Walker and Litwhiler, sending Hopp and Garms to their respective outfield positions. Then, to show how things break on a ball team when matters go badly, neither Hopp nor Garms hit, while both Walker and Litwhiler lined out singles when used as pinch-hitters. Walker Cooper, who had a mediocre series after his great play in the league season, split a finger, and Ken O'Dea, his successor, cracked out two hits in as many times at bat.

3

The stunning Cardinal World's Series defeat of 1943 was as much of a national surprise as was the great victory over the Yankees the previous autumn. A million voices asked: "What happened to the Cardinals? And, why didn't they run as they did in 1942?"

The answer always must remain one of those baseball mysteries. In 1942, the club was "hot," and still was under the momentum of their great August and September pennant drive when they pushed the Yankee juggernaut into the gutter. Everything the 1942 club did in the series was right; in 1943, everything Southworth tried went wrong. And, despite the '43 team's easy pennant victory, the crushing World's Series defeat proved that replacements Walker, Litwhiler and Klein did not measure up to the standards of Moore, Slaughter and Jimmy Brown. Especially did the club miss the inspirational play of the 1942 captain and great center fielder—Terry Moore.

Unlike 1928, when Breadon demoted McKechnie to Rochester for losing a World's Series to the Yankees in four straight games, Singing Sam found no dissatisfaction with his manager. Though he had nothing to sing about, he handed Billy the Kid a few verbal bouquets: "Southworth still is the man who took the club when it was hopelessly mired in the second division in 1940, and finished third. He came in a good second in 1941, despite injuries which could have wrecked any other club, and he won two pennants with a total of 211 victories. Could anyone ask more of a manager?

"There is another thing I would like to say about Billy Southworth. He is a gentleman at all times and you never have a moment's worry about any of his activities outside of baseball. Billy and I never have exchanged an unpleasant word since he became manager of the club."

Before the 1943 season was tucked away in camphor, Walker Cooper, the last captain of the club, visited Breadon's Sportsmans Park office carrying a bundle. When Sam unwrapped it, it contained a black marble desk set, with a bronze swinging ball player for the center piece. Etched into the copper plate was the inscription: "Presented to Sam Breadon as a token of good will and loyalty and with our congratulations on your success. With our hopes for many such years to follow. From your 1943 Cardinals." Underneath were the etched signatures of the 1943 Redbirds.

The gift brought tears to the eyes of the former West Side boy from New York, the man often accused of being hard-boiled and mercenary in his dealings with ball players. "This is the first time I ever heard of ball players giving club owners anything," he said proudly.

So far as the author knows it established another Cardinal record.

As for Southworth, after the sting of the World's Series defeat, he was his own amiable self. "We simply never played our game," he said. "We never got started, but we were beaten by a fine ball club and by McCarthy's great pitching. In baseball, you've got to take the sour with the sweet. Well, last year, we enjoyed the sweets—so this year we've got to take the sour."

As for his brush with the sports writers, Billy said he hoped it wouldn't happen again. He said that McCarthy had suggested reporters be kept out of the clubhouses before games, and he had agreed, but added: "So long as I am manager of the Cardinals, our clubhouse door never again will be closed to baseball writers."

The Sportsmanship Brotherhood voted Billy their annual sportsmanship award, which formerly had gone to such distinguished American sport figures as Alonzo Stagg, Walter Johnson, Connie Mack, Jack Moakley, Lou Gehrig and Mell Ott. And shortly after the Series, Billy further forgot his baseball woes in the joy of a visit from his son, Major Billy Southworth, Jr., a former Toronto out-.

fielder, but now one of the Army's crack flyers, with as many decorations for pestering Nazis from European skies as the Cardinals have won pennants. In his bombers "Bad Check" and "Winning Run," Major Billy made twenty-five successful missions over Nazi Europe.

4

Two teams of All-Stars, freely sprinkled with Cardinals, were gathered to play exhibition games for the soldiers in Australia and the South Pacific war theater. After permission for the trip was granted, and the teams picked, it was called off by high War Department officials. Instead, Frankie Frisch, the former Cardinal manager, who was to have managed the National League team, chaperoned a band of speaking ball players to Alaska and the Aleutians. His band included Cardinals Stan Musial and Danny Litwhiler, the Yankee Borowy and the Dodger, Dixie Walker. Everywhere they were accorded a warm welcome, with Corporal-Sports Editor Howard T. Kosbau, of the *Sourdough Sentinel,* Alaskan Army newspaper, writing: "The soldiers here would rather talk with big league players than with Betty Grable." Frisch's gab was preferred to Betty's gams.

The inroads of the war again cut heavily into the Cardinal ranks as the 1944 season approached—to such a degree that Breadon declared: "I've got a far better club in the Army than I can put on the ball field." Center Fielder Harry Walker; the emergency second baseman, Lou Klein; and Pitchers Al Brazle, Ernie White and Howard Krist of the 1943 National League champions had entered the services. Marty Marion, the great shortstop, and Catcher Walker Cooper were accepted for limited service, though the Army later discontinued this classification. At one time Southworth seemed in danger of losing his entire starting 1944 outfield, as Stan Musial was accepted by the Army and Danny Litwhiler by the Navy. But neither was called up during the playing season, and Johnny Hopp, the new center fielder, was put in 4-F because of a back condition, the aftermath of football and baseball injuries. Other important 4-Fs were Mort Cooper, the hefty pitcher, and Ken O'Dea, second string catcher, big Mort because of an old trick knee and Ken because of a hernia.

However, back in April, Branch Rickey, the Dodger president, who knew the St. Louis organization, was saying: "I wish I had Sam Breadon's replacements," and other National League clubs realized the Cardinals were the club to beat. Yet few of the critics foresaw what a romp it really would be. With their 4-Fs and new material brought up from the farms in Columbus and Rochester, Billy the Kid's boys again tore the league wide apart. Even though their final winning margin over the second place Pirates was 14½ games—3½ games less than in 1943—the eighth Cardinal pennant was the easiest of the lot.

The club chalked up its 80th and 90th victories on the earliest dates on record, and seemed all set to go after the 116-victory record of the 1906 Cubs, when they went into a late August and September tailspin in which they lost 15 games out of 20 and dropped eight straight games to the runner-up Pirates.

Even so, the Cardinal champs of 1944 hit the totals of the 1943 pennant winners right on the nose—105 victories and 49 defeats. In their three championship years, the club varied only one game. And Mort Cooper was as consistent as the club, winning 22 games and losing seven, a duplicate of 1942, and only one away from his 1943 record of 21-8. The Cardinals also came out of the race with a flock of new records. Not only was Billy Southworth the first National League manager since McGraw in the early twenties to win three straight championships, but he was the first N.L. chief in the 68-year history of the old major to win 100 or more games three years in succession. Only Connie Mack had done it in the American League—in 1929, '30 and '31. And the Cardinals set a new record for spanking opponents twice in an afternoon, winning 17 double-headers.

High up among those deserving praise in this new victory for the Breadon arms was Marty Marion, ol' Mr. Shortstop, who excelled even his former great years and was voted the most valuable National League player for 1944. Though Stan Musial was beaten out by Brooklyn's Dixie Walker for the batting championship, the clouting Pennsylvania Pole was the leader of the Cardinal hit parade with a .347 average. Hopp, playing inspired ball all year, wasn't too far behind him with .335.

Shortly after Fourth of July, the Army took George Munger, the big redhead, at a time when he had won 11 games out of 14. It looked as though that might give the club a setback, but a chunky little righthander, Ted Wilks, brought up the previous winter from Columbus, stepped into the breach and became Southworth's third ranking pitcher, in back of Cooper and Lanier. Chunky Ted, out of the Army because of stomach ulcers, had the remarkable freshman record of 17 victories and four defeats. Another 4-F—with a perforated eardrum—Emil Verban, an Illinois Yugoslav, also advanced from Columbus, filled in acceptably at second. Pepper Martin, the old Wild Horse of the Osage, was brought back to the Cardinals' main show after three years as a farm manager, and Dizzy Dean, his old Gas House companion, rooted for him over Station WEW from the radio coop at the Sportsmans Park rookery. After collecting his World Series check, Pepper finally said good-by to the Cardinal organization by accepting the management of the San Diego club.

5

The 1944 World's Series opponents of the Cardinals were their fellow tenants at Sportsmans Park, the Browns, who won their first pennant in American League history in a ding-dong race, clinching the flag on the very last day of the season in a furious finish in which they bowled over McCarthy's famed Yankees four straight.

It was only the seventh time that a World's Series was played entirely in one city. Back in 1906, the Hitless Wonder White Sox defeated Chance's famous Cubs, four games to two, in an all-Chicago series, while the Yankees and Giants met in New York in 1921, 1922, 1923, 1936 and 1937, with the Giants taking the first two series and the Yankees the last three. The Yanks also met and defeated Brooklyn in 1941, and while Brooklyn is a borough of greater New York, it always has retained its identity as a baseball city. The all–St. Louis series, however, was only the third played entirely in one park, the other being the all–Polo Grounds affairs of 1921-22.

The Cardinals continued to be the club to bring the greatest joy to the hearts of National League partisans. By beating the Browns, four games to two, they became the first National club to win five world's championships. Of the seven blue ribbons to go to the old league since 1926, these high-flying Redbirds accounted for five. Old St. Louis, often knocked as a ball town, did itself proud staging its private baseball party, as the six games drew 206,708 and a gate of $906,122. With the $100,000 paid for broadcasting rights, it made it another million-dollar series.

The impetus with which the Browns finished their league season carried them to victory in two of the first three games, but from there on the Cardinals found themselves, and they pulled out the series with three successive victories. It was a pitchers' series, with many new strike-out records being entered into the books. The pitchers of the two clubs struck out 92 batsmen, high for any World's Series, with the Redbird flingers fanning 49 Brownies, while 43 of Billy's boys bit the dust on strikes.

The first game, played October 4, was a heart-breaker for the Cardinals, and there was a lot of griping in the Redbird rookery when it was over. Big Mort Cooper gave up only two hits, but those two bingles beat him. And his old American League home run jinx still camped on his trail. The Browns struck in only one inning, the fourth. Then Gene Moore singled with two out and First Baseman George McQuinn reached the roof of the right field pavilion with a homer, scoring Gene ahead of him. George was hot all during the series, and emerged the batting leader of both teams with a .438 average. His homer bolstered up Luke Sewell's starting pitcher, Denny Galehouse, with a two-run lead until the ninth, when the Birds sidestepped a shutout on Marion's double and the infield outs of Bergamo and O'Dea.

The Cardinals tied it up next day, October 5, in an eleven inning game, which was the most dramatic and exciting of the series. And but for a great relief job by the young relief pitcher, Blix Donnelly, the Birds never could have carried the game into extra innings. With Lanier opposing Nelson Potter, the American League ace, the Birds started off all right, picking up tainted runs in the third and fourth innings. But after Lanier had held the Browns to a bunt single for six innings, the American Leaguers suddenly came to life with two out in the seventh. In a jiffy they tied the score on Moore's single, a long double by Red Hayworth and a pinch single by Frank Mancuso. That left the scoreboard reading: 2-2. Southworth let Lanier start the eighth, but after Mike Kreevich opened with a clean double, Billy quickly yanked Max and wigwagged to the bull pen for Donnelly. The Minnesota youngster, who pitches a tantalizing curve, made one of the great rescues of World's Series history. He fanned Laabs and Stephens, and then after Southworth ordered an intentional pass for the hot McQuinn, Blix blitzed Mark Christman on strikes.

Donnelly had still another hole to dig out of in the eleventh, when McQuinn opened with a two-base hit. On Christman's attempted sacrifice, Blix pounced on the bunt and with a great peg to Kurowski shot down McQuinn at third base and that danger was over. The relief pitcher then took credit for the victory as the Cards won in their half against Muncrief, who had replaced Potter in the seventh. Sanders, the St. Louis home town boy, opened with a single, and took second on Kurowski's sacrifice. Sewell ordered an intentional pass for Marion, but Ken O'Dea, batting for Verban, whistled a hot single to right, and Sanders tore home with the winning tally.

The Redbirds made their poorest showing in the third game, when the Brownies lit on Wilks and batted out a 6 to 2 win, their last victory of the series. After the Cards scored a run off Jack Kramer in the first inning, the Browns showed their only real concentrated offensive of the series with two out in the third, when five successive hits drove Wilks to cover. Three runs scored, and a fourth came over when Schmidt, Wilks's successor, let fly a wild pitch.

In the Saturday game of October 7, the Cardinals got back on even terms with their American League foemen. The crafty left-hander, Brecheen, easily brought this one in for Billy by a score of 5 to 1; Harry, the Cat, was aided by some tidy support, including a sensational catch by Hopp in the first inning and an acrobatic stop by Marion in the eighth, which converted Laabs's bid for a hit during a Brown rally into a double play. Stan Musial enjoyed his best of 16 World's Series games, as he hit a homer, double, single and drew a walk in five times up. Sig Jakucki, hero of the Browns' pennant-clinching victory, was the victim of Musial's heavy artillery. In the first inning, with Hopp on base, Stan hit Sig's first pitch to the pavilion roof for a homer, and his single in another two-run Card uprising in the third helped drive Jakucki out.

With the series deadlocked at two-all, almost everyone appreciated that the Sunday ball game, October 8, would be decisive. It brought out the best crowd of the series, 36,568, and the game established a new World's Series strike-out record. The opening game pitchers, Mort Cooper and Denny Galehouse, squared off again, and this time big Coop won a 2 to 0 shutout as he struck out 12 against ten for Galehouse. After the third inning, the Cards made only two hits, but what hits! This time it was Galehouse who threw the home run balls. In the sixth inning, Ray Sanders cracked one to the right field pavilion roof, and two innings later Litwhiler hit a terrific clout into the grandstand in deepest right center. Just to rub a little salt into the wounds of Brown partisans, Mort Cooper ended the game by striking out three of Sewell's pinch-hitters—Byrnes, Laabs and Chartak—in the ninth.

With the Birds enjoying a three to two edge, Southworth felt he had his second world's title and the fifth for the Cardinals in his grasp. And he didn't let go. His team put on the clincher, October 9, by a score of 3 to 1, with Wilks, pasted out in the third game, doing a Donnelly relief job in this final contest. Lanier and Potter, the starting pitchers of the second game, again hooked up in this wind-up battle, and neither was on the job when it was over.

After the Browns scored a run in the second inning on Laabs's 422-foot triple and McQuinn's single, sloppy Brown fielding helped the Cardinals get three runs in the third, when Potter was given the bum's rush. Walk Cooper walked with one out and advanced to third on Sanders' single. Kurowski rolled to Stephens, but in his haste to start a double play, the Brown shortstop's throw pulled Gutteridge off second, and everybody was safe. Then singles by Verban and Lanier, at the bottom of the batting order, drove in two extra runs and Potter out of the picture.

The Browns had a chance in the sixth when Lanier walked Laabs and McQuinn with one out. The first pitch to Christman was wild, advancing both runners. Southworth then summoned Wilks, who not only retired Christman and Hayworth in this inning, but blotted out the 11 men who faced him in order. And, taking a tip from Cooper in the preceding day, Teddy ended the game by striking out Pinch-hitters Byrnes and Chartak.

After the third game, the first "home game" of the Browns, the wife of Cardinal Second Baseman Verban told him she had been sitting behind a post. Trying to get the tickets exchanged before the fourth game, Verban endeavored to get some satisfaction from Don Barnes, the Brown president. "You ought to be sitting behind a post. Ha! Ha!" was Emil's version of Barnes's reply.

From there on, Verban was a Yugoslav partisan thirsting for revenge. From being the ugly duckling of the Cardinal line-up, lifted for a pinch-hitter in the first three games, Emil became a veritable batting terror. As the result of closing the series with three hits in the last game, he brought his average up to .412, tops for his team. And, as soon as Wilks struck out Chartak for the last out, Emil rushed over to Barnes's box and yelled: "Now, you are behind the post."

6

With three better-than-100 victory teams and two world's championships in three years, the Redbirds are not through soaring. Only three major league clubs, the Browns of the 80's, McGraw's Giant champions of 1921-2-3-4, and Joe McCarthy's Yankee winners of 1936-7-8-9, have succeeded in putting together four straight winners. But that's the goal Breadon and Southworth have set for 1945. And many of their rivals already ask: "How can we stop them?"

Breadon also has planned a new postwar rookery for his Redbirds, a $1,250,000 project at Grand Boulevard and Chouteau Avenue, some three miles south of Sportsmans Park. It will be the most centrally located ball park in the majors; it will seat 40,000, and according to Lucky Sam will be "the last word in baseball construction." For nothing is too good for his Redbirds.

Despite war conditions and uncertainties, Breadon again has engaged his full staff of scouts for 1945 and nation-wide Cardinal tryout camps again are planned from ocean to ocean and from the St. Lawrence to the Rio Grande. When the great conflagration burns itself out, and a distressed world again returns to the happy days of peace, boys now marching in Boy Scout troops, collecting scrap and rubber—and playing a little baseball on the side—from little tobacco burgs of North Carolina, wheat towns of Kansas, the coal mine districts of Pennsylvania, will be riding the Cardinal Cavalcade to fresh pennant and World Series victories.

INDEX

Bob Boynton of the Society for American Baseball Research prepared this index.